AF378017

There's a Crocodile in the House

There's a Crocodile in the House

The Itinerant Ecologist Series

Malcolm Marks

Coeur de Rose Publishing

CONTENTS

CONTENTS

This book is dedicated to my lovely family:

Véronique, Mélanie and David.

The most important people in my life and a family that continually makes me proud.

A special big thanks to my daughter Mélanie who wore her editorial hat throughout the writing of this book and the others in the series. How she ever managed to work full time, raise two beautiful children, edit my work and keep me to a tight writing schedule, I will never know but will be always grateful.

But I do wonder if 'Dedication' is quite the right word, and perhaps the section should instead be entitled 'Apologies'!

Apologies not only for leading my family through the myriad adventures revealed in the Itinerant Ecologist Series but also for making them put up with me while I have been writing and researching the text for my books!

Cœur de Rose Publishing
162 Chemin de la Touvière
Rix, 01680 Lhuis, France

This book constitutes part 2 of a four-part autobiography series, The Itinerant Ecologist, by Malcolm Marks. The description of events has been honestly portrayed to the best of the author's memory.

This is the First Edition of "There's a Crocodile in the House".

Copyright © 2023 by Malcolm Marks

All rights reserved, no part of this book may be reproduced in any manner whatsoever without written permission except in the case of brief quotations embedded in critical articles and reviews.

Cœur de Rose Publications, paperback edition and first edition, October 2023
Edited by Mélanie Marks Purnode
Manufactured in Europe

By the same author in the Itinerant Ecologist Series:

Book 1: 'From Nigeria to Cracking Walnuts'

Available in hard copy (ISBN: 978-2-9590283-0-4)
and electronic version (ISBN: 978-2-9590283-1-1)

Book 3: 'Sapphires, Monkey-Bread and a *Coup d'Etat'*
(in press)

Book 4: 'Of Cows, Chars and Beautiful People'
(in preparation)

All published by Cœur de Rose Publishing.

A Brit in Every Village

Our overnight flight from Lagos touches down in London, pretty much on time, and we are back on European soil after four interesting years of living and working in Nigeria. Yesterday I was on the payroll of the University of Calabar as their senior lecturer in ecology while today I am arriving in Europe, unemployed for the moment and delighted to be so; at least for the next few months. With me are my bubbly French wife, Véronique, and our cute little 14-month old daughter, Mélanie. This is July 1983, and most of the summer lies ahead of us at our home in eastern France.

We make our way through the arrival formalities of Heathrow Airport passing quickly through passport control and then into departures for our onward flight. We join a short queue for the x-ray machine that checks our hand baggage for the Lyon and final leg of our trip. The two processes take only around forty minutes in total, and it would have been even quicker if the young lady in charge of our x-ray machine had not spent ten minutes talking to Véro about all things baby. We go straight to our gate for the onward flight to Lyon-Satolas with British Airways.

Waiting in the cool of the departure lounge, sitting on comfortable padded seats and drinking another 'wake-me-up' coffee, we reflect on the difference between here and the steamy south-east of Nigeria from which we have just arrived. We both laugh, clearly a little too loudly, when Véro reminds me that not once during our passage through Heathrow were we asked for 'dash' (bribes in Nigeria). Our youthful chuckles obviously disturb the elderly gentleman to my left because he looks at us harshly but receives a warm smile from me in response. He, of course, is not privy to our joke nor does he know its context. Our familiarity with Nigeria, gleaned from four years of experience living there, taught us in contrast that it was a rarity not to be asked for something during either our frequent trips through Lagos airport or necessary meetings with government officials while in Calabar. How pleasant then it feels to be back in a country where such events are almost non-existent and, when they do crop up, justice is normally served quickly and severely.

After only a short wait, our flight is called and we are beckoned forward by the young hostess who will soon start to check boarding passes. Once we have moved closer to her and said our 'hellos' and '*bonjours*' she announces into her microphone in English and then in French that the flight to Lyon-Satolas will soon be boarding at Gate 23 and that priority boarding will be given to families with young children.

We are soon on board and our hand baggage stowed in the overhead compartment just, well yes, over my head. I wonder why it is that we Brits generally only ever use the verb 'to stow' when on a plane. Could you imagine answering the question 'what should I do with the cheese?' with 'Oh, just stow it in the fridge'? No matter, I guess, but I notice that there is a considerable part of our vocabulary that we reserve strictly for flights. We are, for example, told to leave the plane by the fore and aft stairs – what is wrong with front and back? When the plane moves on the ground, it 'taxis'. Then there is the exclamation 'Brace-Brace' just before an aircraft crashes. I always think that 'Pray-Pray' might be a little more useful.

The short, ninety-minute flight to Lyon passes quickly with an early lunch being served as soon as practicable after take-off followed by a strong cup of Nescafé; but when will airlines learn that people would really prefer the real thing?

We pass across Paris and then, soon after seeing Dijon, the capital of Burgundy and all things red wine, pass below us, we are told by the pilot that we are starting our descent to Lyon's Satolas Airport. Apparently the sun is shining there and the temperature on the ground is a pleasant 24C. As we gaze left out of our cabin window, we are just in time to see the beautiful and ecologically significant area of la Dombes (the area really is a singular with an s). This so-called 'region of a thousand lakes' lies in the northern half of our new Département de l'Ain and sits equidistant between Bourg-en-Bresse to the north-east and Lyon to the south-west. La Dombes is an interesting area with a rather unique agricultural system that was developed, apparently by monks, in the middle ages and in which fish-rearing forms part of its crop-rotation system. The lakes (or *étangs*) are periodically drained into neighbouring fields, and then become *étangs* for the next few years. The larger fish are netted and harvested with the carp going mostly to Germany, where they are considered a festive delicacy rather like turkey in the UK. The predator fish such as pike (*brochet*), zander (*sandre*) and perch (*perche*) find a ready market in French restaurants where they are filleted and sold for a very significant mark up. By the way, if ever in a restaurant in France in a tourist spot like the Lac d'Annecy or the Lac de Bourget and you want to ensure that you will eat the fish from that very lake, the tip is to read the menu very, very carefully. If it says *poisson* (or *brochet, perche* or *friture*, etc.) *de lac*, avoid because the fish may come from any lake in the world, except the one you are sitting in front of. However, if the menu says *poisson du lac*, ahhh, then you know that it is the real McCoy and comes from the lake outside the restaurant window.

Many of the pike from la Dombes find themselves purchased by the food industry and used in the flavouring of *quenelles* (dumplings to us Brits). Most of the larger remaining fish, usually termed white fish (roach, tench, bream, and so on) are sold to fishing associations to stock their own waters while all the small examples, regardless of species, are transferred into the newly flooded field so that they may grow and eventually be harvested in their turn. Soon after the draining of an *étang* is complete, the farmer ploughs the old lake bed and sows the next crop, often maize.

A few moments after crossing la Dombes, we glimpse the beautiful city of Lyon complete with its twin rivers, la Saône and le Rhône which converge at the heart of the city and, after their confluence, emerge as simply le Rhône.

Lording over the city is the imposing Basilica of Notre Dame de Fourvière that was built on the site of Lugdunum, the original Roman city. Fourvière also boasts the ruins of Roman baths and an amphitheatre. On hot days, it is advisable to reach *Fourvière* from *le Vieux Lyon* (the old town) by cable car (*funiculaire*) rather than attempting to climb the almost six hundred steps that separate the two areas.

As we make our final descent into Satolas, we cross low over the A43, the motorway that links Lyon to the picturesque mountain town of Chambery, famous for its elephant fountain that celebrates the adventures of Benoît de Boigne in India. Locals have nicknamed the statue as *"les quatre sans culs"* (the four without butts) because only the front halves of the four elephants are shown. In reality the nickname is a pun on a famous French film entitled *Les quatre cents coups* (the four hundred strokes).

The plane lands with several bumps and then a rush of engines in reverse to brake our landing speed, inspiring an English wit in a neighbouring seat to remark to his partner "so they even allow the air hostesses to land British Airways flights!"

We taxi to a halt just outside the terminal building and the plane fills with a series of clicks as seat belts are released. The stairs are quickly placed fore and aft and there is the usual mad rush of visitors heading for the exits. We remain seated, watching them jostle for their bags and push and shove their way along the crowded corridor towards the exits. We are in no hurry because this is, after all, Lyon Satolas and no matter how fast anxious passengers can get off the plane, they will inevitably join the ever-slow passport queues inside the terminal building. Lord help us if one of the many flights from Northern Africa happens to have landed immediately before us. When the turmoil calms down, I pick up Mélanie, and she snuggles into her familiar place in the crook of my left arm, head on my shoulder. I manoeuvre one of our cabin bags from the overhead container with my right hand while Véro picks up the other inflight case and struggles with all the remaining paraphernalia that young parents feel obliged to hoick around with them on trips. A friendly air hostess takes pity on us and offers to carry Mélanie down the stairs while we share out the baggage, as usual rather unequally, and follow her rapid descent to the tarmac.

Taking our time and appreciating the relative coolness of Lyon after the steam of Nigeria, we follow the rushing tourists towards passport control and are met with the familiar sight of only two officers on duty and long lines of eager faces waving their passports ineffectually as they queue in the rat-maze. Mother luck is on our side today because a third officer spots us as he enters a neighbouring passport booth and calls out to us *"venez par-là monsieur-dame"* allowing us to seriously jump the queue. A Brit, holding out his dark blue passport, attempts to discover whether mother luck is also on his side, by trying to cut in front of us, but he is met with a Gallic glare and a sharp rebuke of *"attendez monsieur."*

Are we embarrassed by our shameless queue jumping? Véro most certainly not, this is a French custom after all, but me? Well, I have to admit, a little.

Our friendly border agent stamps our passports, wishes us '*bienvenues madame et mademoiselle* and welcome sir', and ushers us through the gates and on to baggage collection. I spot our cases already on the revolving carousel, number 3, and Mélanie's pushchair just popping out of the hatch and down onto the belt.

Customs Officers are nowhere to be seen as this is an internal European flight and so we pass unhindered through the green channel and emerge immediately into the bustle of arrivals. Standing waiting for us are Belou and Mic, Véro's parents. After the customary two cheek kisses all round, Belou takes charge of Mélanie who seems not concerned in the least that this 'stranger' whisks her up into his arms and starts to chatter away to her in French. We are lucky to have such a calm, friendly and cute little girl. Belou is the perfect grandfather (*papy*) and absolutely adores his three grandchildren. Mic (please do not call me *mamy*), on the other hand, is the most un-maternal mother of four that I have ever encountered! Soon my wife and her mum are nattering ten to the dozen as I follow along behind pushing our overloaded baggage trolley. We walk across the road, into the underground carpark opposite and take the lift down to the second floor where Belou's Renault awaits. Our suitcases just about fit in the boot. Then Mic tells me to sit down in the back and lifts Mélanie's folded pushchair and places it between my knees followed by the large carryall bag loaded with baby's gubbins that she balances across my knees. Mélanie gets a cuddle from her mum sitting next to me; no child seats are required in 1983.

We leave the carpark, direction Crémieu which is only a twenty-minute drive away. We soon pass by the turning for the little village of Satolas-et-Bonce with the first part of the village giving its name to the airport; into Montcul, a name that always gets Véro's little brother Nico roaring with laughter because it is pronounced *mon cul* (my bum) and then through or near a series of villages with their names ending in 'ieu' as in Chamagnieu, Tignieu, Jameyzieu, Dizimieu, Crémieu, and so on.

I ask why the villages around here all seem to end in 'ieu' and am told by Mic "*c'est comme ça*" basically meaning 'because they are'.

I am a little suspicious that no-one in the car actually has a clue why and it has taken a foreigner to ask a very obvious question. Given that the place names date from several hundred years ago, I wonder if the spelling has not evolved over time and that originally the word ending came for 'eau' (water) or 'lieu' (place), but to this day I do not have the reason to share with you – it's just like that!

We arrive at their beautiful home just outside of Crémieu, called Bourbouillon, and after a respectable period of conversation, Mélanie yawns in tandem with me and so we excuse ourselves and go off for an afternoon nap. Véro stays to continue chatting with her mum while Belou has already taken refuge in his workshop on the side of the house where he is certainly wiring lamp switches or producing lamp bases from an accumulated antique's stockpile. Mic uses the bases as her inspiration to design and sew beautiful matching lampshades that will then appear in her boutique in Crémieu.

My parents-in-law are amazingly talented people and both come from very artistic families. Mic purchased in 1974 what is a narrow, medieval town house with one room on each of its four floors. She and Belou spent the next several months converting the downstairs into a most magnificent, olde-worlde boutique in which she displays and sells the aforementioned lamps and lampshades along with many other tasteful items that appeal both to passing tourists and to a large following of upper middle class ladies from neighbouring towns as far away as Lyon. The house is handily located next door but one to the church and so is sure to attract tourists through its door. I am in awe of my mother-in-law; her incredible tastes, cultural knowledge and general sophistication.

Since we have just finished four years in Calabar, and it has been almost a year since we were last in France, I know that Véro and her mum have a lot of catching up to do, especially about family gossip. I see that Mélanie is already fast asleep in her old cot, a family heirloom that we had used last summer when she was a new born, while I yawn as I pull off my clothes and get into our bed. I had managed to sleep very little on the overnight flight from Lagos and so really need this siesta. As I gently drift into the arms of Morpheus, I hear clearly, through the old floorboards that separate us, the ladies chatting downstairs about our future plans; which to be honest, at this precise moment, are rather vague. We simply want to enjoy the summer, and come up for air after all the hectic recent events of Nigeria. We both have many bitter-sweet experiences since we returned to Nigeria from our vacation, after the birth of Mélanie the previous year. Despite the offer of accelerated promotion at the university, we had both been concerned about the changing mood of Nigerian politics and so had easily made the decision to leave Calabar University and return to Europe. The only problem we faced with this decision is that I have come back without a job.

Our last vacation from the University of Calabar was mostly spent in France and actually stretched from May through to early October last year. It was, without doubt, the most enjoyable period of our lives to date. It started with the birth of our daughter and continued through the summer months spent in the idyllic little village of Rix in the Canton of Lhuis, bordering the River Rhône. We were lucky to have been able to rent a small stone house from a local farming family because our own, recently purchased house in a nearby village was in a state of total disrepair; read 'ruin'. On most days during that perfect summer, I had travelled the fifteen or so kilometres separating our house in Cordon from our rental in Rix and tried to do as much work as possible to make our ruin habitable in time for this, our current, vacation. This had involved attempting to undertake a crazy amount of building work including uncovering a near perfect "*plafond* à *la française*" and hand scrubbing all the newly exposed beams, changing floorboards on the first floor, installing a toilet upstairs and a working kitchen sink downstairs all connected to the drains via a septic tank that had been sunk in the garden to the side of the house. Given the original hazardous state of the electrics, my kind English brother-in-law had used some of his vacation the previous year to make initial running repairs. Outside help had come in the form of our friendly builders cum roofers, the Franco Brothers, who had promised to fix the leaky roof during our absence and add three skylights so that we could see our way around the fifty-metre square attic. A local carpenter should also have installed a window in our future bedroom on the first floor – so closing us off from the elements – and a staircase so that we could reach the first floor without using a rickety wooden ladder! Hopefully that ladder will now serve for us to climb from the first floor into the large attic. We are both anxious to see whether our workers have lived up to their promises because we will be moving in for the entire summer the very next day.

We wake up early the following morning to a beautiful sun shining through our bedroom window that announces the lovely day to come. Mélanie wakes with us, stands up in her cot and holds her arms up to me so that I can pick her out of her cot and bring her to our bed. The odour of toasting baguette and percolating coffee comes in through the open bedroom door, heralding the perfect start to the day, courtesy of Belou. After a quick breakfast, we load our bags into the tiny Renault 4L with its odd hand gear-change that sprouts from the dashboard. Véro's mum is lending us her car for a couple of days, and so we head off towards the little village of Rix where our own car has been parked up for the winter.

Our old Renault 6 that I had bought two years previously has spent the last nine months or so stored in the barn of our kind neighbours in Rix, M. et Mme Joly, and we have fingers tightly crossed that the engine will start without too much trouble; just like it did last year. Our thirty minute or so trip from Crémieu to Rix is mostly on small country roads that take us via Trept, Morestel and Brangues, crossing the Rhône on the suspension bridge at Groslée. The drive is a moment for us to chat about the beauty of the region we have chosen to live in, and how nice it feels to be finally back in France. Yes, we enjoyed our stay in Nigeria but life was never as one could anticipate and there were always horrors and drama awaiting the unwary just around the corner. From a crocodile lurking next to our washing line, to dead bodies mounting up in the botanical gardens where I had been the director, and on to a frightening, nocturnal burglary at our guesthouse; we were never really at ease and that disquiet had grown with the birth of Mélanie and the fear of tropical diseases.

Now looking out of the car window as I head away from Crémieu, I remember back to the first time I came to this area of France in September 1975. I had fallen in love with the area, its botany and river systems and also, not to forget, with a particular young French lady who is now sitting next to me. On that first trip to meet Véro's parents at the end of the summer, I had been amazed to find colonies of Lizard and Bee Orchids growing in my future in-laws' back garden. Since, I had just received my BSc in Botany from the University of London and was about to embark on a PhD in Physiological Ecology, finding dozens of these two red-list orchid species growing on the edge of their lawn was surprising, to say the least.

My mind comes back to the present as we drive through the medieval town of Morestel and we can see, in the near distance, the foothills of the Jura mountains that run from the northern end of the Alps and up into Switzerland. Immediately in front of us, almost due east, is the mountain that has Lhuis tucked into its belt, with Rix and the Rhône at its base and the beautiful, crystal clear Lac d'Ambléon near its summit. Off to the right, to the south, we can make out the Mont de Cordon, our final destination this morning.

We next pass through the little village of Brangues that has, literally, housed two giants of French literature in the form of Stendhal and Claudel, and then across the Rhône on the suspension bridge, turning immediately left on to the D19. Finally, our day-dreaming and chatter come to an end as we drive up the steep little lane into Rix, marked simply by a tiny enamel sign that someone in the distant past has used for target practice – almost scoring a bullseye on the 'i'. We turn left at the ancient communal washing place or *lavoir* and then right into the courtyard of our rental property of last year. We immediately see our car, and it is already outside the barn that opens onto the far side of the courtyard.

Charles Joly, the 80-year-old patriarch of the village is humming away as he brushes inside the car boot.

"Hi you three", he says as we step out of the Renault 4L and into his courtyard, "I thought I would save you some time and get the car started before you arrive. She started almost immediately and is ready to go."

We drink a quick coffee with Charles and give our thanks with a small present from Nigeria, and then say our goodbyes. We promise to come back and see them when their son Claude is in town and introduce Mélanie to Claude's young son Stéphane. A quick stop to see Marie-Rose, from whom we had rented our holiday home last year, and off we drive to Cordon with me now behind the wheel of the Renault 6 and Véro driving the 4L.

The final purchase contracts on our house in Cordon had been exchanged at the tail-end of 1981, a couple of months after we had finished our summer vacation and returned to Calabar for the third year of our stay in Nigeria. The house was very close to being a ruin when we had seen it and decided to put in a speculative offer of the equivalent of £6,000. This had been rapidly accepted, perhaps too rapidly, by the three Billiemaz heirs. On several occasions during the following spring and summer, we had doubts about our choice of 'vacation home'. Indeed, I had some initial and serious doubts about our overall sanity to have taken on such a challenge. That challenge was made even more difficult because Véronique had given birth to Mélanie the following May and so had been obliged, and only too happy, to look after our little girl while I got on with trying to make the house more habitable. Clearly, Véro could not provide a great deal of help with the rather major renovation tasks that were urgently required if we were to pass the following summer – this summer – in Cordon. Until we took on this renovation project, my most ambitious DIY chores had been either to put up shelves or to change a plug; and do not forget that my spoken French was rather iffy (this from the pupil who scored the lowest possible Grade 9 in his O level and was told by his French teacher, Mr Horne at Sutton

Valence School, "Marks, with all the best will in the world, you will never speak this beautiful language!"

No matter, logic is my forte and so I naively assumed that I could apply logic to the renovations. Of course, this is partially true but not entirely so, as I had already found out on several occasions. Nonetheless, by the time we left France in the late summer last year, we had managed to install some essentials as I have already mentioned. For this summer, we have equally ambitious plans that involve changing the floorboards between the first and second (attic) floors, adding a shower and washbasin to our bathroom, and building walls on the first floor to separate off our bedroom, Mélanie's room and the bathroom. Someone at the local DIY store has recommended using 'carreaux de plâtre' which are basically interlocking rectangular blocks of plaster each weighing some 20 kg. I also want eventually to make a start on decorating the downstairs which will first involve a lot of wall re-plastering as several areas of lime plaster (chaux) have fallen off the walls to reveal the limestone underneath from which the house is constructed. Lots, therefore, to keep us active over the next three months or so.

Before getting going on the larger work, we are looking forward to a visit from my mum and dad, who live in the UK. We have finally convinced them to stay in a local hotel, not camp in our little field as my mum kept insisting she wanted to do. My sister and her family are also due to come a little later in their camping van with my brother-in-law, John, kindly offering to spend a few days with me to complete the wiring of the house. Lots planned for the summer.

The fifteen-minute drive from Rix to Cordon takes twenty minutes as we decide to stop in Glandieu and show Mélanie the waterfall (or cascade) that is Glandieu's only claim to fame if one overlooks the couple of marble producers displaying their garish funeral headstones in front of their factories. Then we drive through Brégnier, passing the Mairie and the eponymous café next door. We have been advised that should we ever need to find any of the village council workers, better to look in the café than waste time going to the place where they are *supposed* to be working. At this time, *le petit blanc* (glass of white wine) is a far better attraction than work for many of these functionaries. We pass by the village primary school with its two small classes of children and into la Bruyère noticing that our old swimming lake, *le lac de Pluvis*, has disappeared and been replaced by a sinuous canal of milky Rhône water. We turn left across the new bridge that spans the new canal, spotting our neighbour's small vineyard on the right, then pass the remains of the XIV century Chateau de la Barre off to the left. All that remains visible of the chateau is a fortified tower that is inhabited by an antique dealer of, err, dubious repute, so we are told by local gossip.

Finally, we drive into our communal courtyard, after being away for ten months. As soon as we lift Mélanie out of the car and put her down on her feet (she had celebrated her first birthday in Nigeria by standing up and walking), Thérèse, our next door neighbour, comes across to greet us closely followed by her sister Yvette who lives in the house opposite ours. They are followed at a more leisurely pace by the Pépé Parcouret, Yvette and Thérèse's sprightly ninety-year old father carrying his '*faux*' (or scythe), just like Old Father Time, that he seems to be permanently sharpening with a whetstone. Then Lili (really Louis), Yvette's husband and my frequent aperitif partner, arrives to greet us. Of course, no-one is interested in Véro and me; everyone is goo-goo-ing and gaa-gaa-ing at Mélanie who was only a few months old when they last saw her. Now she is a real little girl, and loves the attention of all these smiling faces.

Once the two cars are unpacked, we take a walk inside the house to check on the progress of our work. The first thing we notice is that the stairs are in place and so we can proceed up to the first floor without having to climb a ladder; ah real progress. Because of the prohibitive cost of fitting perfect stairs (ones that turn and are made of oak), we have gone with a so-called '*échelle à meunier*' which is a straight staircase, and rather too steep I have to admit, and made of pine. On the first floor, our carpenter has also fitted a window into the stone frame of our '*fenêtre à meneaux*'. We believe that he could have made the window frame less bulky but we are happy nonetheless to have the window installed and the elements now excluded. We then proceed up the rickety wooden ladder to the attic and note the clarity of the room since the Francos have made good on their promise to add three roof lights (called *Velux* here, their tradename) and, thank goodness, they have also completely overhauled the roof. No more shafts of lights coming through the gaps where tiles had slithered down the roof because of ancient broken battens.

Feeling that some real progress has been made, we take a leisurely picnic lunch in the sunshine of our tiny side garden. Actually we are perched on top of the sunken septic tank that had been installed last year with the help of my friend, Alan, now an ex-colleague from the University of Calabar.

As we eat, we discuss next steps in our home renovation. Our initial and urgent priority is to get a shower and washbasin installed in our bathroom both for our own needs but also for the imminent arrival of my mum and dad followed by my sister and her family. Currently, on our first floor of fifty square metres, the only occupant is the lonely toilet standing proud in what must be one of the largest loos in France. Does even Versailles boast a WC in such a large space? We have decided to go for a circular shower that we have seen advertised in a do-it-yourself shop in Morestel that comes as a kit. Decision made, I go off to the shop at 2pm, make my purchases and come back to Cordon. By 7.30 pm the shower is working and ready to receive the sweat that I accumulated during my travail building the shower; never as easy as it says on the pack! I fit the hand-basin the following morning and we have a functional bathroom but it does lack a little privacy. We have to learn how to build the separating walls (or *cloissons*) and decide which building materials to use to partition off the bathroom from the two bedrooms we plan for the first floor. Eventually we will tackle the attic and add two more rooms if or when our little family grows in number.

The time for the visit of my parents arrives and I drive off to Satolas airport in my little Renault-6 to collect them while Véro stays home with Mélanie and coaxes a meal out of our old bottled gas cooker that a kind friend has given us. I make sure to arrive in good time at the airport because my parents are very nervous country mice and would be panicking if I am not already waiting at the exit gate to meet them. Of course, what makes matters even worse for them is that they refuse to speak a single word of French!

Their plane from Heathrow arrives more or less on time. I first spot my Mum, walking at six miles an hour, as is her habit, and then my dad lagging behind, pushing the trolley with their new suitcase on, as is his. My Dad has already acquired his summer, nut brown complexion and that after only mowing the lawn twice this summer. We have a faint and exotic rumour in the family that my paternal grandmother may have been half-Indian. Her father, so he would have been my great-grandfather, had been an officer in the Raj army at the tail-end of Queen Victoria's reign but despite this and having a rather posh surname, my gran and her younger sister ended up in service, as small children, back in the UK immediately after her father married a second wife. Could she and her sister have been born the wrong side of the blanket? It is certainly strange that the two girls came from a quite wealthy family but ended up in service.

Does that explain my dad's complexion? No one knows for sure but my blood group of B is very prevalent on the Indian sub-continent ... Oh, those family secrets!

After an hour's drive we arrive back to Cordon and my parents see our folly for the very first time. When we had explained our purchase to them a couple of years ago, my dad had been horrified that we had taken so many risks in buying a ruin and getting a small mortgage to help do so. During the drive back from the airport I set his mind a little more at ease by explaining that the mortgage was only for a two-year duration and is now about to finish although the renovation work will go on for many years into the future. After spending the afternoon and early evening together, I drive them to *La Vielle Poste* in a hamlet just outside the little town of Les Avenières where they will spend their nights in this very quaint hotel. As luck has it, the host speak passable English.

The following morning, I awake feeling very strange indeed. I have a high temperature, am very thirsty and, try as I might, I cannot seem to focus my eyes while the merest hint of light makes my head spin. I manage to get out of bed and on to the sofa downstairs but that is my limit. I feel absolutely dreadful, and I know that mum and dad are waiting at the hotel for me to pick them up. Véro asks whether I should try to see a doctor but I know exactly what is wrong with me – I have a bout of malaria. Indeed, it is only about a week since we left Calabar but like an idiot I had stopped taking my Paludrine prophylactics and here I am with the sobbing malaria. Véro drives the 10 km or so to pick up my parents from their hotel – as they will certainly begin to panic if we do not show up on time – and then swings past the pharmacy in Les Avenières to pick up some anti-malarial pills. Of course, my mum is anxious as soon as she sees me lying on the sofa. My dad, on the other hand, is less concerned having been a marine in the Second World War seeing action in Burma and the Middle East where malaria was the least of a Tommy's concerns. Suffice to say (because, after all, I am actually writing these lines!), after taking the chloroquine-based treatment for the first twenty-four hours, I am feeling much more myself and able to pick mum and dad up from their hotel the following morning. After three days, I am as right as rain and have never experienced malaria again.

Our vacation continues and we are blessed with the beautiful summer weather that we expect in this part of France. On the day that I drop mum and dad at Satolas for their flight back to the UK, I swing past the cargo terminal to collect our luggage that has just arrived from Nigeria. A couple of weeks earlier, just before leaving Calabar, we had sent forward a couple of duffel bags stuffed with clothes, sheets and pillows plus a large green travel trunk filled with more valuable items and my lecture notes and research data. Véro had been given that trunk by *La Compagnie Française de Pétrole* as a going away present when we left London four years ago. The trunk has protected our more valuable items from dishonest customs officials in Lagos, leaf-burning burglars in Calabar and now, we hope, from the wear and tear of international travel. I knock at the door of the cargo office and introduce myself to the two officials, show my passport, copies of the bill of lading and the inventory, translated into French.

One of the officers takes me outside his office and into a warehouse and nods to my luggage sitting on a palette.

"*Prenez-les*", he tells me, "*au revoir.*"

I am so surprised at the rapidity of this transaction that I stand looking at him with my mouth open. This induces a roar of laughter and he asks me whether I would prefer that he searches through my baggage before I leave.

"Err, no, but since the baggage has come from Nigeria, I had assumed that you would want to check it."

"You mean to see if you are smuggling drugs or something? We, in Customs, know everything that is shipped out from Nigeria and we know that your baggage contains nothing more than what you have listed on the inventory. Goodbye sir."

In a couple of weeks, my sister and her family are due to arrive. My brother-in-law John, a professional electrician, and I have plans to wire much of the house and so there is a lot of work that I need to do to get things ready for his electrical skills. Chief among them is to cut channels in the walls for routing the cables to future plug sockets and also to run cables along the large ceiling beams so that they are hidden away but accessible. The first task simply requires a club hammer, a stone chisel and considerable elbow grease. The second is more difficult and requires me to remove the old, rotting poplar floorboards that form the ceiling of the first floor and the floor of the second floor, the attic. When the old boards are up, I need to run electric cables across the top of the large beams because there is a perfect gap between the smaller beams that run across the ceiling and rest at right angles on top of the supporting large beams. Changing floorboards no longer holds any mysteries for me as I had replaced the boards between the ground and first floors during our previous vacation.

Early the day after my parents caught their flight back to UK, I drive to the local do-it-yourself (*bricolage*) store in Les Avenières and purchase the fifty square metres of pine boards and the rest of the material I need to do the work and arrange for it all to be delivered the following day. Back in Cordon, Véronique places plastic sheeting over our bed and Mélanie's. She knows just how much dust is generated by pulling up these ancient boards. By 10 am, I start removing the old boards and, by the end of the day with a break to allow Mélanie to have her nap after lunch, I have managed to lever up all the old boards with a crowbar. These I throw out of our bedroom window down to the ground below and then move them by making numerous wheelbarrow trips to our little field that lies some seventy metres away from the house. While this last part might seem an enormous task, given that I have fifty square metres of board to move, it was not as time consuming as it might seem because the old boards are both large and long. Some measure at least half a metre across with many being three or more metres long.

My intention is to find the time to saw them into short lengths and use them in our (soon to be installed) wood burning stove; a pretty green *Mirus*. This means that we can even consider making winter visits and not be obliged to use only electric heaters.

During one of the wheelbarrow trips, Yvette asks if she might have some of the boards '*pour faire mes bocaux*'. She and her elderly father tend enormous vegetable gardens in which they grow massive amounts of vegetables, far more than their families can ever consume in a single year. Therefore, she either freezes the surplus in two massive chest freezers that provide a continuous hum in Thérèse's cellar or she bottles it in sealed jars (*bocaux*) that are stored in their cellar. Since I have never seen the bottling process, I give her all the boards that have snapped to shorter lengths and asks that she let me see her do the cooking.

"*Encore mieux, tu peux nous aider ce soir*", she replies. So, once I have swept up all the bits of wood and rubble, passed our old hoover to get rid of the remaining dust, and taken a quick shower, I find myself seated at a long table placed in the courtyard between our two houses. Together at the table with me are Yvette, Thérèse, le Pépé Parcouret and Lili, and we are faced with a gigantic pile of green beans and an even larger one of a vegetable that resembles white celery. Yvette informs me that this is *blette,* or chard in English.

Lili's son makes an appearance to say '*bonjour*'. He is a couple of years younger than me. Lili notices him too and says "*si tu ne vas pas nous aider, tu peux comme même nous servir à boire !*"

With our laughter ringing out, he goes off to the family wine cellar that lies below Thérèse's house and returns with a bottle of his homemade sparkling wine and pours, I have to admit, a generous glass for each of us. Véro and I have nicknamed this brew 'instant hangover' because we both experienced headaches not after drinking too much but actually while in the process of downing a single glass of the wine last year. This year the wine seems to have improved because I do not get an instant headache!

The first task in the bottling process is the preparation of the vegetables. Lili and I are told to get going on topping and tailing the beans while Yvette and Thérèse start to peel the chard and cut the lengths into bite-sized cubes. All the discarded parts of the beans and the chard are kept to feed Yvette's numerous and ginormous rabbits. Meanwhile, the Pépé Parcouret leaves his glass of wine on the table and walks down to a soot-blackened part of the stone wall in front of his house and begins to prepare a fire using a few screwed up pages of '*Le Progrès*', our local newspaper, and some broken pieces of my old floorboard. He soon has a fine blaze going thanks to some colourless liquid – I suspect petrol – that he squirts onto the wood which speeds up the burning process. From across the yard we can hear the old boards crackling and Lili informs me that this noise comes from the resident woodworm that are tonight being barbequed! Once the fire is well underway, I help the Pépé lift a large dustbin-like container onto two stone blocks standing either side of the fire and then, using his watering can, he pours in several litres of water.

As we rapidly get into the swing of topping and tailing the beans, Yvette loads them into 1 kg jars, adds salted water and closes the lids with a wire contraption that clicks an orange rubber seal tightly in place between the jar and its lid. I help her to carry the first batch of sealed jars to the dustbin, load them in and replace the lid that has a thermometer poking out the top. She tells me that as the dustbin heats up, the water inside the jars will boil and cook the beans. As water boils, it expands, and this is sufficient to force most of the air out through the seals. And once out, it cannot get back in; thus preserving the cooked vegetables inside. We then begin to prepare the next batch of vegetables for cooking and conserving.

Luckily, I am saved further vegetable peeling by Véro shouting "*à table*" out of the kitchen window to let me know that dinner is ready (and probably to save me from further work).

I say "*bonsoir, à demain*" to the neighbours and gratefully stop work for the day.

The following morning, we take a leisurely breakfast, in our small side garden, of fresh baguette, purchased from the little bakery in La Bruyère that resides in the old tram station building, and black coffee poured piping hot from the coffee percolator. Mélanie is sitting quite contentedly in her high chair merrily chewing on a piece of crusted bread and taking occasional swigs of milk from her baby cup. What an easy child, we feel that we must be the perfect parents.

At a little after 9, the delivery lorry arrives with my new floorboards, electric cable and the rest of my order. The driver and his assistant join us for, we assume, their second breakfast of the morning. In rural France people tend to be friendly and laid-back; which is just how we like people to be. After a cup of coffee with three sugars – workers in France cannot match the sugar consuming capacity of my old colleagues in Nigeria – and a '*tartine*' of butter and jam, the two men get busy unloading my purchases.

Quickly finishing, they say a cheery "*salut et à bientôt*" and get back into their van and drive off to make their next delivery, and possibly consume another breakfast!

The new floorboards are sitting on a pallet outside the house and the whole is wrapped in thick and transparent plastic; great because the weather is supposed to turn to rain sometime tomorrow. But better to be safe than sorry, I will try to bring everything inside today.

However, my first task is to follow John's instructions and run lengths of the two types of cable along the large beams. He will then tie them into connection boxes and run cables from the boxes to various lights, switches and plug sockets. I complete this simple electrical task in less than a couple of hours, allowing me to stop for a late-morning coffee and play for a moment with my little girl. Véro is in the kitchen cleaning the lettuce for the obligatory midday salad that in France always seems to precede the main dish. Today we are having grilled lamb chops (my favourite), tomatoes and a generous helping of French beans, the latter kindly donated by Pépé Parcouret in recompense for my efforts of the previous evening.

Before we sit down to eat, I have time to carry, on my shoulders, a dozen bundles of floorboards from the pallet outside, up the stairs and then up the ladder to the attic. Each bundle contains ten floorboards, each 2m30 long and six centimetres wide covering an area of close to 1.4 square metres per bundle; so I have around 36 bundles in total to bring up and to lay. After lunch, I manage to work quietly while our princess sleeps and get another fifteen bundles into the attic along with my saw bench, saw, tape measure, spirit level, favourite hammer and a '*chasse-clou*' plus a few kilos of small headed nails. All set. At 3pm the miss wakes up and so I am ready to go.

I knock quickly on Thérèse's door to apologise in advance for the noise, and begin to work.

Last year, when I laid the boards for the floor beneath, I learnt that the walls of the house are not straight and that the two sides and front and back are not exactly parallel to each other either; after all this is a house that was already showing on the 'Napoleonic' cadastre of 1830. The secret to make the result look good – and to save a lot of sweating later on – is to start nailing the first line of floorboards five centimetres or so out from the wall, and to ensure that they run in a perfect straight line. My progress seems pretty slow as the boards, only being six centimetres wide, do not cover much more of the floor as each line of board is added. I need seventeen lines of board just to move a metre out from the wall, so slow going balanced as I am on the beams with a glaring drop open beneath should I lose my grip on a hammer or nails. However, once a wide enough section of beams is covered for me to sit comfortably on, progress accelerates and, to cut a long story short, five days later I knock in the last nail and the floor is finished. We now have a fifty square metre attic, accessed for the moment by the old wooden ladder that proudly bears the initials of Véro's paternal grandfather.

The room is currently lit by the three *velux,* has a sound roof, that should need no further work for the next thirty years, and insulated by slabs of expanded polystyrene covered by plasterboard that are fitted between the main beams. At least the space is functional and we can use it for storage and as an emergency bedroom.

As it is Sunday morning, we plan a tour of two *marchés aux puces* or *vides greniers* (flea markets or car boot sales) that are being held in our area. These are always real opportunities to pick up interesting items, paintings and small pieces of furniture at really low prices. And when we feel that a seller is exaggerating with the opening price, there is no one more adept at haggling than me; after all we have just survived four years in Nigeria! The first flea market is in the little mountain town of Belley, a twenty kilometre drive away. We manage to purchase two pretty paintings of local beauty spots and a small wooden stool for our little girl to sit on. A total expenditure of twenty francs and no need to show our bargaining skills. We leave Belley and go via the backroads through the little village of Brens and into the even smaller village of Péyrieu.

Péyrieu is an interesting place. It was 'discovered' in the 1930s by a rich American who loved the wattle and daub architecture that he had seen in Alsace and so decided to decorate the outside of several houses in the village with strips of wood, imitating this architectural style. These can still be seen on the main road towards the village and on several houses within the village itself. The *marché aux puces* we are visiting today is scattered around the *Mairie*, and spreads from the parking bays in front of the council offices, down the lane, on to the football pitch and then around the tennis courts. As we look through the eclectic offerings of child's clothes, games and furniture with a smattering of antiques and quasi-antiques, I notice several English language paperback books sitting on a small table.

I whisper to Véro "ask the price for me because I do not want the lady selling the books to hear my English accent."

The seller replies *"cinq francs each, madam"* in an accent that is even more British than my own. I select four and hand over the twenty francs note and thank her in English.

"Ah, so you are English too?"

We introduce ourselves and say that we have just moved into the village of Cordon that sits three villages further down the road to which the lady replies "that's interesting, I know Brits in several villages around here."

"Oh, really", I reply, "so just like in India where every mountain has a tiger; here in France 'there's a Brit in every Village'?".

"Didn't Richard Dawkins write that about tigers?" she asks.

"That's quite possible", I reply with a laugh, "but the quote about the Brits is purely mine."

And it seems that my words are true almost everywhere. Our part of France, in the East, does not have wall-to-wall Brits like the Dordogne or the Normandy and Brittany coasts but there are a surprising number tucked away discretely in our beautiful region of the Bugey.

Our summer continues at a leisurely pace. We split our time between continuing to work on the house, relaxing, or seeing family and new friends. Our leisure time is often spent at the new lake that has been provided for the commune by the *Compagnie Nationale du Rhône* in exchange for the destruction of our tiny and muddy Lac de Pluvis. The new lake is at Glandieu. It is much bigger and has a proper beach of pebbles and sand and is split in two halves by a swimmers' barrier. The half with the beach is exclusively for swimmers and the other side is reserved for fishermen. The new lake has become incredibly popular with the young and not so young generations from all our neighbouring communities, especially as the summer days get hotter and hotter.

We do miss our little Lac de Pluvis that disappeared last year when the CNR dug a canal straight across a meander of the river Rhône and the poor lake got in the way of their construction work. However, where the canal re-enters the Rhône further downstream, the CNR have installed a hydroelectric plant. For this privilege, they are obliged to pay a rent to the commune and, thanks to this piece of green engineering, our local rates are kept artificially low for many years to come.

One day while the two of us are splashing in the water at Glandieu with Mélanie, a slim young lady with large sunglasses and a friendly smile comes over to say hello and introduces herself as Claudette. She tells us that she lives just across the road from us in the beautiful old house, standing in an enormous garden and tucked away towards a small forested hill. Claudette works with the mayor of our village, while her husband Gérard is a biology teacher at the state school in Belley. Gérard is *sauvage* (meaning insular or reserved not savage by the way!) and so tends to keep himself to himself. On learning that I am a university lecturer in biology, she tells us that we really should meet Gérard because of the biology connection, and also *Monsieur le Maire*, because he is also a lecturer but in geology, at the University of Grenoble.

We finally get to meet *Gérard-le-sauvage* in a most roundabout way. A few days after chatting with Claudette at the Glandieu lake, I am re-plastering a ground floor room and I suddenly hear our little girl give a squeal. I run over to her and see that she had been playing with an old house brick and had managed to drop it on her thumb nail. The nail turns blue as I cuddle her and her tears begin to dry. What to do? We had heard about a young doctor in the neighbouring village of St-Genix-sur-Guiers so we all jump into our old Renault-6 and head off to his house where he has his medical practice. Our ring of the doorbell brings a young woman to the door. This turns out to be madam Faure and, after explaining the issue, she sneaks us in to see her husband between two patients. Dr Faure, takes one look at Mélanie's thumb nail, lights a small alcohol lamp with a match and gets a paperclip (the French call them *'trombone'*, how cute is that?). He holds this in the flame until red and then quickly touches the nail where it has changed colour. A little blood squirts out but our girl makes no noise, simply looks at the doctor as he works. A quick swap with cotton wool soaked in alcohol and a sticking plaster in the shape of a butterfly, and all is ready to go. As Dominique – for that is what he tells us to call him – works on the thumb, he asks about us and Cordon life and whether we have yet met Gérard, our neighbour. When we say no, he replies that Gérard and Claudette are coming to eat with them the following evening and so we should come too. As simple as that we make new and what prove to be life-long friends with the Faure and the Dubiez. Gérard turns out to be a dab hand at bricolage and quickly turns into my *conseiller technique* (technical adviser) for all things DIY. He is also a keen fisherman and we are to spend many beautiful summer days fishing together for *fritures* (freshwater whitebait), usually wearing only swimming trunks and standing waist deep in the cool Rhône as it rushes from Switzerland, past Cordon and onwards south to the Camargue and then into the Mediterranean. During these occasions we get to know each other's likes and dislikes and the only arguments we ever have are either over England versus France rugby matches (*le Crunch*) or who should get to clean the keepnet full of tiny fish!

Summer begins to merge into autumn, the days begin to become noticeably shorter, the grapes are ripening on the vines, and Lili asks if I would like to try my hand at grape picking, joining a group of villagers and family – why not? He and his son have only a couple of thousand vines and so by the end of a lovely day in the field we have picked all the grapes into wooden buckets. These are emptied into larger containers on the trailer that is pulled by Lili's tractor. Of course, his son has volunteered to be the one who sits down all day on the tractor while the rest of us do the bending work. Most of us end up with blisters on various fingers from snipping the bunches of grapes with secateurs, and we all secretly wish that our tractor driver has at least a blister on his nether regions.

When the picking is complete, we return to our communal courtyard and it is time to tread the grapes. Now, I know at this stage there must be gathering images of sleek-legged maidens with flashing long hair dancing in the grape buckets. The reality is sadly rather different.

Lili walks over to Véro and me and says "show me your Wellington boots" and when he sees that they are relatively new and clean, orders "jump in the first bucket and begin squashing the grapes."

We climb on to the trailer and are both soon inside walking up and down on the grapes. Lili notices Mélanie holding on to Thérèse's hand and so picks her up and plonks her into the bucket with us. We are, all three, soon covered in grape juice while the level of grapes in the bucket has gone down by some fifty percent as we tread the grapes flat. When Lili is happy with our efforts, we move on to the next bucket being joined in neighbouring tubs by some of the other youngsters who have been picking with me.

When all the buckets have received the boot treatment, we carry them individually into Lili's barn, pass them up to two older men each standing at the top of a ladder and they tip the contents into the large, circular grape press. This is the first time that I have seen the design and the actual workings of a press up close. At the bottom of the press is an enormous square, flat stone with deep runnels cut into it. These lead the juice towards a wide lip where the juice runs off into plastic buckets positioned beneath. Above the stone are closely packed slats of oak wood forming a tightly packed ring and these stand over two metres high. Coming out of the centre of the slats is a thick, metal pole with thread running down as far as I can see and topped by a metal press with four metal handles sticking out of it.

As soon as the men tip the grapes from the first wooden bucket into the top of the press, grape juice begins to appear on the stone and follows the runnels into the waiting buckets. As they fill up, so we carry them to semi-transparent, plastic fermenting barrels that stand nearby. Progressively we hand the wooden buckets of trodden grapes to the waiting men and progressively the juice appears at the bottom. After the contents of the final bucket are tipped in, we hand up a pair of thick semi-circular wooden pieces and these the two men put either side of the metal pole and allow them to slide down the inside of the slatted circle. They come to rest on the packed, squashed grapes lower down the press.

Lili tells me that the job of the two villagers at the top of the ladders can be dangerous because the natural yeast on the skin of the grapes has already started to work and is creating considerable carbon dioxide down inside the press. Since carbon dioxide is denser than air, it remains inside the press and, on occasions, people have fallen inside and they must be pulled out quickly to prevent suffocation. My mind wanders to a book by Dennis Wheatley in which the hero manages to lure a villain into a grape press where the carbon dioxide did its work before the press made sure that the wine that year was extra red.

Talking of the press, once the two wooden semicircles are in place, the metal press at the top of the central pole is slowly wound down towards the grapes. When it reaches the wooden circle and begins to exert a modest pressure, juice starts to flow again and it continues flowing as the men at the top of the ladder turn the handles of the press. By now the fermenting barrels are full and our work is over.

Lili hands me a glass of a cloudy, sweet-smelling liquid and says "*goûtes, c'est du vin nouveau*" (taste it, we call the juice 'new wine').

I am surprised to see that the juice has no real colour and that the red grapes have not given a red juice.

"Ah", Lili tells me, "this juice will give us white wine. If we wish to have red wine, we must let the juice stay with the skins because it is not the juice that gives the wine its colour but the tannins and other natural chemicals in the grape skin." We learn something every day.

At 8 pm, Yvette and Thérèse poke their heads out of the window and shout together "*à table*".

We all troop into their dining room and find the long table surrounded with at least a dozen chairs, more than enough to seat all the helpers. The ladies bring us steaming bowls of onion soup – surprisingly, a first time for me – with hunks of bread covered in cheese floating on top. Absolutely delicious but rather hot.

My neighbour at the table was one of the men at the top of the ladder who had done some serious lifting this afternoon. He introduces himself as Jacques Feybesse and tells me that he lives in the second house on the right as one enters the village and that he loves the English as he has a daughter married to a Brit who lives in the UK. Jacques is a very tall, broad gentleman of around fifty with an enormous sense of humour that matches his gigantic handlebar moustache.

When I mention that the soup is rather hot, he tells our young host to fetch a good red wine, not his usual *piquette* and, with bottle in hand, he pours a generous dose into my soup and then into his. That does the trick and the soup is immediately at a much more suitable temperature to eat! The soup is followed by an incredibly tasty and large portion of home-grown chicken served with potatoes, beans and chard from Yvette's garden. An enormous platter of cheese is served next followed by a large pear tart that Thérèse has cooked using fruit picked from the Pépé's elderly trees. Finally, and of course strictly as a digestive aid, Lili places a litre bottle of *Marc de Bugey* on the table. Jacques explains to me that the *marc* (pronounced without the 'c') is obtained by distilling the fermented remains of the wine pressing process and then storing it in oak casks for up to thirty years.

Speaking of Jacques and his sense of humour, one day two of our oldest friends – Barbara and Gilbert – come from Lyon to visit us in Cordon. As this is their first time to our village, they consider it prudent to stop their car at the entrance of the village and enquire where we live. They spot Jacques standing by the side of the road. The conversation between Gilbert and Jacques goes rather like this:

Gilbert leans out of the window of his ancient Mercedes and asks "Excuse me, but can you tell us where the foreign couple live? They have just moved into the village."

Jacques (and do not forget that he is a very tall, imposing gentleman with an impressive Gallic moustache) steps around to the front of the car, looks down at the licence plate and says *"69, Rhône hein?* From where I'm standing you're the foreigners but if you mean Malcolm and Véro, they are in the courtyard behind the water fountain. Good day."

We are now getting towards the end of September and our summer in France has been close to perfect. However, one beautiful evening when Mélanie is asleep in her cot and we are drinking a glass of iced rosé wine, Véro gently says "you know sweetheart, we have to think about picking up the threads of our life again. Our time since leaving Nigeria has been close to perfect but I think we should go back to London and start rebuilding our life. Especially, you need to start looking for a new job."

A week later we get hugs and kisses from Mic and Belou at Satolas Airport and we are off on an Air France flight, direction Heathrow.

2

There's Work if you Care to Look

Six years ago, just before we got married in a beautiful summer ceremony in Crémieu, fortune had smiled and persistence paid off when we had been able to buy a small, one-bedroom apartment in London in the up and coming area of de Beauvoir Town, just off the Balls Pond Road in Dalston but still in the prized N1 postcode area. Although this ground floor apartment in Culford Road had only cost ten thousand pounds, we initially had serious problems with obtaining our tiny mortgage from the Halifax because of my status as a postgraduate student at London University and Véro's as a junior receptionist for the oil company, Total Oil Marine. After two years of scrimping and scraping to save up a significant deposit, the local branch had laughed us out the door and told me to come back 'when you have a proper job'. That response from a spitting image of Dick Dastardly had both embarrassed me and got my goat sufficiently aroused that I wrote to the Chief General Manager of the Halifax about the incident. To his credit, he quickly wrote back with an apology and the telephone number of the manager of a central London branch. After an interview of an hour over tea and chocolate biscuits, we were offered a mortgage, and the rest is history. We moved into our beautiful little apartment the day after we returned from our wedding in France.

Now we are back in London after four years in Nigeria. Our family has grown from two to three and we have the additional luck that the tenants in our apartment moved out just the previous week, allowing us to move straight in, rediscovering our old furniture. We quickly settle into the familiar territory of Dalston except that our upstairs neighbour, Vanessa, has sold up and moved to Gozo (well, why not?). She has been replaced by a couple even younger than us. John is a handsome guy with the most carroty hair that I have ever seen. He is a journalist for a motorbike magazine and each evening he seems to come home on larger and yet larger motorbikes. We broke the friendship ice when one of his bikes toppled over and he needed extra muscle to help to stand it up again. If my memory serves me correctly it was a beautiful BMW 1000 (or something like that), and wretchedly heavy that we struggled to lift upright.

A couple of days after settling back into Culford Road, I make a strange trip to the Biology Department of Queen Mary College to have a chat with my former PhD supervisor. I arrive at coffee time and so accompany him and my old buddy Richard (now Dr as he passed his PhD during my time in Nigeria) to the third floor departmental tearoom. There, I meet up with the two prominent professors who had helped me so much during my research years and, especially, following my infamous PhD viva exam in a Mile End transport café. This most unusual spot for an external exam had been brought about by an IRA bomb scare back in 1979 that had driven us out of the university buildings.

Most of my old PhD student friends have gone off to other jobs but many of my old lecturers are still at QMC including dear Peter Wanstall, who had helped to build my love of ecology as an undergraduate and then had recommended Nigeria to me. I also found Andy, my erstwhile squash partner and stamp collecting friend, Bryn, the animal ecologist, and several others who had made my undergraduate studies so interesting and had then become firm friends during my postgraduate years.

Question after question follow from everyone who walks through the door about my time in Nigeria and an equal number of queries about what I plan to do next. When I mention that I am looking for a job, my old supervisor immediately reiterates his offer that I can help out during his practical classes and this brings other offers from lecturers in the botany and ecology fields. Before I leave the tearoom that morning, I manage to pick up work for three afternoons per week. A reasonable start.

My next port of call is the college library but, of course, no longer being registered at QMC, I cannot gain access through the automatic barriers. Luckily, I am recognised by a senior librarian who has recently married one of my old student friends and she kindly slips me into the basement of the library where I can collect the information I need. An hour or so later, I emerge with a list of every college in London (there are, surprisingly, rather a lot) together with their postal addresses and the names of the head of each biology department. My chore during the following week is to type out and post letters to each head, offering my services either as a lecturer or a 'demonstrator' (a lecturer's assistant during practical classes). I do not expect too much in the way of response to my mailing but I prefer to play the numbers' game.

The third thing I do is to sign up to local, private tuition agencies. There are several listed in the adverts' section of the local Hackney and Islington newspapers and, within two days, have three sessions with A- and O-level students in place. One student lives in

Hampstead and shares my surname, one in Islington turns out to have a dad who is a Tory MP and a party whip, and one lives near to Highbury Corner roundabout. Without personal transport, it is difficult to fit in my afternoons at QMC and the tuition hours that I have to accept either in the evenings or at the weekends. The government can say what it likes about the quality of public transport in London but I can assure them that while their chauffeur-driven cars may be highly efficient for taxiing them around central London, taking buses and tubes to the outer reaches of London most certainly is not … but beggars cannot be choosers and I find that Shank's Pony is often the best means of transport if I want to arrive on time.

However, luck soon smiles in two very different ways. First, my sister Sandra invites us over for Sunday lunch at their home on Harrow Road and, during the meal, her husband, John, asks if we would like to borrow their little camping car until we save some cash to buy a small run-around. Perfect. The second is that the following day I receive a letter from the West London campus at Whitelands of the University of Surrey asking me to attend an interview for a potential demonstrator's position in biology. After a quick phone call, I set an appointment for the following day and go across London to meet their ecology lecturer. Surprisingly, he turns out to be as young as me and new in his job. He admits that I am better qualified in ecology than he due to my four years of teaching experience in Nigeria and multiple scientific publications – now numbering ten – but I reply that it is he who has the lecturer's job! Being concerned that I may lose this opportunity by being 'over-qualified' (what a stupid term when one is desperate for work) and a threat to him, I say that I see this opportunity as short term and I offer to work on a term-by-term basis if that is more suitable for the university. I get the job.

Anyone having only a fair inkling of the geography of London will now be realising that I have managed to find work in East,

West and North London; and London is a big place to get around quickly. With all my work contracts signed and sealed, I sit down to work out how I can be in the right place at the right time, and this throws up an issue. On one of the afternoons, in order to meet my engagements, I need to get from Whitelands College in the West of London to Hampstead in the North using first British Rail, then the tube and finally a bus; and the timetables will just not allow it. Step up Véro. She comes to meet me at the exit to the train station and drives me to the bus stop, cutting out a couple of changes on the tube. Only then can I arrive on time to provide some private tuition in chemistry to an O-level pupil. We are young and not over-worried by such events although the situation of running around London does last for more than six months and my income barely covers our needs.

However, one morning I am flicking through the Times Education Supplement and see an advert for a temporary lecturer in biology and microbiology at South London College. I apply, am invited for interview, and get the job. My interview is with the head of the college in Tooley Street, in the shadow of Tower Bridge and screaming distance from the London Dungeons. All passes well and I am offered a minimum six-month contract. My new role is to replace a sick lecturer and to teach HND-level biology and micro-biology to dental technicians. (I now understand why there are literally hundreds of plaster casts of upper and lower jaws complete with teeth dotted around the college!). While this work is a step down from university work, it does pay a relatively attractive salary, provides our income with a modicum of stability and means that I can stop running backwards and forwards across London. I decide, however, to keep all my tuition classes and to block them into an extended Saturday morning. They provide us with a bit of extra pocket money.

I arrive early in the classroom for my first lecture at the college. I am to teach a group of thirty dental technicians in introductory microbiology; a relatively simple start. As I unpack the lecture notes from my briefcase, a young lady of perhaps 19 or 20 comes into the classroom, says hello and sits down on the front bench. After replying to her greeting, I tell her that she must come from Benin City in Nigeria.

Her mouth drops open and she asks "how do you know that sir?"

I explain that I have just spent four years in Nigeria and recognise her facial physiognomy and accent. That little stroke of 'luck' is to prove important for my future teaching in this inner London college. Next to arrive are a couple of young ladies who go into a whispered huddle with the Nigerian student. As they giggle together, a group of young men with accents that suggest Mediterranean origins (Greek and Italian, I learn) come in and play the macho card so typical of young men in this age group. Finally, my class is complete and I am delighted to see such a racial and ethnic mix: African, Mediterranean, western and southern Asians and even a few real Cockney Londoners.

After introducing myself and explaining that I will be seeing them through to their exams at the end of the following term, we settle down to work; or at least try. An Adonis-headed young man, hailing from Cyprus via Turnpike Lane and head of the macho group, decides to claim some tough guy points with the group of girls.

He stands up and calls out to me "I bet you will be as useless as the old fart you are replacing."

While Adonis sees the look of shock on my face, what he does not see is the open palm of the lady from Benin City that slaps him soundly around the ears.

"You leave doctor alone, he is a nice person and far better looking than you."

I allow Adonis to receive a few moments of gentle ribbing from the rest of the machos and then take my preferred stance, or rather seat, which is atop the laboratory bench that acts as my desk, facing the class. I begin to talk about microbiology and the different fungi, bacteria and viruses that we will be studying and the class settles down and sits and listens to me.

The hour-long session is over before I really get started but I know the ice is broken because as the students leave the room, Adonis comes across and apologises to me.

"You're OK sir and not at all like the old fart." Praise indeed!

My next class is a small group of final year HND biology students. I walk into their room and they fall silent and open their notepads with biros poised. After quick introductions, I explain that today's lecture is to cover floral biology, and I start to explain. After talking for several minutes, I note that their pens are still poised over notepads but not a word has been written by anyone in the class; odd. I ask if they have perhaps already covered the topic in previous classes and am assured that they have not so I suggest that they might like to start taking notes and at the end of the lecture we can use a few moments to discuss any issues.

Hands start to write as I speak, explain and provide examples and draw illustrations on the board. As always happens in front of a class, time runs out quickly and I note that we only have five minutes left. I stop and ask if they have any questions about the topic so far. The remaining few moments are taken up with a questions and answers session until the bell rings to tell us to go on to our next classes.

As I pick up my briefcase, the ten students in my class begin to applaud. A second shock on my first day at the college. My quizzical look brings a laugh from a young lady at the front.

She provides an explanation: "the lecturer you're replacing has been teaching us for over a year and never, ever talks to us. He has reels of overhead projector film that he slowly turns in the machine and we copy and copy and get bored. Today is the first time that anything has been explained to us, and we really enjoyed it." She turns to her classmates and receives nods in response.

"But what does the lecturer do while you are copying? He must be bored too," I reply.

"He reads and makes notes on horse racing newspapers. He enjoys a flutter." The class all join her in laughing out loud. I do not like what I am hearing on this first day at work.

My six months as the replacement at South London go far too quickly and I am told by the Head of College that the old lecturer is almost recovered and so my contract is nearing its close. Just before I finish up my stint at the college, I am having a coffee with Jim, the sociology lecturer, and we are talking about the 'class divide' in the UK.

He looks straight at me and says "of course you are most definitely middle class while I am working class."

Not that I care too much what category I am put in but I do want to fish around for his logic and so I say "but Jim, you know very well that we have exactly the same lecturer position, similar qualifications, similar salaries. My dad worked in a quarry breaking stones and then as a labourer in a paper mill and I grew up in a council house. If that isn't a working-class background, I don't see what is."

His reply is to tap the side of his head with his finger and say "class is not about background or riches; it is what you feel in here. Now tell me that you are not striving to become more affluent." I have to agree that he is right and he adds with a grin "so you are actively seeking to leave the working classes behind."

Thus I now know – to the very minute – when I apparently graduated to the middle classes. What a foolish country remains Great Britain with its emphasis on the class divide.

As a final note on my short but enjoyable time at South London College, one nice memory that I carry with me is the success of my small, final year HND biology class. They all did well, better than they had individually hoped and, one among them, the young lady who had explained to me about their boredom with the previous lecturer, went on to get excellent results. When she told me that she had not bothered to apply to any universities because she never imagined that she would get high enough results to obtain entry to read biology, I made a quick call to the professor responsible for admissions to biology at QMC, he called her for interview during Clearing, she obtained a place and eventually an excellent honours degree.

We try to get back to France as often as possible but the flights offered by Air France and British Airways are horribly expensive and so only allow a single trip a year, during the summer holidays. Also, because of my different part-time jobs, I receive no pay throughout vacation time but still have to pay all the bills on our London flat and a few on the Cordon house too, so funds are tight. We realise that we need to find another source of income ... and where there's a will there's most certainly a way.

Véro finds the way, thanks to new friends we have made called Anne and John. They live in a large house just over the road from the famous Arsenal Football Club. Véro's new money-making scheme is to buy cheaply small items of 'junk' from a house clearer that owns a damp-ridden shop just down the road from our new friends. She has been snapping up attractive, typically English vintage and antique items such as teapots, milk jugs, teacups, silver-plated Victoriana, bone-handled knives, old cameras, and the list goes on; never paying more than two bob (ten pence) each. Initially, she started buying these items for us but she soon amasses an excess, and these we decide to take to France and try our luck at selling them in the flea markets of Crémieu and Morestel that are held each summer. I add in packets of stamps that are excess to my collection and price 100 different at ten francs. Any trip we now make to our home in Cordon sees our suitcases packed with our 'antiques' carefully wrapped in clothes. Our first foray as 'antique dealers' is at the 14th July flea market in Crémieu – and we clear enough on that single day to pay for our three return flights. The next is at Morestel for the 15 *août* and, even with our now reduced stock, we still manage to make almost three thousand francs. We both love selling in the flea markets and we always make a joke to browsing people about us selling genuine English antiques with accent and all.

One hilarious incident that occurs is when a couple of British tourists approach our stall and start to handle and appreciate pieces of ceramic that they could so easily have bought back in the UK.

The wife picks up an old 'Mason's teapot' that we have priced at an excellent mark up and says to her husband "don't you think that this would make a lovely present for my mum's 60th birthday?"

Her husband looks at the price ticket and says "yes it is very pretty but I will bargain down the price." His wife looks sideways at us while she shushes her husband. Meanwhile, we smile and look and behave as though we do not understand a word of English. "Yes, but I am going to try to get the price down by 50%, just watch me deal with these froggies. That will make a cheap present for your mum."

I nudge Véro under the table and she squeezes my hand in response before I say in English to Véro, "you know, I would be so embarrassed to want to bargain for a beautiful object like that if I was going to give it as a birthday present to your mum!" and we both roar with laughter.

The poor lady goes bright red and says to her equally blushing husband "I told you that one day we would find French people who speak English as well as we do, now get your wallet out and pay these nice people the ticket price on the teapot."

The husband pulls out his wallet and reels off ten fifty francs notes and hands them over, with his face still shining bright red in embarrassment.

I hand him back fifty francs and say "that is a discount for giving us such a good laugh. Have a lovely vacation."

Buying in the UK, mostly at car boot sales, for selling at flea markets in France becomes a source of fun and extra cash that we do for many future years. As soon as Mélanie is old enough to make the rounds of car boot sales early on Sunday mornings she comes with me to help buy stock. Several years later, she takes over the 'business' when she is old enough to add up and bargain her prices, just like a seasoned trader.

Back in the UK we see a lot of Anne and John. Anne is French and comes originally from the Beaujolais region, just north of Lyon. John is of Irish origin, has the most pronounced Cockney twang when he speaks French (even I can criticise him!) and calls his wife 'Cherry Pie' so badly does he pronounce *chérie*. By coincidence, he has a Master's degree in economics from Queen Mary College and we must have overlapped there while I was completing my PhD; but we never knowingly met. John is the most single-minded person that I have ever known and currently is focused on nothing else but the London Stock Exchange. And I mean nothing, if one excludes smoking a very stinky pipe and sharing bottles of red wine with me. We get on very well indeed and spend many Sunday lunches and afternoons together. The ladies talk about lady subjects, Mélanie plays with their daughter Chloe, and John and I talk companies on the stock market, especially small caps (companies with low market values).

John is voluntarily unemployed and the couple live on the dole, receiving vouchers for almost everything, including the laundrette and cinema tickets. Luckily they live in an apartment owned by John's parents and so save on rent but this situation is a great source of embarrassment to Anne who comes from a very bourgeois background in France. She confesses to Véro that she has tried everything to get John to look for work but he insists that he will only work on the stock market. I try from my side because South London College is crying out for maths teachers but receive the same response as Anne. However, what John does do is to show me a series of economic analyses of small companies trading on the London stock market. Knowing so little about the economic side of company accounts, I cannot say whether his analyses are good or bad but they do look impressive to an untrained eye. He also shows me his *curriculum vitae*; a very threadbare document that finished four years previously with the award of his master's, then nothing because he has done nothing.

I state in a friendly tone of voice "that will be an issue for any future employment, John. You really must do something to begin catching up for lost time. Are you sure that the maths job is not of interest; the pay is not bad either?"

"Err, Malcolm" and he puffs on his pipe sending an acrid cloud into the air, "no ta, because my next job is going to be on the stock market, you know that." He takes a sip of red wine and then continues "next week I'm sending off a couple of my company analyses along with my CV and covering letter to a few City companies and I expect that one will offer me a job."

Well, he did and they did. Of the investment companies that received his package, several called him to interview and one gave him a job offer. He is about to start work as a small companies' stock analyst for a private client firm and his starting pay is impressive. The stubborn bugger! I am so happy for him.

Sunday afternoon exchanges with John, over glasses of red wine, lay the foundations (as well as building a considerable part of the walls) for my own nascent interest in the stock market. I have never been anywhere near as successful as him but certainly by following his advice on the companies I research does now enable us to rely less on selling at flea markets and more on the stock market for our future air tickets.

During my contract at South London, I am never under any illusion that the position is anything other than temporary and this pushes me to continue going after any suitable vacancies – which are few and far between.

I apply for a lectureship at a university in southern England that requires a lecturer in weed ecology with sound and practical experience of West Africa and with the additional requirement to be fluent in French. I simply cannot imagine that many people will be better suited than me, and I say this here with due modesty. After all, I have just spent four years at the University of Calabar as the senior ecology lecturer and director of the botanical gardens, I have published ten papers in aspects of weed ecology in distinguished, peer-reviewed journals and can now speak and write French at a pretty passable level. Can there be an enormous amount of competition?

I write my application, taking great care with the details, and send it off. I wait and wait but receive absolutely zero response. I am hoping for at least an interview ... but nothing, not even an acknowledgement. Being both curious and a little annoyed, I ring the university and ask to speak to the secretary of the head of the biology department; always the person who knows the most about departmental affairs. She informs me that the post has been awarded to an internal candidate, indeed to someone I know quite well from the rounds of ecology symposia that I attend each year. I lost to a nice chap who had just completed his PhD at the university and, as the secretary let slip, has never visited West Africa, has no teaching experience, does not speak a word of French and has only a couple of publications from his England-based PhD research. I may have encountered corruption in Nigeria but, make no mistake, it is alive and kicking at this time in the UK too.

Among other interesting position I try for are with the British Council (I fall at the final hurdle tripping completely over my nerves) and at The United World Colleges for a post in Trieste and lose out to an internal candidate.

I am told with honesty by the head of the college that "we eventually decided to go for 'the Devil we know'."

Decision time then as the summer term and my contract in Tooley Street is almost over. Véro and I sit down to talk over options, made more urgent because we really would like to add another baby to our family and our Culford Road flat is too small to accommodate an extra child. So we need to move. And moving means a bigger mortgage and that in turn requires a permanent position.

I gently say to Véro "I think I may need to look for a teaching job at a private school – not having a teaching diploma means that I cannot apply in the state system."

Véro looks at me and her face crumbles and tears start to roll down her cheeks. While my wife is a very gentle and caring lady, she is also a pretty tough character and rarely lets her emotions slip. Seeing her cry openly is highly unusual but after a few more sobs and a nose blow, she retakes control and explains. "I am so, so sad for you, *mon chéri*. It's not fair, after all the studying you did."

But fair or not, I need to get a permanent job and we left Nigeria almost two years ago, so time is passing rapidly.

I start to scan private school ads in the Times Education Supplement each Friday and find one in a private school in South London that needs a biology teacher and notice another similar position in the town of Northampton. Here I must hold my head in shame and admit that I think, at this time, that Northampton must be near to Sunderland and Newcastle, perhaps a little closer to Scotland. While the advert registers in my subconscious mind, my conscious mind rejects it with no further thought. Coincidentally, on the same day that the adverts appear, we are off to spend the weekend with old friends from Nigeria days, the Ward-Best. Mike used to work for a plastic pipe-making business in Calabar and left to become the head of the Crown Agents in London. His home is close to the Lake District – now I know *that* is in the North-West of England – and he will drive us there and back.

On Friday afternoon at 3 pm, Mike draws up in his car, we load in our bag and Mélanie's pushchair, and off we go towards the M1 motorway. At 4.10 pm I see a sign at Junction 15 that indicates 'Northampton'.

"Hey Mike, is Northampton really so close to London?" I ask.

"Yes, it is about 60 miles away," explains Mike, "as you can see, about an hour from your place."

After passing a great weekend with this nice couple, we arrive back in London at around 7 pm on Sunday evening. I sit down and write an application for the teacher's job in Northampton and get it in the post that night. Tuesday morning my phone rings and I am told that the Headmistress from the school in Northampton would like to speak with me. A gruff and commanding voice comes on the line and I am instructed to attend for interview in the early after-noon the following day. The next morning, I catch the direct train from Euston to Northampton, leaving myself plenty of time for de-lays, and arrive in Northampton just after 11 am. The address refers simply to a street in the town and, once I walk out of the train station and cross the railway bridge heading into town, I ask an elderly lady if she could kindly direct me to the school. Her response is amusing as it is totally composed of shop, bank and finally theatre names – no attempt to guide me with lefts and rights or street names.

"Walk past Brierley's, keep going until you pass Lloyds Bank, continue past the Derngate Theatre and you will find the school, near to the end of the road."

My first impressions of Northampton remind me of my home-town of Maidstone in Kent; not flashy or rich but solid working class and relatively quiet and clean. Although I am very early for the interview, I make my way towards the school as I want to scout out its location before going for some lunch. After walking up a steep hill from the station, I begin to pass the town square, marvelling at its lovely cobbled surface which, unbeknown to me at this time, is soon to be destroyed by a foolish local council in favour of modern paving blocks.

Today is market day and there are a large number of stalls selling fruit and veg, meat, and clothes plus a whole corner occupied with 'almost' antiques, books and various items of 'junk'. On the side of the market square is an estate agents and, out of curiosity, I wander over to get an idea of house prices in the town and nearby villages. I stare in amazement at the houses on offer. They are not luxurious but solid and standard two- and three-bedroom terrace properties, near to the town centre, start at around ten thousand pounds; un-believable, even for 1985. Our little apartment in Culford Road is now valued at slightly over forty thousand pounds and if, I know a very big if, we decide to move to Northampton, we would probably not need to sell the London flat to buy here.

After a quick and non-alcoholic lunch, I arrive at the school door and ring the bell of this cute Georgian house. I am ushered in by a lady wearing a housecoat who sees my eyes looking around the interior of the extensive entrance hall.

"Do you appreciate antiques, sir?" she asks as I cannot help looking at the various and beautiful art deco items. "Do you know of Charles Rennie Mackintosh? He lived in a house that the school owns just next door and some of these items came from there. But best I not keep you as the Headmistress awaits" she says this with a smile and an upward flick of her eyes. Ominous!

The Headmistress turns out to be a short, slightly stout lady probably in her late-50s, I would guess. I am greeted politely and she asks me about my past work in Nigeria and in London. After more of a chat than an interview, a slight gentleman with thinning hair and a lovely Welsh accent comes into the office and greets me as Malcolm and introduces himself as the Head of Biology and of Science. The Headmistress hands me over to him and off we go for a tour of the school. We head through the gardens, down a short flight of steps and towards a newish building that I am told is the Science Department, of which he is also the head. All around are well-behaved young ladies of various ages from eleven upwards who are obviously in the process of changing classes. All are wearing a uniform comprised of a form of tweed skirt in light and dark blue and black with a light blue blouse. I confess to appreciating the UK idea of school uniforms rather than the French system of anything goes.

As girls pass, they all say "hello sir" to the head of science and then turning to me, repeat, "hello sir." Gosh, so polite after South London College!

Biology is on the top floor of three and I am taken into a class of second year A-level girls who are studying the functions of the kidney. The head of science asks them if they have any questions to ask me (meaning about the kidney).

"Sir, did you enjoy Nigeria. Was it hard to live there." And once the questions start about Nigeria, there is no way these eighteen-year old girls are going to ask about boring nephrons and tedious renal arteries!

After fifteen minutes of chatting, the head of science tells me "clearly the girls took to you. They were hoping to have a handsome young man coming to the school! Now let's see if you can charm this lot."

We enter another room and are met by the school's second biology teacher. She comes straight over from the blackboard to greet me. Her class is composed of some twenty-odd little ones, 11 or 12-year olds, I assume. They are currently trying to make mushroom traces by placing large field mushrooms down on white paper and waiting for the spores to fall on to the paper. The head of science tells me that he needs to talk with his colleague in the prep room next door and could I handle the class for ten minutes or so. Why not?

I start off by asking the girls if they could describe what they are doing and twenty-odd hands go up in the air and there is a whispered *sifflement* of "sir, sir." After getting two or three good replies, I ask if they know how the spores get off the gills, and they logically tell me that they must simply fall off due to gravity. But no, they do not just fall off, they are actually fired off by miniscule popping water droplets and so are called balistospores. I do a simple diagram on the chalk board to show them. Well, the young ladies' imaginations run wild on hearing that ballistics was invented by a mushroom and they sit almost spellbound in their seats. At this point, their two teachers re-enter the room and one of the girls begins to explain to her teacher how the spores get off the gills.

She gives me a big smile and tells the girls "we are trying to get Dr Marks to come and teach here. I am sure he has many interesting items to share with you."

As the head of science and I make our way down the stairs and continue the tour of the school, heading towards the staffroom to the east of the old Georgian building, he says to me "you did that very well with the little ones. I can tell you now that we have another candidate that has a lot of experience with the younger age groups and we were concerned about your lack of experience at that level. However, both of us agree that you handled that class very well and, off the record, we are recommending you to the Headmistress."

The next day, I receive a telephone call from the Headmistress offering me the post with the job to start in early September.

I tell her "I am delighted, thank you, but would you please give me a few minutes to confer with my wife and then I will call you back, say in ten minutes?"

I am later to learn that apparently, the Headmistress was flabbergasted by my need to talk the job offer over with my wife and her shock and horror rapidly did the gossip rounds of the school with everyone concluding that I would be in her bad books from day one!

No matter, after a chat with Véro we decide to accept, and so next stop for us will be Northampton. There is even an apartment in the Rennie Mackintosh House for us to occupy until we find other accommodation in the town. But we will not be moving to the Midlands until after our summer vacation in France.

We head off to Heathrow, catch our flight to Satolas and are met by Véro's mum, Mic, just after we pass through customs. A couple of days in Crémieu and then we head towards Cordon via our Uncle

André where our car awaits us outside his garage, battery charged, tank filled with petrol and ready to go. The summer passes quickly as we continue to work on the house, and see what our lovely builders, the Francos, have achieved during our absence. This includes opening windows on the west side of the house. They were sufficiently caring to have recovered windows and the supporting oak beams during the demolition of an old barn on the Isère side of the Rhône. They kept them for us and have now installed them in our house. Apart from a few broken panes that I quickly replace, the windows look like they have always been there. A second positive is that they hand us back the equivalent of £200 telling us that the work was easier and quicker than they had originally estimated. How many builders do you know who are that honest? The only negative to the work is that they leave me two enormous piles of stones in the garden that were taken out of the wall to make room for the windows. I spend several days building a dry stone wall around our little garden as a protection for the septic tank against marauding tractors.

We manage to set up stall in three flea markets: Morestel and Crémieu, like last year, and in Les Abrèts on what must have been the hottest day of the summer. Nonetheless, we make a reasonable number of sales over the three days and manage again to cover the cost of our air tickets and with a bit left over. Our summer holidays are quickly over and we return to UK for the next chapter in our lives.

3

Of Saints and Cobblers

We arrive back in Culford Road in mid-August and begin the process of packing and renting out our apartment, ready for the start of the new school year in early September. Before leaving for Northampton, the three of us make a weekend trip to see my parents in Coxheath and, while there, my dad proudly shows me his new car.

"Malc, would you like my old Ford Classic? It still runs very well."

Well, of course we would and this allows us to hand the camper van back to my brother-in-law. While I have been grateful for the loan, it has always been a nightmare to park in London.

We take a pre-term trip to Northampton. The school's accountant, hands us the keys to the little apartment at the very top of the Rennie Mackintosh House which we will occupy until we can buy a small house in the town. We are to be neighbours of a new English teacher of indeterminate age. She takes an immediate shine to Mélanie, who is now just over three years old and still a little sweetheart. Since the apartment is furnished, we do not need to move much furniture out of Culford Road and so can let our little apartment furnished, at a higher rent.

We start visiting houses with estate agents in Northampton, to get an idea of the type of houses that are within the budget of a schoolteacher and find that similar three-bedroom terrace houses to those I had seen on the day of my interview in June have now risen to around fifteen thousand; that makes an approximate fifty percent jump in less than four months. We will have to move fast to catch this market and so I chat through possibilities with the estate agent who has his office near to the town square and clarify that we are soon moving to the town with a job as a teacher.

He explains that as first-time buyers – I quickly forget to mention our London apartment with a small mortgage – we can easily get a loan through the Bradford and Bingley especially if we take an endowment policy that can be provided through the agency's financial advisor. We next meet the aforementioned F.A. in his first-floor office near to the magnificent Lloyds Bank building. He explains at great length the way that the proposed mortgage will work. It is to be an interest only mortgage so the monthly repayments will be lower than a traditional repayment mortgage where an amount of capital is also repaid each month. The principal of the loan is only repayable at the end of the 25-year term and the repayment will be made from a parallel endowment insurance policy. This policy is to be taken out with an assurance company. The financial advisor draws two graphs with a twenty-five-year timescale. The first shows the repayment of a traditional mortgage and the second shows the effect of having the endowment policy. The second graph illustrates that at the end of the mortgage term we will end up with an excess amount, after repaying the capital, predicted to be up to thirty thousand pounds. Well, we would be fools not to go with the endowment policy, wouldn't we?

We find a little three-bedroom house at the bottom of Edith Street for just under sixteen thousand pounds and get a ninety-five percent mortgage from the B&B and an endowment policy from the assurance company. The rental of our London apartment not only covers its own mortgage and that of Edith Street but leaves us around a hundred pounds per month surplus.

(But first, fast forward to the end of our mortgage term in 2010 and the famous endowment policy from the assurance company. It did not return us the promised thirty thousand pounds excess; it did not even return us an extra thirty pounds. After all those years of payment, it effectively returned us the same amount of money that we had paid in during all those years – only around ten thousand pounds. There was absolutely no excess and so in reality, given several intervening years of mammoth inflation, the money we had contributed over twenty-five years had lost a considerable portion of its real value. This type of scam investment, for a scam it was and only people like our financial advisor and the assurance company made a profit, was eventually heavily punished by the UK Government. Endowment policy issuers were forced to compensate people like us that had been led astray by so-called financial advisors. When I challenged the assurance company for compensation, I was told that the compensation scheme only functioned for policies taken out after 1987 – we had signed up two years too early to benefit and so were fobbed off and received nothing.

To add insult to injury, when I wanted to cash in my matured policy after twenty-five years of contributions, I was forced to go through a foolish telephone interview with another so-called financial advisor from the assurance company. This lady had the audacity to ask me if I would not prefer that the assurance company continue to look after my investment for me. During that phone call, and the receipt of this final insult, I was looking at the graphs that the financial advisor had drawn for me, all those years before, and the lady received my response in a long line of expletives!)

A few days before we are to move to Northampton, Véro says to me with a big smile on her face "you remember that I told you yesterday that my period is rather late? I decided to stop at the pharmacy and get a pregnancy test kit. Shall we go and check the result?"

And, what joy, we are to be parents again and our new baby will be a Cordon baby, 'put in place' during our recent summer vacation and awaited, with a little impatience, for next April 1986. What a delight for us and also for Mélanie who is finally to become a big sister, and what lovely news to be taking with us to Northampton.

The weekend before the new term and academic year starts at the school, John, my brother-in-law arrives at Culford Road with his work's van and we load in suitcases, cooking equipment and as much furniture as we can honestly take while still leaving a furnished rental in place. Our 'infamous' travel trunk is stowed in the boot of my sky-blue Ford Classic. We drive in convoy on to the North Circular and around to the M1 entrance. Our luck is in as the M1 is not its usual parking lot, and we arrive in Northampton a little more than an hour after leaving Culford Road.

Once installed in our new apartment and John has taken his leave, we hear a knock on our door and find the new English teacher with a small gift of welcome for us. She espies Mélanie and immediately starts to play with her while Véro and I get started on unpacking. Mélanie being a highly talkative young lady provides our neighbour with a potted history of the Marks family including the news that she is going to be a Big Sister.

After my new colleague leaves our flat, we decide to explore the Mackintosh House that is to be our home for the next few months. Our first surprise is our bathroom – which is outside our apartment and down a flight of stairs; shades of Tabley Road, we laugh.

Our first home together was a rented apartment in Tabley Road, in the shadow of Holloway Ladies' (*sic*) Prison. We lived there for our first two years together, before we saved up a sufficiently large deposit to buy our Culford Road *bijou*. Just as now, our bathroom in Holloway was on the floor below our flat but then was shared with numerous other occupants of the house, including a Guinness-loving gentleman with a terrible aim!

The Mackintosh bathroom is altogether different with a stunning art deco design. The walls are tiled in miniscule orange and black tiles and the bath is served by *errr* three taps. The usual hot and cold, of course, but with a third that is for rainwater stored in a rain-capture tank up in the attic. Apparently rainwater was considered in the 1920s and 30s as excellent for hair washing although I have to wonder if this was before scientists discovered the existence of acid rain or the damage that lead pipes can cause to the nervous system.

I arrive early on the first day of term. This is rather easy since I now live only two doors down from the school entrance. I walk up the stairs to the staff room and join the six other men who occupy, on block, the rear of the room that is otherwise full of ladies of all ages and appearances. The Head of Science, and biology colleague, who had interviewed me a few months previously introduces me to the Head of French, the Head of Art, the Head of Physics, a Chemistry teacher, and the school accountant. I cannot believe the hum of voices that fill the room nor of the clouds of cigarette smoke that blanket the air from numerous puffing teachers. I make a mental note to visit this room as little as possible and to make use of the prep rooms, that the science department has aplenty, for lesson preparation and marking.

The Head of Science walks me through my early morning duties of taking the registrar – I have a second-year group, twelve / thirteen year olds, to manage – and lead into the morning assembly.

As today is the start of a new school year, the Headmistress walks to the front of the large assembly hall, accompanied by her Deputy. They make an interesting pair. While the Head is, for want of a better description, short and round, her Deputy is tall and gangly. Together they climb the few steps up on to the stage.

The Headmistress, as is her manner, stares down on the assembled five hundred or so girls, greets them to a new year and announces that there are four new teachers. First she introduces my new neighbour, who will be teaching English and completes her 'welcome' by shouting "oh for goodness sake, do stand up and let them see you!"

This very shy lady gets to her feet and tries to smile. Next on the hit list is me.

"Mr Marks is joining us from Nigeria to teach biology. Some of you will have heard that he is sometimes called Dr Marks. But no, here he will be simply Mr Marks."

Not wanting to get harangued on my first morning, I stand up from my chair so that the girls can identify me. A round of giggles, that only girls can produce, starts echoing and grows louder as it circulates around the room.

This is quickly stifled by the Headmistress who says "Girls, really, I am sure you have seen a man before." Her Deputy quickly moves forward and whispers in the Head's ear which prompts the latter to explain "of course Dr Marks, I mean Mr Marks, is not from Nigeria. He was teaching there for several years."

With that misunderstanding settled and the other new teachers introduced with no further mishaps, we get down to say the Lord's Prayer and then the assembled pupils go off to their first classes.

I am never to be very popular with the Headmistress. I guess the sins of being male and slightly non-compliant, although I do have a respectful enough relationship with her deputy. My biggest concern during this first term, shared with all the other new teachers, is to pass the one term of probation. Until this is completed, all of us are only too aware that we could rapidly become 'jobless in North-ampton'; and on the whim of a single person. But I only have three uneasy moments during my probationary term.

The first is when an apparent staff secret is inadvertently 'leaked' to a third form class. There are three such classes with me looking after one of them. The first thing I know about the leak, and the on-going investigation, is on arriving in the morning, and being told by the Deputy that the Headmistress wishes to speak with me urgently. Not imagining the fury that awaits, I knock on the Head's door and walk in. I am immediately met with a tirade of accusations delivered in a very loud voice that could be heard down the corridor by the gaggle of nosy teachers that are gathered with the sole intention of overhearing.

I allow the Headmistress to finish her angry tirade. Then, feeling that I now possess the moral high ground because it is her that has lost her temper, I say to her very gently "Good morning Head-mistress" and allow her the time to reply.

I secretly thank my early Nigerian experience where the correct greeting is always needed, no matter the circumstances. I then add "you say that the girls were told this piece of information at the end of yesterday afternoon? Yesterday was my afternoon off, so I was not in the school and so there is no way that I could have spread the secret. Might I suggest that it is better to ensure that all facts are in hand before accusing people of doing such things?"

She gives a harrumph and a curt "you can go Mr Marks."

I walk out the door being pleased that I had remained calm and reasonably polite but hope that I had shown that I will not be pushed around. The same cannot be said for the next person to be interviewed over the secret. This time, a new and very young maths teacher enters her office, receives the same tirade and reappears a few moments later sobbing her heart out. All I hope is that the Head will feel some guilt and remorse when she reflects on her achievements of this particular day.

My next confrontation during probation proves to be even more foolish as I am quizzed at length over why I am not using red ink to correct pupils' homework books. This is a nonsensical battle from the school hierarchy and they know it.

However, the third ordeal does have me worried for a little while, despite it occurring in a rather humorous manner. Today I have the upper fourth class, the fourteen going on fifteen-year-old girls, for biology GCSE and the subject is birth control.

Just before the class starts, one of my biology colleagues, hands me over a small cardboard box with a closed lid and says "this is today's goody bag, Malcolm. Now don't get embarrassed in front of the young ladies!"

I open the box and find it crammed full of the wonders of 1980s birth control methods. After eight years of marriage, I'm quite used to some of them!

The girls arrive well on time, as is the habit within the school, say good morning and settle into their usual places in the biology laboratory that we use as a classroom. I take my place at the front of the laboratory and have my 'goody bag' in plain view.

"Hi girls, yesterday we finished looking at human reproduction and how babies are made; today we are going to look at the different means of stopping unwanted pregnancies by using contraception. Some people might believe that contraception is sinful, perhaps some of you believe that too. I will not tell you that you are wrong, I am only going to show you the methods that are available should you enter into a relationship where you and your partner consider that now is not the time to start a family. Having once been a young man (*pause for their laughter to die down*), I would recommend that you young ladies do not put too much faith in your eventual boy-friends to be properly prepared! I am sure you are all aware that there exists contraception for ladies and for men. Can you give me one or more examples of each?"

Hands are raised and I receive the expected answers of 'the pill' for ladies and condoms for men. One girl, very honestly says that she has seen the pill that her mum takes but has never seen a condom.

I open the 'goody bag' and first draw out a condom still in its foil cover, holding it in the air "this is how they are sold, and usually in packets of three."

I then take out a pink condom that has already been extracted from its foil, and to all intents and purposes looks like a deflated party balloon, and hold it up in the air.

One girl asks why they do not burst, an excellent question and important to reply honestly to them. To show the strength of such objects, I hold it aloft in my two hands and stretch it width-wise and then lengthwise for all the girls to see. As I am standing at the front of the class with thirty quite mesmerised young ladies paying careful attention to me and with the pink condom stretched to over fifteen inches long, the door bursts open and in walks the Headmistress.

She makes her trademark 'harrumph' and says in her flat bitter voice "I will see you later Mr Marks."

I fear that I will be taken to task for being so open with these young ladies. And they fear the same for me with one saying "We hope you will be OK but don't worry, we will support you Mr Marks."

When the bell rings to mark the end of the lesson, I walk across the beautiful gardens from Science to the main building, climb the stairs, knock on the head's door and enter.

As is her manner, she immediately spits "I was not impressed this morning Mr Marks, I was insulted by what occurred." Oh dear I think, here it comes, she is going to ask why I was stretching a pink condom. But no. she splutters through her rage "why on earth did the girls not stand up for me when I entered the room?"

Ooph, oh Lordy-Lordy, is that all, I think?

"I am sorry that the girls offended you but perhaps you did not know that we have a safety policy in Science that during classes we have instructed the girls not to stand up automatically for visitors. Imagine, for example, that the girls were heating acid over a Bunsen Burner and, when you walked into the lab, they jumped to their feet and knocked the acid over each other. How would we explain that to parents?"

"Ah, an excellent policy Mr Marks, carry on. I will not keep you further."

My probation period ends and my job is secure.

Halfway through my first term at the school, we sign contracts on our little terraced house near to the bottom of Edith Street, at number 15, and quickly move in. The house was built in the 1890s, has three bedrooms upstairs and a single, rather large room downstairs at the front of the house where a dividing wall has been knocked down. This room opens at the back to a kitchen with a second door that leads to a separate bathroom and toilet. The toilet was clearly once the outside privy but has been connected to the rest of the house by a downstairs' extension back from the kitchen. There is a miniscule backyard where Mélanie can play and washing be hung to dry. There is also a third door from the kitchen that opens onto a short flight of wooden stairs that leads to, oh my goodness, a large cellar room. There is some light from a grated window that sits at the bottom of the front wall and opens onto the pavement outside – this would formerly have been a coalhole.

The house is one of about twenty-five on each side of the road and all open directly onto the street pavement via two or three concrete steps. We quickly nickname this our Coronation Street house and, in reality, we are now living in an old shoe factory house. Northampton was, and still is, the premier shoe and boot making town in the UK. Not for nothing is the Northampton Town football team called the Cobblers (although their on-pitch performance is often likened to a load of old cobblers). But they did enjoy one golden run when they rose from the fourth to the first division in consecutive seasons and then, to prove that this had not been a fluke, repeated the process, this time downwards.

In Northampton, however; the noble world of rugby differs from the football rabble, not least in the fact that the team is known far and wide as the 'Saints'. The Saints' rugby talent equals Respect, right across Europe and the team remains in the top five of English clubs, year after year. But if only we could occasionally beat the Tigers of Leicester.

Near the top of our road lives Jimmy, ex-army, and the owner of an incredible wine shop. We quickly become friends and I spend considerable time providing him feedback on the wines he kindly recommends to me. Did we choose our house well or not?

There is also, at the top of the next street, a general store owned and manned 24 / 7 by a lovely Indian family who take it in turns to provide everyone with almost anything that they might need to buy, even at 2 o'clock in the morning.

Indeed, Mr Patel, the kindly patriarch of the family, once asked me a very interesting question. "Doctor, do you know why we

Indians do not play your football?" My answer was to assume that they enjoyed cricket more than football. "Oh no, no, no" he said while nodding his head vigorously "we have been banned by FIFA because every time we play and an Indian gets a corner, he builds a convenience store!"

Well, you can believe me, this was the first and only time that tears flowed down my face in Northampton!

Our house, in estate agent jargon (does that equal 'untruth'?) is in need of some TLC. In reality, it was 'modernised' in the 1950s and (luckily, as it turns out) has remained unchanged for the next thirty-odd years, that is, until we buy it. From the cellar looking upwards, I could see the original floorboards that lie beneath a dirty blue carpet with black foam underlay sitting on top of several layers of lino of questionable vintage. The front door dates from the sixties, is glass-panelled and, to be honest, ugly. This goes on our 'needs to be changed' list. The doors inside the house have been modernised but luckily only by tacking hardboard onto both sides and then being painted. A quick flick with a sharp screwdriver and we find the Victorian doors in all their original splendour underneath. The original, porcelain door handles were obviously lost in the modernisation – but I know where to find them next time we are in Islington. At some time in the near future, the doors will need to go to be dipped to remove the indeterminate number of paint layers, some certainly containing lead. One nice discovery is the presence of an original fireplace in the sitting room complete with its grate. This will soon contain flowers, if I know anything about my wife.

The kitchen is of dubious vintage with the cupboards sitting on a lino covered floor that has been lain over a concrete base. On removing the concrete, I discover a perfect quarry tile floor. The bathroom has an original lion-footed cast iron bath that, on closer viewing once the side panel is removed, proves to have lost three of the four paws and has a hairline crack that is quite invisible from above. Sadly, then, we will have to change it (but if we are honest, Véro always complains that caste iron is cold to sit on). The toilet must be very old, even original, as it still has a high-level flush made of cast iron and a piece of string to pull. That will have to be changed too.

The three upstairs bedrooms each have fitted carpets and all the carpets are worse for wear and need to go. Our bedroom also has an old coal fire hidden behind a hardboard panel while at the top of the stairs is a laundry cupboard that contains the immersion heater and the central heating pump (this temperamental beast is often to receive hearty clunks from a heavy piece of wood that I keep for just that purpose when it decides to go on strike). Finally, there is a hatch to the attic that we can use for storage. In a later life we would almost certainly have extended into the attic but not in this incarnation.

Lots of work is therefore needed to turn this terraced house into our home and we start off quickly on modifications before we get too much furniture into the place. The first thing we do is to hire a skip and an industrial sander. The skip receives all the old carpets from around the house, the lino off the sitting room floor and sheets and sheets of hardboard that we have prised off every door and fire-place in the house. Sanding the floorboards in the sitting room is going to be child's play since I have already sanded one hundred square metres of flooring in our Cordon house. What proves not to be child's play is lifting the industrial sander out of the back of my Ford Classic. Indeed, as I lift it up and out of the boot, I feel a distinct muscle stabbing, I can only describe it as a bubble popping in my back. My weekend is painful but successful as we sand all the boards back to the raw wood and then paint on two layers of resin that brings out the beautiful yellow and pink highlights of the pine wood's patina. We are both even successful in not managing to paint ourselves into a corner! While this work is underway, Mélanie spends the day with her new friend Amy who lived just round the corner from us in Woodford Street.

Once we pay the deposit on the house plus solicitor's fees, we do not have much in the way of savings but then neither did we have much in the way of furniture. One day I am telling the head of art, about our move into Edith Street and he comes up with the perfect solution. He and I have quickly become friends and he is proving to be a mentor to me. He is also a fount of knowledge about everything, and I mean everything. When I mention that we are on the lookout for furniture for our new home. He says "why do you not go to the auctions?"

Interesting, and it turns out that there are two auction houses in Northampton: one in the old brewery building down from the town centre and the other tucked in the Cattle Market and only a five-minute walk from the school. Since Mélanie is now in nursery school a few mornings a week, Véro can use these moments of freedom to attend the auctions and bid on furniture. I am also known to be capable of sneaking out of the school on a few occasions to try to buy interesting lots.

The auctions rapidly provide us with wardrobes, dressing tables, chest-of-drawers, dining chairs and table. Nothing costs us more than a fiver and many items are knocked down to us for the starting price of 'a quid to the gentleman in the back row!'. We even buy a series of Lloyd Loom chairs for a pound a piece. All we end up having to buy new is our bed, so my colleague's tip saves us a fortune.

Mélanie loves being at nursery and, as a calm child, she is liked by the teachers. That is, until she meets up with one Alex Coe, a most boisterous, cheeky and unruly child of three! Alex's parents, Brian and Diane are destined to become very dear and lifelong friends. 'Auntie' Diane and Mélanie soon develop a terrific bond. After all, poor Diane does have to share her home with three men ranging from 'Boisterous Alex', his older brother 'Studious James' and her long-suffering husband and the world's number one Francophile, Brian. Brian works for the Milton Keynes Development Corporation. MKDC's one enormous claim to fame and worldwide renown is for *planting* life size concrete cows on a grass verge along the main artery of this new town. For the record and in contrast to popular opinion, Milton Keynes is not named after a famous economist or even two of them!

Time passes swiftly during this first academic year at the school. I find that I really enjoy teaching at the school level and do not consider lesson preparation and exercise book marking too onerous; certainly far, far easier than preparation and marking at the university level. I quickly get myself into a rhythm of making use of free periods to hide away in a biology prep room and do class preparation and marking; only making occasional visits to the staffroom for the morning coffee breaks. This leads a few of the staff to talk about me as being unfriendly and this inevitably gets back to the Head and her Deputy. On their suggestion, I make an attempt over a few days to use the staffroom and not the prep room but find that I cannot concentrate due to the permanent chatter of staff with nothing better to do and cannot breathe due to the multitude of 'fag-ash-Lils' who chain smoke their cancer sticks for everyone to enjoy.

My solution is to invite the Deputy Head to sit in the room with me and, after only a few moments, she declares "point taken Mr Marks!"

We approach the end of April 1986 and Véro's appointment with the Northampton Sausage Factory (aka the maternity ward) arrives with some stomach-churning contractions. Our beautiful baby is born and much to our surprise is boy; we had been so sure that we would follow the family tradition of only having girls. After all, the male members of my maternal line, starting with dear and late grandad Ted and passing via various male cousins plus myself have managed to produce a run of fourteen (or is it fifteen?) girls on the trot. The odds that such a sequence will occur due to chance alone run into the thousands to one and so we had come prepared with a name … Charlotte, but none for a boy.

When the wiggly and slimy little creature appears and I spot an appendage that we had not expected, the midwife's question of 'what name have you chosen' goes initially unanswered until I suggest "what about David?" and so David it is. We add the second name of Edward, in memory of the aforementioned grandad Ted whose run of girls we have now broken. For the record, a second boy appears in the family courtesy of a male cousin but girl production still far, far outnumbers the boys.

With the arrival of David and the fact that we now have the 'King's choice' in children, we decide that two kids are to be our sum contribution to the human race. This decision proves to be wise when we take our next flight in the summer to Lyon and have to struggle with the paraphernalia of two little ones. We reach a decision there and then at Heathrow as we struggle with a pushchair, a baggage trolley, various bags, a new baby and a four-year old that flights are out until the kids become more independent. However, we have been looking forward to this break from the school so that we can see the French side of the family and relax, in our own particular manner, in Cordon.

This summer we have an important event to organise; the christening of master David. As we did four years previously for the christening of Mélanie, we go to visit the priest at the church in Brégnier-Cordon and he provides us with the time and date for the ceremony. We can now tell my parents and sister when they should book their trip as they will be coming for a visit. Our little niece of ten, Alexandra, is to be David's godmother (*marraine*) while Véro's brother Jean will be the godfather (*parrain*). The day of the christening arrives and David is duly welcomed into the Christian family by the sign of the Cross drawn on his brow in Holy Water.

We hold a party at our home in Cordon, overflowing into the garden, and invite several members of Véro's family in addition to our parents as well as some of our close neighbours.

The priest also kindly makes an appearance for an hour or so and, as he takes his leave, he says to me "perhaps see you in another four years then Malcolm!"

"Point taken, apologies for not being a very regular visitor to your church."

For the first time in Cordon, we are happy to show Véro's elderly relatives around our home that has been – we say with a certain amount of pride – transformed over the four years that we have owned it. As we are helping two octogenarian great-aunts to descend the rather steep *échelle à meunier* that leads from the first to the ground floor, I hear a lot of chatter and laughter coming from my mum and my mum-in-law. Like all good English ladies, my mum stubbornly refuses to speak a single word of French, despite having learnt bits of the language during several years at school. My mother-in-law, follows the hearty French tradition of never uttering a single word of English, except those that they believe are French like weekend and baguette (only kidding on the second one).

However, the two ladies are sitting down together with Mélanie having, what looks from across the room, like an interesting and lively conversation.

After about fifteen minutes, as I am serving drinks from behind an improvised bar, I hear Mélanie say "no more, that's enough" and she comes over towards me closely followed by her two grand-mothers.

My mum says "it's incredible."

My mother-in-law says "*je ne peux pas le croire*"

"What's happened?" I ask.

My mum explains that for the entire fifteen minutes, before Mimi got fed-up, our little girl had been translating the conversation between the two grannies, switching from French to English and back again like an experienced translator. The English side of the family have always heard our little girl speaking in English and the French side in their language but this was the first time that they had heard her switching at ease from one to the other.

In some awe, my mum asks the obvious question "how do you translate so easily, my love?"

To which my four-year-old answers, as only a four-year-old would "it's easy nanny, I know there are two words for everything but you only understand one of them and my *mamy* only understands the other. When someone speaks to me with '*bonjour*' words I know which words they can understand and when they speak to me with 'hello' I know I must use the other words."

We both feel so proud of our little girl and it is a pleasure to know that, now as adults, both our children have two maternal languages and the right accent in both (unlike their parents)!

We return to Northampton a little early because our next-door neighbours have phoned to tell us that our house in Edith Street has been burgled. The police have been to the house and taken finger-prints, leaving powder scattered over every surface, and then the kindly neighbours have repaired the forced front door and tried to straighten the contents of drawers and cupboards that were tipped out on the floor. To cut the story short, the thief – we learn that he is well known to the local police – made off with all the jewellery that Véro has not taken to France plus a few paintings that were hanging on the sitting room wall and other odds and ends that took his fancy. One of the paintings is a lovely oil painting of the artist Ravier's House in Crémieu by Véro's uncle Ferdinand. Ferdie is a well know local artist and frequent award winner. The others are a coloured etching of a famous Victorian English racehorse and a watercolour beach scene. As we belong to the neighbourhood watch scheme in Edith Street, we had followed police advice by marking the picture glass and frames with our house number and postcode using 'invisible ink' that can only be seen under ultraviolet light. The thief is arrested soon after our burglary, and much booty recovered from his store, but we are never to receive a single stolen item back.

Soon after this incident, we become the target of some sort of revenge cum hate campaign over a two-week period. It initially starts with a fire engine arriving at our front door one autumn evening and some pretty irate firemen asking first where the fire is and then threatening me with dire consequences for calling them out on a false alarm. Slowly it dawns on the fire chief that this has been a hoax 999 call, especially when I ask him to check the phone number that had dialled in the 'fire'. This proves to come from a phone box on the other side of town and, as the fire chief then admits, I could not have made the call and gotten back home – and into my slippers – before the engine arrived.

The next incident is a hail of tomatoes and eggs pelted on to our front window and door and this is followed several days later by a dart thrown at the glass panel of the front door. By a miracle the glass does not shatter, the sharp end of the dart simply penetrates through the glass.

At this point, our sweet but very embarrassed next-door neighbours at number 17 come up with a likely explanation of mistaken identity, or rather mistaken address. It transpires that they own a second property; on the other side of town. This is rented to prime candidates for the title of 'tenants from hell'. The tenants have refused to pay rent for several months leading to our neighbours starting an eviction process through the courts. They believe that their tenants are seeking revenge against them and are targeting our house by mistake. I go with my neighbour to the local police station and make a formal complaint against 'person or persons unknown' while my neighbour provides his theory. The hoax 999 call is used by the police as a pretext to call on the unruly tenants, as part of their inquiries, and the attacks cease.

Time passes quickly in Northampton; I teach Mélanie how to ride a two-wheel bike in the carpark of the shoe factory at the bottom of our road. David grows fast, will soon be a year old and so should soon start to walk. Véro takes on some private tuition pupils who are looking to improve their French grades and she is also asked to come into the school to replace one of the assistant teachers during a pregnancy leave.

The results of my different classes of biology pupils at both O and A levels have been excellent, a reward in itself for me. We are relatively comfortable now. Life is good but ...

Are our feet starting to itch? Am I really getting a little displeased with my salary from the school that moves little at the end of each year since I am stuck at the top of the scale? Something does not quite feel right despite our cute little house that now has a new kitchen and bathroom, that I fitted. We have also rewired the house – thanks to my brother-in-law – changed our dart-ridden front door by recycling our neighbours' original Victorian door that he has replaced with a lovely plastic version. We have also traded in my dad's old Ford Classic for a more recent Vauxhall Cavalier.

Véro and I chat through my gut-feeling that something is not quite right; that my career is lacking sufficient challenge. She suggests that I should speak to the Headmistress about my future at the school. There is, for example, a Careers Advisory position that the school wishes to appoint internally, starting the next term, and this would add challenge to my work and 20% to my salary; if I can get the nod that is.

The following week, I make an appointment to speak to the Headmistress and explain why I feel that the careers advisory position would be very suitable for me but I get completely blown off by her and the blunt statement that "Mrs H. will get that position".

Now, I have nothing but respect for Mrs H. but she is pushing 60 so will be looking to retire pretty soon, has been a teacher all her life, mostly spent at this school, and is one of the Head's closest staff friends. I feel that I am being fobbed off and, due to Mrs H.'s lack of experience outside of the school environment, this is a not a good appointment for the pupils.

As I get up from the chair in front of the Head, I tell her "Thank you for your time. I would like you to know that I enjoy teaching the pupils at the school and their exam results are excellent. We are happy in Northampton but my career feels that it has come to a halt and I now believe that it will not progress further at the school. After our chat this morning, I really have no other option but to look for another job."

She retorts back "you will not do better than you have here, Mr Marks."

I feel that battle lines are really drawn. She clearly does not respect me and the feeling is becoming mutual. My two biology colleagues are sympathetic but both tell me that the order of things will not change until she retires in a couple of years. Do I want to wait that long?

4 |

Africa calls: I'm Going Back

Fate steps in, as it seems to do throughout our lives; this time heralded by a simple phone call. It is the early evening of 2nd July 1987. This is our tenth wedding anniversary. The children are in bed and asleep and we are just in the process of polishing off the bottle of champagne that had escorted us back from France. We are both in that nice state when the alcohol has relaxed the mind and we feel cosy together, just before sitting down to a celebratory meal. The ring of the phone stops our chatting and I step into the kitchen where the phone hangs on the wall.

"Northampton 739827, Malcolm speaking," I say.

"Hi Malcolm, Cesar here from ORT, we met in Calabar ..."

My head clears of champagne and my mind flicks back to a lovely evening in Nigeria that we had spent as guests of our great friends, Roger and Catherine Cornish. At that time, Roger worked for a Swiss consulting firm called ORT and Cesar, the managing director of the company, was on a work visit to his training contract with the Mercantile Bank in Calabar. We had been invited not only as close friends but also so that I might entertain the boss who Roger had told me was a little difficult to talk with. His boss was, I guess, in his early 50s and sported a razor haircut. We had immediate empathy and managed to chat through the aperitif, then at the dinner table and continued afterwards too. No-one else got too many words into our conversation and I had feared that I was over-monopolising their boss. He wanted to know about everything related to my academic and professional life. Why ecology? Why university teaching? What research was I doing? What consulting work had I carried out? What were my plans for the future? What languages did I speak? What does Véronique think about this life? and on and on.

After we left Nigeria, we had continued to correspond via occasional New Year greetings cards and updated CVs but nothing much more. This is the first voice contact for four or is it five years?

"Malcolm, I am calling because we need an Ecologist to do some work on our US-funded project in Chad. Would you be able to go as soon as your term in UK finishes?"

After some exchange on the type of work involved – basically to test the quality of soils and well waters in the 'wadis' (these are inter-dunal valleys) of the project area in northern Chad – I say yes to the six-weeks of work.

With the phone on speaker, Véro is able to follow the conversation and is nodding her head and making 'thumbs up' as the conversation proceeds. Will this exchange help to lead us back to the life we hanker after?

Two days later I receive a letter in the post from the London office of ORT giving far more details of the work involved, an offer package for salary, per diems, details of eventual air tickets, and so on. There is also a request that I travel to the London office for an 'informal interview'.

Véro and I sit down and discuss how to make the consultancy work for us. My summer vacation from the school is exactly eight weeks long while the mission to Chad is for a total of six weeks.

The best way to proceed seems to be to drive to France the moment the school closes, get the visa process for Chad started as soon as we arrive in Cordon, book the flights and travel to the Chadian Embassy in Paris on the day of my outward flight to pick up my visa before flying out to N'djamena direct from *Charles de Gaulle*. At the end of the trip, I will have a short week in Cordon to recover before we drive back to Northampton for the start of the new school year. Obviously I will not get a great deal of vacation but this is not an opportunity I want to miss. Meanwhile Véro and the children can enjoy their vacation in Cordon, surrounded by her family and our local friends.

But first the 'informal interview' that could scupper all our hopes if it does not go well. As Wednesday is my afternoon off from the school, I book my appointment with ORT for 3 pm and arrive at their offices with ten minutes to spare.

The interviewer starts off in English and asks about my career to date, especially the time we spent in Nigeria and then how I had met their big boss.

After chatting for about 20 minutes, the interviewer says in French "so, you have proven that you can speak English, let's see if you can speak in French!" We switch to French and continue the interview.

As a final question I am asked *"comment tu as appris à parler français ?"* (how did you learn to speak French?).

My reply is the joke that many people use in response to such a question: *"sur l'oreiller bien sur"* (on the pillow, of course). With that joke of a response and laughter shared, the mission is sealed and contracts signed.

Before the term ends, I use many spare moments to read up on desert soils – after all, apart from a short trip to the Sahel region in northern Nigeria around the cities of Kano and Zaria in 1981, I have never visited an arid zone. I also send the London office a list of soil- and water-testing equipment that I will need for my work in Chad. I make a mental note to go through some research papers that I have left in the attic in Cordon because one thick booklet deals specifically with desert soil characteristics and how to test their fertility; a document produced by the US Department of Agricultural.

The end of term arrives at midday and Véro and the two children are already sitting patiently in the school carpark in our fully laden car, ready for the trip south. We pass the night at my parents' house in Coxheath, taking our leave at five am the next morning, direction the Hoverport in Dover.

The crossing only takes around forty minutes and so we arrive in France at just after 8 am, are quickly on to the Calais motorway and heading south towards Reims and then Dijon. The children sleep as we speed south on a perfect and empty motorway. This allows us to knock over 200 km off the journey before David stirs, waking his sister, and time for breakfast is signalled. The rest of the journey goes without a hitch and we arrive in Cordon in time to settle in, make the beds, have an aperitif and feed the children before tucking them in bed.

The next morning, we travel over to the home of André and Paulette, Véro's uncle and aunt, who live in a village just outside of the small town of le Pont de Beauvoisin in the neighbouring department of Isère. When we tell them that I am soon off to Chad, they are very excited as they had lived in the country pre-independence and have many fond memories of Fort Lamy, the capital's colonial name. But André warns me to be careful as the country has regressed during the past decade or so with first a civil war and then Libyan meddling and aggression in the country, promoted by one Muammar Gaddafi. I have to confess to being very ignorant of recent Chadian affairs.

A couple of days after that pleasant visit to close relatives, I receive a call from the Chadian Embassy in Paris informing me that my passport and visa are ready to be collected. Without further ado, ORT books my return flight from Charles de Gaulle to N'djamena, and I travel to Paris on the TGV. Hats off to the French for their excellent infrastructure. The motorway network is comprehensive, of excellent quality and rapid and, in my view, certainly worth the motorway tolls. Equally, the TGV or *Train à Grande Vitesse* is comfortable and very fast, if a little costly.

After stopping at the Chadian Embassy to collect my passport and have a chat with the *Chargé d'Affaires*, I travel on to the airport at Roissy. Here I go, on another adventure in Africa which, unbeknown to me at this time, will change the future direction of our lives.

At check-in with Air France, I request and receive an aisle seat for the overnight flight. One thing I learnt from flying regularly between Nigeria and Europe is that getting out from a window seat in the middle of night is particularly difficult as well as disturbing for others. An aisle seat provides a little more room for reading, and this I intend to do as I have brought the desert soils booklet to read through and annotate.

Sitting next to me is a very young, red-headed lady from the UK who is making her first flight – ever. She tells me that she is more nervous about taking the flight than going off to Chad to spend several months living with a local family; part of her gap year. I do not tell her that I feel that the flight is probably the easiest part of this adventure, especially as she hardly speaks a word of French.

The seven-hour flight goes without issue in our workhorse Boeing and, after an almost sleepless night while I try to read through the booklet on desert soil characteristics and testing of fertility, we begin circling over a very dusty looking N'djamena. Below, I can see the usual patterns of arid Africa begin to unfold: the reds and oranges of bare soil and dry vegetation, the grey and rust-banded iron sheeting that serves as the roofs of most 'richer' households, and the serpentine green that signals the Chari River that forms the border with the neighbouring Cameroons.

As the plane begins to make its descent, it hits a zone of turbulence and begins to bounce and shudder. First I hear a whimper from the young lady beside me and then she grips me tightly by the arm and pushes her head against my shoulder. Tears are streaming down her face.

She tells me "I am so frightened, are we going to crash?"

I make the right noises and tell her "turbulence is normal; we will soon be below the upwelling. It's only air currents rising from the desert as it warms in the early morning sun."

"But I read", she sniffles, "that the most dangerous moment in a flight is the landing."

"I can put that theory to rest as it is take-off when the plane is loaded with aviation fuel that is by far and away the most dangerous moment. So by rights, you should have given me this hug at take-off, not when we are about to land!"

The poor girl suddenly realises that she is still gripping me tightly and that my slightly ruffled blue shirt now has damp patches from her tears down the right-hand side.

"Oh gosh," she apologises, "I am so sorry, and I have rather wet your shirt too. Sorry, sorry" and the poor ginger-haired young lady proceeds to blush even redder than her usual rosy complexion.

We are both soon laughing as the plane clunks down onto the runway, and we have arrived in N'djamena.

We pass together through passport control without an issue but then are called over to a table standing to the right and manned by two ladies wearing white-blouses; nurses, I presume.

"Vos carnets de santé s'il vous plait" (health certificates please).

In France, everyone has a booklet that lists all the vaccinations they have received throughout their lives; in the UK, of course, we have no such thing. Instead, I hand over four vaccination certificates that I had received before going to Nigeria which include yellow fever, cholera, typhoid and gamma globulin jabs (and ouch again to that last one).

The young lady whispers to me that she has no such certificates, what should she do. I suggest, in a returning whisper, that she should say nothing. One of the nurses counts the certificates, checks the first one which is for yellow fever and obviously satisfied that the certificates are for both of us, hands them back to me with a *'merci monsieur / dame'*.

We find our baggage going round on the carousel with a hundred similar items. I lift the young lady's suitcase on to the trolley that she has brought over and I grab my sports holdall. We walk together through the green channel of customs and emerge into the turmoil and organised chaos that is a common scene in most African airports. At the exit gate are a sea of faces, many holding aloft sheets of paper with various names of hotels or the persons they have come to collect. I spot the notice with my name written out in block letters held high by a chunky Chadian and wave across to him, receiving a smile and a wave in return.

However, I do not feel comfortable simply leaving my travel companion in this new country. I ask if she can see her name on any of the boards and am astonished when she replies that she had not sent her name to the hosting family.

"How will they know who you are?" I ask.

She laughs out loud and says quite logically "I told them that I have ginger hair!"

And she is right, of course, as the only young lady in the whole airport with such stunning hair colouration. Almost immediately, a slim and handsome young man comes across, introduces himself in impeccable English as Ibrahim, the son of her host family. I breathe a sigh of relieve and we say our goodbyes.

My sign holder comes across and introduces himself. "My name is Abdoulaye, sir, but you can call me Doo-doo. "I am your driver during your stay in Chad."

Handshakes completed, we walk over to his white Toyota pick-up truck and off we go, direction down-town N'djamena where the project has its offices. As the car picks up speed, Doo-doo first switches on the air-conditioning unit at full blast, releasing a cloud of dust from the air outlets, and then fiddles with the radio until he finds a French language station with popular songs.

The car is soon freezing and my head is aching slightly as I am tired and dying for a coffee.

"Eh, Doo-doo are you feeling hot because I am very cold? And can you switch off the radio please?"

"Sorry doctor," he says, "I thought you would need the A/C as you are from Europe and Chad is very hot for you."

"Ahh-ha", I laugh, "but I lived for four years in Nigeria."

The A/C goes off and the windows are opened and I can breathe in the special smells of Africa again. The mixed odours of dew-covered soil, of spices and of clean but dusty air.

At the office I am met by the chief-of-party (or team leader) of this US-funded programme. He is an old Chadian hand who has worked in the country for many, many years and he tells me that he has few intentions of leaving anytime soon. He previously worked for AfriCare-Chad, a very large and well-respected international NGO, before moving over several months ago to lead the project for

ORT. Also on his team are Firmin, a Senegalese from the town of Saint-Louis in Northern Senegal and a young American on his first international assignment. Firmin is in charge of the agricultural and training sides of the project while the young American, a graduate engineer, is working on mechanical issues, looking after items such as irrigation equipment.

The team leader calls for coffee and this arrives two minutes later, piping hot and brimming with sugar. Shades of Nigeria in Chad with incredible sweet teeth! We chat through my mission and the team leader has a confession to make. While he had received my list of required equipment in good time for ordering, he did not have sufficient budget to cover all items and so had made an executive decision to cancel the Conductometer.

"But after all, where you will be working there is no electricity, so it does not matter!"

Only it does. This was the most important item; how do we get around this issue?

At 2 pm sharp, I see everyone in the office starting to pack away their papers and begin leaving.

"Is it lunchtime?" I naively ask.

"Well, yes, it is lunchtime but it's also the end of the workday. Didn't you know that we do a '*journée continue*' that starts at seven and ends now with no break? Most people spend the afternoon napping or catching up on personal issues. If it's OK with you, I'll take you back to my place for lunch and then we'll drive over to your hotel to get you settled in. You must be exhausted after your flight. Tomorrow, we have an introductory meeting at USAID where you will meet the Mission's Pedologist, their soils specialist. He is new and a bit keen but I hope you will get on OK with him."

And off for lunch we go. The team leader proves to be a truly very nice guy and we are destined to be friends for many years that see us meeting up or working together, not only in Chad but also in future years in Niger, The Gambia and Guinea.

In the early evening I am taken back to my hotel, I check in and pretty quickly crash out until my alarm call wakes me early the following morning for the 7 am office start. After a very basic breakfast, I collect my briefcase from my room and stand outside awaiting the arrival of Doo-doo with the project pick-up truck.

As I look around at the hotel surroundings, I see several round holes in the hotel's outer walls. Curious. They are sufficiently large for me to poke my little finger in and they seem to go all the way through; even more curious.

Doo-doo's arrival first stops my exploring and then he puts my curiosity to rest by informing me "Libyan bullet holes, sir".

The morning goes well in the American Embassy building where the team leader and I spend a good couple of hours chatting through my upcoming mission. The Pedologist knows his stuff pretty well but did not know one of the newly gleaned techniques that I had picked up by reading that booklet on the plane. I offer to make him a photocopy!

As I have gone through life, and indeed this is something that I learnt while teaching ecology in Nigeria, I am not very good at 'off the cuff' talking, especially about technical issues. Far better that I prepare thoroughly and in advance rather than try to 'wing it' with my technical knowledge. Come to think of it, I'm also not very good at debating or arguing either. I never seem to think of the right thing to say on the spur of the moment – my winning arguments always come many hours later when the debate is already lost.

This is in stark contrast to my dear wife. She always (with a capital 'A') has a reply that I can never wriggle around and this means that in the twelve years that we have been together, I have never won a single argument; which all must agree is rather unfair.

But as she often reminds me, "that is because you are always in the wrong"; *touché*!

Firmin and I spend a lot of time together over the next couple of days, getting ready for our trip to Ngouri sub-prefecture in north-central Chad. While the distance we must travel is 'only' around three hundred kilometres as a bird flies, the time required across desert tracks is in the region of twelve hours. Firmin has only visited this small town on a single previous occasion and is using my trip as his opportunity to move permanently to the town for the duration of the project. He has been out purchasing everything that a single man could require in a town where there is no electricity, and precious little else. Doo-doo comes back to the office on my second day in Chad with the back of the Toyota pickup loaded with enormous cardboard boxes. On closer inspection I see that one large box has a picture of a chest freezer on display.

Yes, I thought the same ... but there is no electricity!

On looking more closely, I can see that this is a paraffin freezer that somehow works with a heat exchanger that burns paraffin to cool the freezer. Noting my curiosity, Firmin declares that, on arrival, he is nominating me to get the freezer working. And while I am at it, I can do the same with the full size oven and rings; this time running off bottled gas. I also note three large squares of thick foam rubber, rolled up and tied with string; here then are our beds, together with some packs of pink bedsheets with Chinese writing on them. The list goes on and, I also note, includes several cases of Chadian beer that should keep us going for a while.

The next day, Firmin and Doo-doo pick me up from the hotel at six am and we begin our drive northwards. The first hour or so is on a relatively good tarmac road, and I think to myself that twelve hours for the whole trip must be an exaggeration given the speed we are currently making. That is, until the tarmac suddenly ends and we plunge into thick sand that requires a frequent switch into 4-wheel drive. Our speed reduces from a healthy seventy kilometres an hour down to fifteen at the best. Now I can see why this journey may well take so long.

The drive across the sand is not unpleasant. The vegetation is relatively sparse, as one would expect. After all N'djamena is on the same latitude as the beautiful and historic town of Kano in Northern Nigeria where I had spent a little time a few years previously. And, we are heading due north towards the outskirts of the ancient boundaries of Lake Chad; now a mere puddle of its former self.

Just as in the north of Nigeria, the trees are dominated by the beautiful parasols cast across the sand by Acacia trees and there are also numerous *Balanites* trees, most filled with birds' nests of different sizes and vintages. The African *Balanites,* or thorn trees or desert dates, are an interesting group of plants. They possess a sparse number of small dark green leaves, that look a little like the leaves of olive trees, and long, sharp thorns. Some religious historians have suggested that the crown of thorns fashioned by the Romans both to torture and try to humiliate Jesus Christ before His crucifixion was made from the twigs of the thorn tree. As an ecologist, the interest to me of these species lies in their fruit which are highly concentrated with many good things. In the North of Senegal, for example, lies the Djoudj National Bird Sanctuary and a goodly proportion of our familiar summer birds in Europe, overwinter in Djoudj and the surrounding Sahelian bush right across the Ferlo. They spend our winter months in the sun of Senegal literally stuffing themselves with the berries of both *Balanites* and the Jujube tree before attempting to make the hazardous flight north, across the deserts of Mauritania and Morocco.

Our journey continues northwards and although the trees begin to become less dense, many retain their impressive height and shade. Testimony to the lack of human interference in this now remote area of Chad. While we see very few traces of human life outside of scattered villages, these are replaced by the most magnificent birds. They are too numerous to list here but among the most beautiful in the trees are the rollers and carmine bee-eaters as well as my old friends the weaver birds. Among the most spectacular of the ground species are the bustards and a single example of a secretary bird; a first sighting for me.

The morning passes and we are well into the afternoon when Doo-doo tells us that his calculation of a twelve-hour drive is a little off and we will not make Ngouri until after eight pm, even nine. That means at least two hours after sunset; a little worrying since, for the last several hours, we appear to have been running across virgin sand.

I ask the obvious question "will you be able to find your way in the dark?" to which Doo-doo informs me that this is not a problem because he will continue to follow the road with his headlights. I do not want to appear stupid by asking 'which road' because apparently there is one, even if I cannot see it.

Dusk falls at six pm and full Stygian blackness follows a few moments later. Nightfall in the Chadian desert is the time when it really comes alive. As we continue driving slowly across the sand, all wonders of magic desert life make an appearance. From my seat in the rear of the car, I spot two beautiful sandy-coloured foxes with very large ears standing guard outside their burrow – Fennec foxes my memory of zoology courses at London Zoo tells me. Our headlights catch them in its glare and, just as we pass, only a few metres away, five lovely little bundles tumble out of the burrow to see this strange nocturnal passage. A little further on it is the turn of the feline race to appear in our lights. I spot what, for all intents and purposes in size and colouration, looks like a domestic tabby cat but is in fact (at least I believe) an African Sand Cat; a species only discovered in the second half of the twentieth century. To make up the trio of interesting nocturnal species, we frequently see Jerboas hopping along the sand like miniature kangaroos. These cute little creatures are one of the reasons that tabby and foxy are out on the prowl.

Eight pm comes and goes and still we plough on through the desert sand. At one point, Doo-doo admits that he is a little unsure exactly where we are; no GPS at this time. Luckily, a few minutes later, we spot a faint glow, a soft glimmer in the distance which can only be of human origin. We head towards it and come across a tiny nomadic camp of three or four temporary structures and, after the correct number of greetings, questions and answers between Doo-doo and the camp leader, we head off at a slightly different angle. Nine pm comes and goes before we spot another faint glow in the distance, and finally we arrive in Ngouri. Fifteen minutes later we draw up into the compound that will be my home for the next five weeks or so. We are all so tired that we agree that the best thing to do is to unwrap our mattresses and sleep fully clothed. Tomorrow we can worry about unloading the truck and getting ourselves settled into our empty house.

The next morning comes far too quickly for Firmin and me but we are pleasantly surprised on struggling out of our rooms to see Doo-doo marching into the house with two baguettes under his arm and plastic mugs of strong and very sweet coffee held in his two hands. He has managed to unload a small gas burner from the back of the car and set water to boil while he had driven into the centre of town and found a baker's stall with fresh bread. Kudos to the French who managed to seed excellent baguette makers across their entire old African Empire although, here in Ngouri, sand does appear one of the main ingredients of the dough that is used.

After our first 'bush' breakfast, Firmin tells me that our arrival late last night has been noticed and that we are obliged to go and say hello to the town dignitaries. As we set off in the Toyota, Firmin informs me that there are several people to speak to. The most important, as far as the government is concerned, is the *sous-préfet* or sub-prefect, a formal government appointee as the most senior civil servant in the department.

The French have a multi-layered government structure which most of their former colonies like Chad have adopted. Chad, like France, is therefore subdivided into regions, containing departments, in turn containing arrondissements, then communes and then villages and hamlets. This complex government structure – the French with considerable humour and a typical Gallic shrug of the shoulders call it the '*mille feuilles*' after a rather more delicious cake composed of multiple layers. At least the government structure provides employment to a multitude of *fonctionnaires* (civil servants).

The *sous-préfet* is the head honcho for the whole department and he reports to the *préfet* who is based more centrally and comfortably in the regional capital. Ngouri town, despite its small population of, I would guess, a couple of thousand people, is stretched out over several kilometres.

We arrive at the *sous-préfet*'s office that is identifiable by the nation's flag hanging limply in the still morning air and are shown immediately into his office; government business must be slack today. After making our '*a salam malikum*' greetings, the *sous-préfet* tries out a few words of greeting in his local language – there are over a hundred in Chad – and is rather surprised when I make a correct but slightly mispronounced reply.

The *sous-préfet*'s mouth drops open and Firmin asks "what was that?"

Strangely, the *sous-préfet*'s greeting was almost identical to the few words of Hausa that I had learnt during my time in Nigeria. And in truth, the Peul, Fulani, Hausa and many other ethnic groups across the dryer Sahelian region from Mauritania and Senegal in the West to Kenya in the East are able to understand each other in a rudimentary fashion by a common language root that has evolved regional particularities.

The upshot of that lucky response is that the *sous-préfet* offers us the use of a spare government-issue generator for the duration of my stay. When we take our leave, being escorted to the car by the *sous-préfet* himself, I can see that the generator has already been loaded into the back of the pickup and a jerry can of fuel kindly offered by the official too. We can at least run a few lights to help us cook in the evening, and now if only I can find a conductometer ...

Our next stop on the grand tour of Ngouri is to the main mosque and a presentation to the Imam himself. After a brief discussion, ably translated by Doo-doo, the Imam says a small prayer for us.

I have learnt that when joining a Muslim prayer, one stands with palms outstretched to catch the wisdom of Allah and at the end of the prayer to say '*a hamdallah*' (thanks be to God) and at the same time raising the palms to the face to allow the wisdom to wash over one's head. I may not be the most devout person but I do respect the religious practices of others.

Our final stop is at the home of the local teacher that has his state school close to our compound. He speaks very passable French and so we do not have need of Doo-doo. Instead our driver excuses himself, needing to go to the market to purchase food for midday. We chat at length with the teacher while drinking the (by now) ubiquitous strong and very sweet coffee, and I explain the contents of my mission to the area around Ngouri.

The teacher tells me that it is school holiday time at present and so he would like to spend time with me in the wadis but unfortunately he has to travel to be with his family because the important Muslim festival of *Eid-al-Adha* or *la Fête du Mouton* is coming up in the following weeks. Eid celebrates the willingness of the Old Testament prophet Abraham to sacrifice his beloved son Ishmael in obedience to God and of the response of God in providing a ram caught by its horns in a burning bush as a sacrificial substitute for Ishmael. During Eid, goats and sheep are sacrificed by Muslim communities around the world as one of the cornerstones of their faith which is obedience to Allah.

One cannot help dwelling for a moment on the fact that Abraham (or Ibrahim) is a prophet for the Jewish, Christian and Muslim faiths but that far too many people who claim to follow one of the three faiths cannot find the love and compassion – and understanding – for each other that is the basis of the three religions. History shows that 'an eye for an eye' is a far more common response than 'turn the other cheek'. Having said that, in all my travels through Christian, Muslim, Buddhist, and Hindu countries, I have, with very few exceptions, been treated with friendship and tolerance.

As we take our leave from the kindly teacher and walk towards a shady tree at the entrance to his compound where Doo-doo will collect us, I notice a young boy in rather raggedy shorts and t-shirt hanging around the teacher's entrance. He looks across at me on several occasions but then looks away when I try to catch his eye to give him a friendly smile. Doo-doo's arrival ends his 'I'm not really looking at you game' because as we climb into the car, his shyness slips and he calls out to Doo-doo in Arabic. The driver laughs and says something in response and puts the car into gear to draw away.

"Attends Doo-doo, il veut quelque chose, le petit ?" (does the little boy want something?), I ask.

"Oui Docteur, il veut travailler pour toi et je lui ai dit 'non' !" (he wants to work for you and I told him 'no').

"Wait, let me talk to him." The car engine is cut and I get out of the vehicle followed by Doo-doo to translate.

But I have no need of the driver because the little boy greets me in passable French and proceeds to say to me "Boss, if you want to work in the wadis, you will need someone to translate from the local language of Ngouri into French. That will be my job. My name is Ishmael but my friends call me Izzy."

And just like that, I hire a guide, interpreter and make a young friend!

Before taking this new relationship further, I go back to disturb the teacher and he confirms that Izzy is one of his best pupils, that he comes from a poor family where the father has died, and that if I can let Izzy help me and give him some coins at the end of the day, his mother will be happy.

Doo-doo tells me quietly that five hundred CFA per day (about a pound) is an adult manual labourer's salary in these parts so I tell Izzy that he can only work for me if he will accept a daily salary of five hundred CFA ... and I will not pay a CFA more! The little boy's smile was so wide that I thought that his face would split in two.

I put him to the test immediately. After dropping Firmin back at our compound, I ask Doo-doo to drive us to the local market because I need to buy a hat to protect my head since its crown is beginning to show some early signs of desertification.

Immediately, one must forget Westerners' idea of the market as, for example, one finds in Northampton. Next one must also forget the bustling souks of North Africa or even the art deco edifices that the French built in Dakar, Niamey and N'djamena. The market in

Ngouri means the open air with herds of camels, roped together and spitting for all they are worth in high bad temper at being made to stand in the midday sun and not quite able to reach the piles of hay that are on sale nearby. It means small homemade tables with little pyramids of tomatoes, onions and the occasional potato that has made the journey from the south. It means rickety corrugated iron sheds that are open to the elements at the front and in which the tradesmen and their families will sleep.

Today, there are only a few stores open and even fewer items on display: some bright red plastic mugs, minute dark blue metal tea-pots that are used to make strong mint and sugar tea, and a pile of plastic kettles held together with string. These latter intrigue me. I ask myself, how on earth can water be boiled in a plastic kettle? My question is answered when we turn the corner of a shop and come to the front of the Mosque and I see the faithful getting ready for midday prayers (*Dhuhr*) using water from plastic kettles for their ablutions.

The next store has a range of artisanal products including desert straw hats, looking more like *cache-pots* than Panamas. I pick one up and try it on and immediately the shopkeeper hands me a broken slither of mirror to admire myself.

Izzy tells me "the shopkeeper is asking for four hundred CFA (80p), but that is far too much. How much do you wish to pay?"

I tell him that the price sounds reasonable and I do not want to haggle over so little.

He turns back to the shopkeeper and rattles off a few sentences. In response the rather elderly gentleman, reaches over to the back wall of his store and, with a big smile on his face, hands me a metal dagger with an ornate sheath of different coloured leathers.

"I agreed to the price," Izzy tells me, "but I told him that he should give you the knife too. Doo-doo just bought a goat and you should baptise your knife today, that is our custom."

(That knife, to my eyes it is really a dagger, has sat in my office since the day I brought it back from Chad – which almost got me into trouble, as will be seen a little later. As I type these lines, it sits on my desk and has retained its original condition. In its sheath, it is fully 35 cm long, has an eighteen-centimetre blade that runs to a very sharp point and its edges are still razor sharp. The handle is ornate and bound with red and yellow leather with fine black stripes, colours repeated on the sheath. And, of the hat? Well, it served me throughout my time in Chad and then, for several more decades, was able to protect an ever-thinning cover of hair while I grew organic vegetables in various gardens in France. That hat finally proved that it was recyclable by disintegrating last winter when I foolishly left it outside in the rain.)

Back to the present, the knife receives its baptism today, not by me but by Doo-doo who is far less squeamish. My role in the passing of the poor goat is after the fact in that I am nominated to butcher it down to meal-size chunks and freeze them in our, by now, functioning freezer.

As Firmin so rightly points out "you are a biologist and a doctor, so you should know how to dissect the poor creature."

However, using a machete really does take the finesse out of dissection!

The time comes for Izzy to take his leave, and he does so with a crisp five hundred CFA note in his hand and another broad smile on his face. I also extract a promise from him to stop calling me '*patron*' (boss) and instead by my first name, Malcolm that he Islamises to Malik.

"*A demain, Malik.*"

In general, we follow the idea of *journée continue* partly because the house has no curtains and so we wake early with the sun and partly because by the time 2 pm comes around the temperature outside is usually over forty centigrade and there is very little shade. My days begin at 6 am with half a sanded baguette filled with a triangle of *'vache-qui-rit'* ('the Laughing Cow' cheese triangle) and a plastic mug of Nescafe coffee. I then spend ten minutes in our latrine cum washroom that sits at the very edge of the compound and is surrounded by a two-metre high wall of millet stalks. This height is sufficient to stop any curious passerby peeking over the top while I am contemplating life over the toilet hole or trying to shave with a mugful of water. It is, however, not sufficiently high to prevent one very curious camel that seems to stop by to say hello most mornings.

Izzy arrives at 6.30 am for his breakfast and Doo-doo then drives us off to one or other of the six wadis that I am working in. He then takes the car back to the compound to pick up Firmin and drive him to his own work sites; mostly in different wadis to me. Firmin works most days with the local farmers helping them to improve not only crop production but also their post-harvest storage techniques, especially for the onions that all farmers seem to produce.

After the first few days, my work begins to take on a standard and routine format. After getting Izzy to introduce me and explain my activities to the farmers working in the wadis, I break the individual wadis down into visually homogenous zones and collect plastic bags of soil from randomly selected patches and at different depths in the soil. I also collect water samples from the well or wells present in the wadis before descending the wells on a rope to measure and map their soil profiles.

After one such adventure, a farmer comes across to Izzy and me and says that he is impressed by my courage. My response is to say that I always test the wooden structure above the well before tying my rope and descending.

The farmer looks rather confused and Izzy translates his words back to me "but he wants to know how that protects you from the snakes?" So those are what live in the holes around the top!

Between 2.30 and 3 pm, after Doo-doo has already taken Firmin back to our compound, he comes to pick the two of us up. First we drive Izzy to his home and then we return to the compound. On the first day as we drive away from the wadi towards Ngouri, we pass a group of young children playing outside of their fenced compound and they begin to wave and shout in unison and with excitement, the words '*abba nassala, leyla*'.

Here I am obliged to spell the words phonetically as I hear them because I know not in which language they were calling. Izzy tells me that I am the first white man they have ever seen and they are saying 'white father, hello'. I am very touched and receive the same enthusiastic greeting each time we pass by young children. I have to say that in my whole time in Chad, I was treated with kindness, politeness and respect. Thank you Chad.

Back at the compound I am building up rather a number of samples for testing and it is my plan to tackle those over the coming weekend. But still I am bothered by the lack of the conductometer, especially now I have the small generator with which to run it. Help is at hand in a rather strange form.

When I get back to the compound after a day in a distant wadi, I find another Toyota truck parked along the millet fence. Inside I can hear a conversation that seems to be switching from English to French and back again spoken with foreign accents. The first voice is clearly that of Firmin and the second, I find as I enter, belongs to a slim, thirtyish man who announces that he is Italian and his name is Emilio. We share a cold beer from the freezer – which basically functions better as a fridge – and Emilio explains that he leads a private-sector road-building team that is tracing out a future road to run from Lake Chad, through Ngouri and onwards to places still to be decided, and joining eventually with N'djamena. The road is being funded by various donors through the United Nations. There is an independent team of two engineers that oversee the road tracing and building work. Emilio grimaces as he speaks about the officials but I decide not to ask the obvious question.

As Emilio takes his leave, he invites both of us to eat with him and his team that evening at their encampment, just outside the town. Indeed, Firmin tells me that you can see their electric lights – the only electric lights visible in Ngouri at night – from our compound. While I say that I would be delighted to join Emilio and his team, Firmin declares that he has another date this evening and so cannot come; odd in Ngouri but not my business.

At 7 pm sharp, Doo-doo hands me the keys to the Toyota and tells me simply to aim for the lights of the Italian compound. I have a dead easy, ten-minute drive across the sand and the remains of stubble left in the fields to their compound; shining like the North Star in the black of the desert. My reception by the team is as friendly as only Italians can be; and I soon have a cold glass of prosecco clutched in my hand and hitting all the right spots. Across the large, air-conditioned shipping container that serves as their common room and dining area, I can see into the kitchen where I know that pasta must be bubbling.

There are five members of the Italian team present, counting Emilio, and they grill me with questions about the project's ambitions and what role I am playing during my consultancy. As I describe my work and explain that I am lacking an important piece of soil-testing equipment, Emilio tells me that he knows that there is a conductometer in the town of Bol, about six hours drive westwards across the desert sands towards Lake Chad. He tells me that it belongs to the supervisory engineers who are based in Bol and oversee the road building work. Again, I notice Emilio grimace as he tells me about the two officials.

I ask Emilio why his face drops each time he mentions the officials, I noticed him do this back at our compound too, and he tells me they are French and very difficult people. I assume that the problem stems from their personalities while overseeing the work of the Italian company rather than any common – and hitherto unnoticed by me – trait of the French nation!

The evening passes pleasantly, and how lovely it is to be completely air-conditioned for a few hours, but eventually I have to take my leave as it is getting late. One of the Italians walks out to the car with me and points out the faint glow of a paraffin lamp that Doo-doo has placed at the entrance to our compound. I set off across the sand trying to keep the faint glow of light in my forward vision while looking down at the tracks that I had made in the sand earlier that evening. The latter was my big mistake because I soon realise that there are more tracks than just mine and, to make matters worse, I have lost the distant lamp glow that was guiding me in. What to do? I decide to stop, switch of my headlights and try to re-find the lamp. Nothing doing, all is dark in front of me. I know that I am lost in the desert outside Ngouri. So, feeling rather foolish, I turn the car around and aim back at the Italian Pole Star still shining brightly thanks to an outsized diesel generator. One of my new Italian friends emerges from the container and kindly points out the direction of my compound and the faint lamp light that is meant to guide me in; and he does this with a straight face too. I eventually arrive back to our compound and receive a teasing from Doo-doo about the White Man who got lost in the desert. I suppose I deserve it!

One too many beers and a few too many glasses of wine mean that I wake in the middle of the night with a bladder fit to burst. I take my torch and start to make my way from my bedroom thinking to visit the latrine. But that is a little far and means walking across the sand so instead I make my way bare-footed through the house towards the back door thinking to water the sand off the back porch. To this day I thank the foresight that made me pick up my torch because as I walk down the corridor towards the door, more asleep than awake, I suddenly notice two very large objects picked out in the beam of my lamp ... scorpions. Not the cute little red-brown ones that we see under rocks at the Mediterranean but big black monsters that have large pincers, just like crabs. No exaggeration, the two animals were at least seven or eight inches long and ready to dispatch yours truly to Ecologists' heaven. I gingerly step over them, go through the back door, water the sand, step back over them, close my bedroom door and drift back to sleep.

Early the following morning, even before the sun has made its appearance, Doo-doo gently shakes me by the arm, back to full consciousness. He hands me a coffee already made and half a baguette spread with a triangle of *vache-qui-rit* and reminds me that we need to hurry to get on the road for Bol and my encounter with the 'difficult French' who work for the donor team and oversee the Italian road building efforts.

As we bump our way out of Ngouri, I try not to spill the steaming Nescafe over my lap, while chewing on my sandy baguette. It is now 6 am and we aim to arrive in Bol in time to catch the French at lunch. No matter where a Frenchman is based, in Paris or Timbuctoo, he will always ensure that his lunch *hour* (from 12 to 2 pm of course) is respected. I am confident I will catch the two gentlemen if we can arrive in time.

With Firmin remaining in Ngouri, I can claim the front seat and spot more quickly the wonders of desert life, especially the birdlife. With trees now being relatively few and far between, birds of several species congregate together and so I spot *Balanites* trees containing Rollers of two or three types, green and red bee-eaters, a few weaver birds and the occasional hawk. Watching out for rarer species with binoculars poised at the ready or chatting with Doo-doo about the recent history of Chad, time passes quickly as we drive relatively rapidly over the compact sand. At around eleven-thirty we begin to spot the occasional village, our first sign of human life since leaving Ngouri over five hours ago. I learn that we are now on the outskirts of Bol and will arrive soon.

We drive into the town with its houses as spread out as those of Ngouri. This appears common in the desert where there is little restriction on space. Our first stop is at the sub-prefecture to announce our arrival and ask where the Frenchmen live. This is also when I suddenly realise that I do not know their names. But no issue, Doo-doo simply asks where the white men live and we receive indications to a small house and compound a few minutes' drive away.

We arrive and I knock on the door. No response – and it is 12.10. I begin to worry that our trip will be for nothing and so ask Doo-doo if there is a restaurant in the town where perhaps the Frenchmen might eat. As I am speaking to my driver, a car pulls up and I am asked in French by the occupant of the car who I am looking for. After an introduction and a quick explanation of my project, which my new contact knows, I broach the subject of the conductometer.

"I wonder if you would lend me your conductometer for a few days so that I can test some soil and water samples?"

"Non, impossible" he spits out which rather knocks me back on my heels both for the two-word response and the venom that those words seem to contain.

Now, please try to imagine: having drunk too much the night before, almost stepping on two very large and mean-looking scorpions, getting dragged out of bed in a slightly hung-over state at 5.30 am, then travelling six hours across the Sahara Desert and all that to be met by a rude, bad-tempered gentleman. Well what would you do? Yes, quite right, and that is exactly what I do too. I cuss that gentleman from hell to high water. I tell him that he is all that is bad in development. That he is only in Chad to make money fast and does not care for the people that he is supposed to be helping. And, of course, all that I spit out in my accented French with every two or three words interspersed with the terribly rude swearwords that my little brother-in-law, Nico, has been teaching me for several years.

As I get to the end of my tirade, my opponent looks at me and then starts to laugh. He guffaws and slaps me on the back and laughs some more.

"Oh my good God, where did you learn all those terrible words? I have never in my life heard an Englishman come out with such filth. With words like that you would be able to take on a Marseille Fishwife!" and he starts to laugh again. "Come in, come in and share my lunch with me."

The meal of rice and goat stew tastes delicious and, as we eat, he explains that he has a difficult boss and that he would get into trouble if he lent me the equipment without permission; and unfortunately, the boss has travelled to N'djamena.

"Except, if ..." and he stops to rub his chin in thought "... you could do some analytical work for me. Would you do that? At the moment we are tracing the route of the road that the Italians are to build and we are trying to go in as straight a line as possible to cut down on costs. Sometimes we need to cut through wadis but do not want to destroy fertile land. What I am thinking is to bring you a few samples of soil from those wadis and get you to test their fertility. If fertile, we will bypass that wadi, if not we can save cash by going through it. What do you think?"

Well of course I will. We shake hands on the deal and I leave Bol at 2 pm with the Conductometer safely sitting on the backseat of the Toyota.

Two days later Emilio arrives in our compound in the late afternoon, accompanied by the Bol-based engineer. He hands over four plastic bags of soil from the four different wadis indicated on the labels. I promise to get them analysed during the next week or so. We split two of our few remaining beers and everyone is happy. Even Emilio no longer grimaces in the company of his technical controller.

The day of the Eid festival arrives and Doo-doo informs me that as a 'dignitary' in town I must go around the houses of the other dignitaries to wish them *Eid Mubarak* (Happy Eid). I put on some clean trousers and shirt and go off to look for Firmin, whom I assume will be accompanying me. But I find poor Firmin confined to his bed and feeling under the weather.

The start of our round is to the *sous-préfet*'s house and he greets Doo-doo and me at the door and invites us in. We sit on a raffia mat placed centrally in the room and are passed glasses of Coca-Cola or orange Fanta. As we chat about the progress of my work, and I do not forget to thank him effusively for the kind and continued loan of the small generator, a young woman comes in carrying a large, round, metal dish covered in pieces of liver and intestine mixed with slices of raw onion. Normally I adore liver as well as tripe – after all Lyon is the renowned capital of all things gastronomic especially

Andouillette (tripe sausages) and *gras double* (tripe and onions) – but before arrival Doo-doo had warned me how the offerings are cooked. In effect, the proffered delicacies are simply soaked in boiling water and left to stand until cool, so while I am honoured to be offered such morsels, I am a little reticent to tuck in too heartily. Step up my trusty canvas bag.

During my stay in Ngouri, I am accompanied the whole time by a workman's canvas bag that contains a closed plastic folder holding my passport, air tickets and money. As our meeting proceeds, I am obliged to sample the delicacies on offer. When our host is looking directly at me, I make a show of popping pieces of onion into my mouth as well as a few pieces of liver; it looks marginally more cooked than the pieces of intestines. Doo-doo is looking at me taking piece after piece and so he too chews on the rather tough meat on offer. After a suitable period of time, we take our leave and go on to the next dignitary. The process is repeated there and again at the third and fourth homes. Finally, Doo-doo tells me that we have done our duty and can go back to the compound to check on Firmin.

We arrive to find our erstwhile *Sénégalais* sitting in the shade of our building, cuddling a glass of beer and not looking sick at all. He asks us how the afternoon has gone and Doo-doo pours compliments on this 'foreign guy's' ability to eat the semi-raw offerings while confessing that he feels quite sick.

He turns to me and asks "doc. how did you manage to eat so much? Didn't you find it horrible?"

I upend my canvas bag and pieces of liver and intestines fall out on the sand, much to the pleasure of the scrawny cat that has adopted us.

The beer stock held in our paraffin-driven freezer (that freezes nothing) is dwindling fast and Firmin jokes that when we are dry, we must go back to N'djamena. Since we are now down to our last few bottles, our departure will be in less than a week; which happens to coincide with when I should be leaving Chad anyway. While we have been very careful in rationing our beer to about a bottle a day between us – and Doo-doo does not drink alcohol – somehow the word has gone around the village that the foreigners have lots of beer. Most evening we are 'kindly' visited by groups of men who just sit outside the house in anticipation of sharing a free bottle. Firmin made the mistake, soon after our arrival in Ngouri, of offering a glass to a visitor who entered the house while we were splitting a bottle after our day in the wadi, and the rest is history.

My days are relatively simple and routine: work in the selected wadi in the morning, carry out soil and water analyses in the afternoon, and help prepare a simple meal in the early evening. The meal is followed by hours spent laying on a large, round raffia mat out on the sand of our compound looking up at the stars and spotting satellites as they cross the sky. We generally chat about our lives back in our own countries with Firmin having his family in the beautiful Senegalese town of Saint-Louis, nestled in the north-western corner of Senegal while I tell him of my past work in Nigeria, my current job in the UK and my love of life in France.

Firmin usually has his radio tuned to a French language Chadian station with the volume turned down to a barely audible level so as not to impinge on our nocturnal conversations. One evening, we suddenly hear the radio commentators speaking rapidly followed by sounds of gunfire from close by in Ngouri. What is happening? Firmin turns up the volume and we follow the amazing news that the Chadian National Armed Forces has, just today, taken back northern Chad from Libyan occupation and so reunited the entire country. The battle for the Aouzou Strip – a small but militarily significant patch of land in northern Chad – has been won against great odds. Over the last couple of weeks, we had been hearing that the occupying Libyan army had suffered a series of defeats and so they had launched a counteroffensive, targeting the Tibesti Mountains. The 3,000-strong Libyan force had attempted to drive south but had been intercepted by the Chadians, surrounded and attacked. They then tried to retreat northwards through the desert towards Aouzou receiving numerous casualties along the way. By the time the battle was won by Chad, the Libyans had lost 650 soldiers, 147 captured, 111 military vehicles taken and at least 30 tanks and armored personnel carriers destroyed. The gunfire we had heard locally came from celebrating Chadian soldiers from a small force based in Ngouri. As the news continues to filter through from the capital, we learn that France, as Chad's main ally, had opposed the Aouzou offensive and had refused to provide Chad with the promised air cover. The brave Chadians had decided to go it alone and had achieved total victory over Libya; much to the embarrassment of François Mitterand's government.

My work is now coming to an end. Izzy receives his final five hundred CFA note and leaves us with a few tears and a big hug for me. I hope that little man will be able to fulfil his potential, hard as that is in Ngouri. He has been a Godsend and, thanks to his translating, I have had absolutely no issues with the many farmers I have met; quite the opposite. It was a rare day that my canvas bag was not bulging with gifts of onions and cucumbers and any attempt to pay for them refused.

The day before we set off for N'djamena, my new French friend stops off at the compound to collect his conductometer. I hand the machine over to him and thank him for his kindness in lending it to me. Without that machine I would not have been able to make such a complete soil and water analysis of the Ngouri wadis. I also hand over to him four A4 pages of handwritten results and analyses from his samples collected in the various wadis between Bol and Ngouri. He looks astonished at my work and tells me frankly that he only anticipated a 'good or bad' against each wadi name.

"This is far, far more than I had anticipated, thank you," he tells me.

The next day we set off from Ngouri early in the morning, direction N'djamena. The drive goes without incident and Doo-doo drops me off at the hotel for a sound night's sleep on a proper mattress. I wake up early, put on a shirt and tie and eat breakfast. The team leader arrives in the car with Doo-doo and we go together to the USAID offices at the embassy to provide a debriefing to the Head of Mission and the Senior Pedologist. They seem happy with the work presented and wish me a safe trip home.

Back at the office, the team leader hands me a bulging envelope containing a wad of CFA notes held together with an elastic band.

"Your accumulated per diem during your stay in Ngouri" he states "can you count it and then sign here."

He pushes a sheet of paper over to me. Once signed, he then takes the pile of notes back with a big smile on his face.

"Of course, although the CFA is tied to the French Franc, there is no free exchange outside of the CFA block. I will send Doo-doo off to the bank to exchange the CFA for you."

An hour later I have several thousand French Francs sitting snugly in my wallet.

My flight from N'djamena back to *Paris Roissy-Charles-de-Gaulle* is due to leave at around 1 pm, getting me back to *Roissy* at about 7.30 pm and leaving me enough time to travel to the *Gare de Lyon* to catch my TGV to the *Part-Dieu* station in Lyon. If all goes to plan, I should get into Lyon sometime just before midnight.

To speed up my passage through the Paris airport I decide to bring my sports holdall that contains all my clothes and papers on to the plane as hand luggage. Doing this will mean that I will not have to waste time at the luggage carousel in Paris.

Given the chance of delay, before setting off from France at the start of the mission, I had promised Véro that I would phone her from Paris when I knew at what time I would arrive in Lyon. From her side, she planned to stay the night at her parents in Crémieu so that they could look after the children while she would drive to the train station to collect me. That all sounded very logical at the time.

The crew of my Air France flight get us all seated for the 1 pm take-off and nothing is said to me as I bring my rather large sports bag on-board. But then again, my bag shrinks into insignificance when compared with many of the items being carried onto the plane today; especially the ubiquitous blue and red stripped traders' bags made out of recycled plastic and closed by an all-round zipper. These enormous rectangular bags seem to be used by every trader from right across the African continent. Most of the bags weigh so much that they cannot be lifted into the overhead compartments by a single person, many are so well stuffed that they will not fit in at all. But this does not seem to faze our Air France crew today, especially as the plane is only half full. Once more I have an aisle seat and to-day I am at the front of the economy section, and so away from the smokers crowded at the back.

The time ticks around to 1 pm but we stay firmly on the ground.

A steward comes through the curtain from business into economy and says to me "we are going to be delayed a bit, the announcement is just coming."

And true to his word, the intercom crackles into life and we are told that we will remain on the tarmac for a short while as we are awaiting the arrival of a VIP passenger. We wait and wait and (well) wait. Minutes pass and they stretch into an hour, then two and still we wait.

The friendly steward wanders back and tells me that in fact we are awaiting the arrival of two groups of passengers; wait for it ... The French Ambassador to Chad and his family who are going on holiday and the Chadian Minister of Defence and his entourage. There seems to be a bit of a diplomatic spat going on whereby neither party wants to board the plane first and have to wait the arrival of the other so both groups have decided to wait in the VIP lounge until the other party boards. Meanwhile this latter day 'mine is bigger than yours' has some 200 passengers being delayed on a hot airplane sitting on the Chadian tarmac.

Given the size of the 'V' in these two VIPs, Air France decides that it would be judicial if we all go through a second security check of our hand luggage. Everyone has to descend the plane and form a queue while three tables are set up, manned by the Air France staff. We are called over to one or other of the tables in turn and, by coincidence, my bag is to be checked by the chatty steward. I unzip the top of my sports bag and warn that it contains six weeks of dirty laundry. He decides not to check too hard.

"And what do you have in the side pocket?" he asks.

I suddenly remember that my goat-sacrificing dagger is in there, blast, here comes trouble.

I unzip the pocket and say nervously "I am so sorry I forgot ..." He spots the dagger, winks and tells me that all is OK and I can get back on the plane.

Finally, at around 4.30 pm, a limousine pulls up to the front of the plane and two adults and several children climb up the stairs. So the French Ambassador has lost out in the diplomatic power struggle. Five minutes afterwards, a military jeep pulls up to the plane and a dapper looking gentleman with several aides in uniform climb on board. This is a very pumped up Chadian Minister of Defence, as he has every right to be after beating up the Libyan army. Since France declined to be involved in supporting the final offensive on Aouzou, the Ambassador had lost bragging rights to the Chadian minister.

At close to 11 pm we land at Roissy. I calculate that I just might make the very last TGV for the night from the *Gare de Lyon* and rather than lose time by taking the connecting train from the air-port, I jump into a taxi using some of the funds I received from my per diem to pay the driver. But all in vain. The last TGV has left and the only way to leave for Lyon tonight is on the 'milk train', departing in fifteen minutes. This proves to be the TGL (*le Train de Grand Lenteur*) version for it will take over seven hours to travel the four hundred kilometres or so to Lyon, meaning that I will get into Lyon at around seven-thirty in the morning. Before boarding, I find a pay phone and call through to Crémieu. Véro answers on the first ring and, after I give a brief explanation, she promises to be at the *Part-Dieu* in the morning to pick me up.

The next morning, as promised, my lovely wife is at the station to greet me. As we drive back to Crémieu we chat about my trip and Véro is delighted that I found the work and the experience interest-ing and so much fun.

We both say simultaneously "if only this can lead ..." neither of us needs to finish the sentence.

We stop in the lovely medieval city of Crémieu to buy bread and croissants for breakfast and, as we set off again towards *Chemin de Prajot* where her parents have a lovely stone residence, Véro tells me that a surprise awaits me at the house, interesting!

As I climb out of the car, a screeching Mélanie runs to me and jumps into my arms.

"My daddy" she says "I missed you so much", followed by a torrent of little girl kisses.

Véro precedes me into the house, carrying the bread, while I carry Mélanie in my arms hearing all her news. As the door opens, I see my little blond boy stagger-walk across the floor with his arms raised to me. The tears of pleasure to be home and of sadness at having missed my son's very first steps run freely down my face.

Going on adventures is always fun but nothing beats a home-coming to a loving family.

5 |

Coincidences fall into place

The new autumn term is about to start at the school and so we arrive back in Northampton from France the day before. David is now almost sixteen months old and ready to get his first taste of school; nursery that is. We sign him up for morning sessions at a small nursery on the Wellingborough Road, just across the street from St Peter's church.

Meanwhile Mélanie, at five and a quarter (as she insists), has already started primary school. Since we benefit from a teacher's reduction on fees, we enrol her in the primary section of my school. It sits on a separate campus to the main school but is conveniently placed on my route to work. So each morning she will walk with me to school while Véro drops David and picks the two of them up at their respective times. On this first morning of the new term and a new school for Mélanie, we dress her in her school uniform of navy blue completed by a gorgeous little blue hat with a yellow ribbon. My Mimi preens herself in front of the mirror and continually pesters me to leave for school, despite it being far too early; no first morning nerves here. Finally, 8.30 arrives and we leave our little house, cross the road and start to turn left to cut through to Ethel

Street and from there on to the Wellingborough Road. Our progress is instantly halted by Archie Morris, our over-the-road neighbour who is one of the nicest people in our neighbourhood. Archie is already retired and must be pushing 70 but he remains sprite and very talkative. Seeing Mélanie resplendent in her new uniform – and she does look cute – he hurries across the road to give her a hug and wish her a nice first day at school.

One of jobs I have been assigned at the school, in addition to teaching duties, is 'Responsible for School Charities'. This lofty title actually means considerable extra work but no extra recognition, all *pro-bono*. The School has an enviable record of raising money for diverse charities, and I am very proud of the efforts put in by the girls to raise money for their selected causes; from cake sales to endurance runs and quizes, to sponsored silences to a whole host of sports matches of girls versus staff. Every class, throughout the school, selects a charity to support each term and organises their own fund-raising events. In my class we have a super fit young lady of fourteen who decides that one of our class events should be a sponsored run around the hockey pitch. The maximum number of circuits is to be twenty (making about 8 km, I later calculate) and the whole class, including yours truly, will take part. Very few of the teachers believe that I am capable of making the twenty laps, especially my beer-drinking partners among the male staff, and so I have some heavy amounts of cash placed on my ability not to succeed. The girls decide that we should all be able to complete the 8 km in around an hour and so set the run to take place immediately following lunch and before lessons begin. We all line up in our running gear and start to run. All the fitter young ladies in the class go steaming off ahead while I puff along behind with the less athletic girls. As the laps are reeled off by the girls, and puffed off by me, some of the youngsters begin to pull out. Slowly the field drops to a dozen runners, then eight and finally we are five. I get lapped once (or is it twice?) by the fitter ladies but finally my twenty laps are complete and the class raises the highest amount of all classes for that term.

Although that was a good effort, the school's best effort during my time in charge comes in response to the Armenian Earthquake in late 1988. During lunch on December 7, a teacher asks me if I have seen the news on the BBC about the earthquake in which it is reported that perhaps fifty thousand people have been killed and many more injured and made homeless. European governments are calling this a major catastrophe and the USSR is asking for help. I have a quick conversation with the Headmistress and get her approval to turn all our money-raising efforts to help Armenia. A quick chat with the Head of Physics, a natural actor, and we set up a pantomime performance for the school assembly the following morning. As the Headmistress, who is in on the act, sits down after saying prayers, the Head of Physics (let me call him *Wilsky*) arrives on stage wearing a heavy fur coat and ushanka hat. He puts on a very good impression of a Russian accent (apologies to Armenians who are, of course, not Russian) and asks the girls "did you 'ear about de terrible earthquake in h'Armenia?" Of course most had seen the news the previous evening.

"Yes" comes the audience response.

"Vill you 'elp us vith your charity vork?" asks *Wilsky*.

A louder "yes" from the girls.

"'ow can you ensure that you vill raise a good sum of money?" *Wilsky* asks.

And here comes the set up ... some of the girls say via cake sales but one cheeky miss simply puts her hand in the air so that *Wilsky* hushes the audience and asks her directly if she has another idea.

"Yes sir, we will sponsor Mr Marks to shave off his moustache!"

This is followed by pandemonium and high laughter in the assembly hall, even by the Headmistress while several of my close colleagues tap me on the back.

"Come up 'ere Mr Marks, come up on de stage" demands *Wilsky* and once next to him in full view of the five hundred or so people in assembly, he asks "vill you shave off your moustache, vill you 'elp h'Armenia?"

"Sorry but I am very attached to my moustache and so, no I cannot help you."

Booing proceeds to rise out of the ranks of the girls gathered below the stage followed by their chant of 'off, off, off'. I swear, even the Head gets involved.

"Ah OK" I say "if it is so important to you girls I will shave it off but you must raise £3,000 before the end of next week or I will not remove my moustache. Can you do that?"

And of course they do. Not only do the girls raise money, so do the teachers and so do many of the parents. By the Thursday of the following week, my accounts show that the school community has raised almost £4,000 for Armenia. The moustache must go.

But before proceeding, let me relate the history of this famous 'tache that has caused so much money to be raised. In my last two weeks at Sutton Valence School after finishing my A-levels (that dates back to 1972) we, the six-formers who were about to leave the 'august establishment for young gentlemen' had decided that we would all stop shaving. Some of my buddies like Nasr, a Persian, had a very noticeable and dark beard within a week while all I managed to achieve was a look akin to a dirty complexion.

Over the summer a soft beard did manage to sprout and eventually turn into a facial adornment that convinced everyone that I had been attacked by moths. I carried that 'beard' during my first year at university, occasionally trimming it. A few weeks into my second year, the prettiest girl in the new intake of biology students told me bluntly that she hated my beard and overlong hair, declared herself a hairdresser, produced some scissors and proceeded to cut my hair and trim my beard to a length that I could then shave off. However, I held on to the 'tache, in a pretence of a 'male show-of-strength' … until now that is, but now it has to go.

I decide to keep quiet about this self-amputation, even to my family. I simply go into the bathroom as usual, take my razor and off it comes. I then walk into the sitting room, as if nothing has happened and where Mélanie is waiting for me to walk her to school while Véro is getting David ready for nursery.

My little girl lets out a screech and begins to cry and sob "my daddy," *sniff-sniff,* "my dad-deee".

Véro looks up to see why the commotion and tears and lets out a roar of laughter and says a few words in French that are not repeatable here. I then explain why the 'tache had to go but promise to let it grow right back.

As part of the scene for the girls at the school, I take a piece of strong black paper, cut out a moustache-shape and stick it with glue to my upper lip. From a good distance, it would appear that my 'tache is still intact. I walk Mélanie to her school and then walk on to work with a scarf wrapped tightly around my mouth and neck – no peeping girls.

Wilsky takes again to the stage and announces in his fake accent "Girls, the people of h'Armenia thank you fe raising de money. You kept your side o' de deal, now did Mr Marks keep 'is? Come up 'ere Mr Marks."

I climb the steps on to the stage with my face still covered by the scarf and half-face the audience while looking at *Wilsky*. I lower the scarf slowly and 'no, no, no' breaks out from the girls and staff gathered below.

Wilsky leans over and rips the paper moustache off my lip in one slick movement (that actually rather hurts because the glue had done its job rather too well). After an initial collective 'ouch' from the girls, they put back their heads and howl with laughter. I think that even the Head joins in.

I am now in my third year at the school and am relaxed about this new term. One positive about being several years at a school is that one sees pupils maturing and developing, not only in the subjects being taught but in their characters. I was lucky to have had a lovely group of thirteen-year-olds to look after in my first year at the school and they have now grown to be young ladies of sixteen. They took their GCSEs last term with almost all doing very well indeed and have graduated into the A-level classes; many opting to do biology. This year I have not been assigned a year class to look after and so do not need to arrive at school quite so early but still like to get in early to prepare for my lessons.

As I wait in the common room, quiet and smoke-free since the noisy teachers and the smokers are in assembly, I switch on the staff computer that usually sits idle on a side table. My trip to Chad has resulted in two notebooks full of data, observations, ideas and quotes. I need to write them all up in a coherent report to present to ORT. Only once ORT has received and accepted my report will I get paid for the trip.

Strange as it might seem to any person under the age of fifty, I have never touched, let alone used a PC. They are new on the scene and pretty rare objects. As the computer boots up, I am asked for a password, and of course I do not have the faintest idea what it is. I am saved by the arrival of the school's computer teacher, a friendly and gentle young guy. He gives me the password and stands back to watch. When the flickering Dos prompt appears on the screen, I am again lost.

"Type 'WS' Malcolm, that will launch the WordStar programme." WS results in a flurry of activity on the screen and several clicks and clunks from inside the computer box. As the screen changes to a page-like appearance, I am informed "Now you are ready to go".

For the next fifteen minutes I begin to write the introduction to my report and then, when I hear the noise of staff coming back to the room, I ask how to save what I have typed so far. My first ever lesson in PC computing is finished and my kind colleague offers to help me more at the end of the school day when the room becomes a little quieter. After a week of trial and error and growing confidence, my report is completed, printed in duplicate and parcelled off to ORT in London. My rather generous salary for the six weeks in Chad is transferred to my bank account; I see that as likely to be the end of Chad's involvement in my career.

Soon after the report is finished, I flick through the business section of the Times and notice that they are calling on schools to enter a share-picking competition that allows senior school pupils to 'play the stock market' with an imaginary £10,000. I wonder if our A-level girls might be interested. At the following day's assembly, I ask the six-formers to stay back and put the idea to them. Out of the hundred or so girls, half are initially interested and, by the time I send in our application to take part, the school will be represented by three teams of eight. This is a nice aside from schoolwork and the teams of girls get excited about having £10,000 to spend! First I give them a few lessons on profit and loss, the value of dividends, P/E ratios and the rest; just as my friend John MacReady had given me several years previously.

Finally, the big day arrives for the start of the competition and the different teams come in with their ideas for investment. Clearly some rather conservative parents have also become involved because most of the choices are boringly normal: Rio Tinto, BT, Barclays Bank and similar. No matter, by the end of 14th October 1987, the three teams have invested their mythical £30,000 in a number of different stocks listed on the London Stock Exchange. However, when we arrive for school on the same day, the following week, the combined value of the shares has fallen to below £20,000; fully thirty percent of the value of those shares chosen by the girls has been wiped off in a day. Welcome to Black Monday, welcome to the dangers of share investment, welcome to a very valuable lesson for these young ladies.

My own share investments have also suffered. I was a typical 'Sid' and had invested small amounts in the many privatisations that the Thatcher government had decided to bring to the market: BT, British Gas and Rolls-Royce plus a few small companies that John had spoken to me about as well as in a tiny offshoot of Racal Electronics … called Vodafone.

There is never any need to panic when market corrections occur – unless the money tied up in shares is desperately needed (but then desperately needed money should never be tied up in the stock market). History shows that once markets correct, they will slowly regain confidence and come back to previous peaks; although this may take some time. So, while Black Monday makes me swallow hard a couple of times, Véro and I decide to add more cash from our limited savings into some of the hardest hit blue-chip stocks rather than panic-sell as some of my friends decide to do.

The crash also makes us seriously discuss what we should do about our little apartment in Culford Road; and here we initially disagree. My logic tells me that, just like in the stock market, a bubble is building up in London property and it will surely burst in the year or so after the stock market crash. Véro's logic is that we should just sit tight. Finally, we jointly decide that we should at least see how much our ten thousand pounds purchase of ten years ago is now worth. We are shaken hard with surprise when the estate agent, who manages our rental tenants, tells us that he believes we could get up to seventy-five thousand pounds. That news causes Véro to change her mind! As soon as our tenants vacate at the end of their contract in December, we put the flat on the market and it sells within a couple of months for seventy-two thousand pounds.

As the estate agent tells us "you did well as the market is starting to come off the boil".

After paying back the Halifax for their loan, we suddenly have more money than we could ever dream of. We place it into a high interest account with the Town and Country Building Society and we sit back and watch the interest rapidly build up.

(However, fast forward to the present day and this little apartment is valued at ... wait for it ... £829,000. Perhaps I should have listened to my better half!).

Also of interest, at around this time, is that the Town and Country starts to discuss merger terms with the Woolwich Building Society. This leads to oodles of excess reserve cash being returned to T&C members, us included. A few years later, the Woolwich floats on the London Stock Market, giving free shares to members and then starts to declare extravagant levels of dividends with their excess reserve cash. Finally, Barclays Bank launches a takeover bid on the Woolwich causing the latter's shares to go through the roof. Each of these market movements entice shareholders with cash on deposit to go along with the deals, meaning that we come out of them rather well. And the missed opportunity to have kept our flat and to have an asset now worth north of £800 K? My philosophy in life is to learn from experience ... but never to regret it.

Given the improvement in our cash situation now the apartment is sold, we look around for other investment opportunities. My favourite is to buy another house (or even two) in Edith Street, do it up and then resell it. During the past year or so, prices have begun to move higher but they can still be bought for around twenty-five thousand pounds. In our street alone there are at least half-a-dozen properties with sales boards up; many have been up for several months and so prices could be bargained down. I consider that most will only need a lick of paint and a refitted kitchen and/or bathroom to make them more 'desirable' and some probably only need the front door locking and a bit of patience before they will rise in price on their own accord.

Chatting over a glass of wine with a Northampton-based friend, I mention the possibility of buying and doing up a couple of houses in our road. I should have kept my mouth tightly sealed (Véro frequently suggests this to me!) because he immediately picks up on the idea and says "let's go in together 50/50. You can do the refurbishment work, because you have more free time and I do not have your skills; then we can split the profits." Yeah, sure!

Véro suggests another idea "let's move closer to Abington Park, that's the nicest part of town. We can probably afford a slightly bigger mortgage too." That seems a nice idea to me and I say so. Never being one to hang around, she then announces "great because we have two houses to visit this evening." And she hands me over the information sheets that she has already collected from the estate agents, roughly folded in eight. Have I fallen into a well lain trap?

Looking at the details of the houses, I notice that they are semi-detached, our current one is a terrace, and have an upstairs rather than downstairs bathroom and more significant gardens. But apart from those three facts, the only real difference with our house is the price – houses around the park start at over one hundred thousand pounds. Even by selling our house and investing some of the cash we had made on Islington, we will still need to up our mortgage to well over forty thousand pounds. I doubt the banks would consider my teacher salary sufficient for this amount. Nonetheless, we start the search for a new property with Véro doing most of the legwork during the day and me making second visits to those that she likes the most.

To cut this story short, we did move to Abington Park but not during this incarnation because fate, again, steps in. Just before leaving for school one morning, the postman knocks on the door and hands me a telegram. This is the first and last telegram that I ever receive in my life. On opening it, I read:

'We offer Ecology post in Senegal STOP Mobilisation soonest STOP call … STOP'

Where on earth has this come from? Talk about being gobsmacked. Nothing to do at the moment because the sender of the telegram is based on the East Coast of the USA and will still be tucked up in bed. My day crawls past as my excitement mounts but finally I get home from school at 4 pm. Our friend Diane is looking after Mélanie and David so that we can make this important call together and without the noise of two children who would just have gotten home from school.

I make the call and get straight through to the sender of the telegram. He has a faint accent that I put down, correctly as it turns out, to Dutch. After a rapid exchange of greetings, he informs me that he is the desk officer for the Ecology Centre in Dakar, Senegal. He goes on to tell me that I have been selected for the position of Technical

Advisor in Ecology, starting immediately. I am a little surprised because he is talking as though I know all about the position and that I am already employed and on my way to Senegal in a few days' time! With our phone on speaker, so that we can both listen in, Véro looks at me with eyebrows raised – as well she might – and I have to shrug my shoulders as I have no idea what he is talking about.

I eventually interrupt and say "sorry to interrupt, but can we take a step back or even start from the beginning? All I know is from the short telegram that I received this morning advising me that there is a vacant position for an ecologist in Senegal but I know absolutely nothing more. Where did you get my name, for example?"

As he replies, excusing himself for speaking too rapidly, he tells me "I am just back from a management trip to Dakar where I spoke with the project leader and he is getting fed up with our slowness in recruiting a suitable ecologist for his team. Then, when I got back to my office on the East Coast, I found a report from a French consultant who is overseeing a road-building project in Chad." Ah, finally the penny starts to drop. "Attached to the report was a short note that says you did some *pro-bono* analytical work for him of very high standard and that he recommends you highly if a suitable position should come up. He even added your handwritten pages of analyses into his report as an annexe. I checked them and am impressed too. But I had no way of finding you until I had a call with your old PhD supervisor who has just done some consulting work for us in Senegal. I asked him if he knew of an Anglo-Saxon trained ecologist, who knows Africa and who speaks French. He told me that he knew of one, and that was you! He gave me your address in the UK, hence the telegram. I have posted a package to you today via DHL with an offer and all the details. Call me back if you need to discuss any issues further. Are you interested in the job?"

I look over at Véro and her head is nodding up and down like the 'Churchill Insurance Dog' "yes, very interested" I reply.

So one coincidence has been added to a second and that to a third. I had been found via my old PhD supervisor now based at the University of Maryland in the US as an associate professor. I knew he had an interest in the Sahel but not that he was actually doing work there. It seems that his recommendation plus that of the French Consultant from Chad were considered sufficient references with the approval of the project leader, to offer me the job.

Well knock me down with a feather.

WE ARE OUT OF HERE!

The first people to know about our likely change of country are Diane and Brian. Brian finds this sufficient excuse, if he ever needs one, to open one of the *piquettes* that he insists on bringing back from France during his frequent booze-cruises. He always believes that this bargain find at less than £3 a bottle surely ranks alongside one of the better Burgundy reds.

"Oh do shut up Brian Coe" is usually his wife's response; said with love but a certain embarrassment too.

Dear Brian, he loves everything French and his enthusiasm for our cousins across the channel is heart-warming in its simplicity.

We decide to wait for the information papers and the job offer to arrive from the USA before saying anything to anyone else. It would be bad to say too much, too soon, especially at the school; just in case the offer does not meet our expectations.

A week after my call with the USA, a parcel arrives with DHL. It contains numerous papers to be filled in but the ones that interest me the most are the terms and conditions, the mobilisation details and, most importantly, the job description.

The proposed salary is more than three times what I currently receive at the school. I am to be appointed at P4-2 level; a quite senior level in their system, I am later to discover. There is also housing allowance over a certain level, air tickets, assistance in paying private school fees for the children, and so on. Mobilisation is ASAP but I have to, and will, respect my school contract that requires one term's notice. A quick call to the East Coast confirms that this is acceptable.

The job description is comprehensive, and in French. Some of the words both Véro and I have never met previously. '*Télédétection*', '*enquêtes aériens*', '*système d'information géographique*', '*désertification*' are four terms that leave us a little puzzled as to what they mean and involve while 'use of advanced computer programmes' has me a little concerned. But I am a fast learner and will make the necessary effort to catch up. Other components like 'leading botanical surveys', 'frequent field work', 'team management', 'occasional deputising for the team leader, cause me less concern.

We fill in the papers – and there are a lot of them – go for a medical (I get the all-clear) and go to a professional photographer on the Wellingborough Road for photos. I need some standard passport photos because I am to be issued with a blue passport while Véro dresses the children very cutely for a 'dependents' photo' as they are to be issued with a *laissez-passer*. We agree on a departure date for me, it is to be at the end of March 1989, and Véro and the children will follow two weeks later in mid-April. This will give me a little time to settle in and get organised before they arrive.

My next task is to meet with the Headmistress to offer my resignation. This proves harder for me than I would have imagined and, as I knock on her door, I find that I have a lump in my throat.

"Good morning Headmistress. I asked to see you this morning because I have been offered a senior Ecologist position with an international agency in Senegal. I would therefore like to tender my resignation to be effective from the end of the spring term."

"Ah, Mr Marks. I am happy that you made this appointment" says the Head "because we have been discussing your merits and want to offer you more opportunity at the school. This will mean a promotion as we want you to stay with us for many more years".

I cannot believe my ears. How can this be after the chewing off I got not too long ago when I wanted the careers advisory position and had been refused and told that I could never expect better?

I find myself saying "I'm afraid this has come rather too late. While I have always been happy teaching at the school, I have never made a secret of the fact that I am ambitious and need to be challenged. Now I have been offered an excellent career opportunity. I cannot say no."

The news spreads rapidly around the school and, soon after, outside of the school too. Several of my original 'class of 85' come in with presents and notes from their parents that wish me luck and offer their congratulations. I am particularly touched by several mums and dads who I look on with fondness and as friends for their kind words. The phone at the school office also starts to ring with calls coming from several county newspapers. They want to interview me about my great news. I wonder who tipped them off? Could it have been the school looking for some free publicity? I do not know but I am interviewed by three newspapers over the next week or so with the worst headline being produced by a local Northampton rag that has me looking through a large magnifying glass so one eyeball is enormous and with the headline of 'Top Marks'. *Très drôle* mister journalist.

Despite the lovely farewells that the girls and many of the staff offer me, not once do I (and will I ever) regret this decision. While Chad may have been the catalyst of the change, Senegal will prove to be the place that changes both my career and my outlook on life. It also deepens my love for Africa, strengthens my character and teaches me not to be so naive. It's the place, if I am honest, where I take several hard knocks and, in doing so, learn some important life lessons and where, if I am being *really* honest, I grow up.

6

A President Weeps

Towards the end of the Spring term, we put our house on the market and hire removal companies. We split our belongings into three parts. The first part – that seems to be predominantly composed of an enormous collection of toys and kitchen utensils – is collected by the packers from my new employers and disappears in the direction of Senegal. The furniture we wish to keep but not take to Senegal goes off with a second company of packers and makes its way across the channel to Cordon. The remainder is either sold privately, given to friends or loaded into a hire van and dropped off at the Northampton auctions. All that we place in the auctions sells and surprisingly we realise a profit on every item.

Meanwhile, we travel over to France and arrive in time to receive the Cordon-bound furniture while the agents get busy on selling our now empty house in Edith Street. We had decided to sell Edith Street for, in my words, "we will never return to live in Northampton."

They put the house on the market at £55,950 – a nice mark-up from the £16,000 that we had paid less than four years previously – and in the end we accept an offer for fifty-two thousand in a falling market. For the record, the value of our old house continued to fall so that in 1995, six years after we sold it, we saw that it had been resold for only £42,000.

The day, or rather the late-afternoon, of my departure to Senegal from Lyon-Satolas comes around quickly. Since I have been sent a one-way ticket, my new employers have to pay full-price and this entitles me to a business class seat; the only time this happens while working for them. I queue up to register my luggage with Véro and the children at my side and soon reach the check-in counter. I place my suitcase and sports holdall on to the scales and note that they add up to 35 kg; five over my allowance. I hand my ticket and sky-blue (and brand new) diplomatic passport to the Air France agent. He informs me with the straightest of faces that my luggage is overweight and so would I mind accepting an upgrade to first class; would I heck?

With my first-class boarding pass in hand, I am whisked through the waiting 'hoards' from economy and escorted by an air hostess to the front row of the plane, seat 1F. As I sit down next to the window – no worries about having to clamber over fellow passengers in this seat – two more hostesses bring a suited gentleman to the seat next to me. They seem to hover around chatting to him for long minutes but eventually he is able to take his seat. We say *bonjour*, shake hands and exchange names. His name means nothing to me, why should it? I assume that he must be an off duty pilot given the attention he has just received.

As we await take-off we are handed glasses of champagne – oh my goodness, Véro will be jealous – and chat together about why I am travelling to Senegal. In return, he tells me that he works for Air France. The flight takes off and, as soon as the seat belt sign is extinguished, my travel companion excuses himself to visit the toilet.

One of the air hostesses comes across and introduces herself with "hello Dr Marks, my name is Jeanine and I will be looking after you on this flight. You seem to be getting on well with our MD."

So my travel companion is none other than the boss of Air France!

The trip goes smoothly; we are served a fantastic meal while the wine list contains many French wines that I have never heard of – so they must be good! Mr MD suggests a particular red wine from Bourgogne that tastes so good that I am tempted to drink the whole bottle. But perhaps I better not.

The plane lands in Dakar at close to 11 pm but being one of the first off the plane and then holding a light blue passport sees me quickly through the police and visa checks and on to baggage collection. A few minutes wait and I am collecting my suitcase, then passing through customs unhindered. What an easy arrival this is proving. That is, until I walk out into the arrivals hall. Now, I have been through arrivals in Lagos and more recently in N'djamena but here in Dakar, 'you ain't seen nothing yet!'

The entire hall is sheer pandemonium with at least half-a-dozen young men trying to grab my bag and suitcase out of my hands. I presume, correctly, that they are taxi touts, and I have to resort to yelling variously '*non*', '*ça va*', '*laissez*' until a young man of about my age comes across and yells at a more persistent tout "*dégages*" (clear off) and I find a little more space appears around me. This is Diagne and he is a driver with the ecology centre. The team leader has sent him to pick me up and take me back to stay at his home.

I have arrived in Senegal, and it's 'Back-to-Africa'.

The team leader lives in a house tucked away off a main artery in the Liberté-6 area of the city. The size and proportions of the house are not evident from the street because the one-storey house is surprisingly large once inside. He has been living in Dakar for a couple of years and is with his partner and her two children. I understand they met several years earlier during his work in the Senegal River valley. Despite the late hour of my arrival, he wants to talk about my future work at the centre. We talk away (or rather he talks and I listen and take notes) into the small hours of the morning. Eventually, I am obliged to tell him that I am exhausted after my flight and need to sleep. This is, I am to find, one of his characteristics, for everything he does, he does well and with 150% effort; and he never seems to need to sleep.

The next morning, we go off early to the offices that the project occupies. They are located in the very beautiful *Parc de Hann.* The Park is occupied, at its northern end, by the newly built Forestry Department; to the East by ISRA; to the west by the Dakar Zoo and to the south by the Livestock Department. We are housed above a livestock research unit in a neo-colonial building. Our offices are on the first floor and are accessed by climbing a metal stairway that runs up the outside of the building. At the top of the stairs are four doors. The first, the team leader tells me, is a communal kitchen with a fridge and a kettle; the second has its door open and I see it is a toilet that does not look over-clean; the third apparently leads to the national project coordinator's office. The team leader laughs as he tells me that the coordinator is not involved in project activities but is at his happiest when given a newspaper, a packet of cigarettes and a computer for playing Patience and Tetris. The final door leads into the main project office that contains seven larger rooms. The first room, at the entrance, belongs to Accounts and is staffed by Mr Keita with help from two secretaries, including one dedicated to the project coordinator, plus a messenger. As we enter, Mr Keita, 'call me Keita' comes over to shake my hand and tells me that I am most welcome.

Senegal is the country of 'Teranga' which translates from the main language of Dakar, Wolof, to 'hospitality' but I soon find means far, far more. It is a word that encompasses the manner, steeped in culture, that one should treat one's guests with generosity, respect, patience and honour.

The second door leads to the team leader's office. It has all glass walls above waist height so easy to know when he is in residence. The third, on the left, leads to a room shared by the computing team, composed of only a Frenchman, who is a few years older than me, and the socioeconomics team of one. The door opposite is to be my office. It is occupied by three other people, and they are the seniors in my ecology team. The first to stand up and shake my hand introduces himself as the national expert for ecology. He seems four or five years older than me and, until recently, worked in the government's livestock department and now is under a similar contract to mine, but the national not international version. He has been overseeing all ecology activities until my appointment. He proves a godsend to me as I seek to settle in and learn the ropes. He is extremely patient and happy to pass on his very considerable knowledge.

His younger colleague, a forester, has been seconded to the project by the government and he heads up the botanical field team. He is a complex but lovable character. Unbeknown to me at this moment as I shake his hand, is that we will butt heads frequently but end up as good friends. The final person in the room, and I notice how cramped it is with just these three people, introduces himself as a civil servant from livestock and he leads, very logically, the livestock activities at the ecology centre, including aerial survey work.

The next and largest room is the project conference room that also contains a nascent library. This is the domain of the self-styled 'head of communications'. Two rooms lead off the conference room. In the first, I meet the other two members of the aerial survey team while in the second, I am introduced to a tall, gangly Dane with a scrawny beard. He is the technical adviser for geography, and he shares his room with some of his team of geographers, including the project's deputy coordinator, and the lead technician for the project's nascent geographic information system.

After shaking many hands, responding to several *nan-ga-def* (Wolof for 'how are you?'), I am led back to the team leader's office for a cup of Nescafe (for me) and a glass of water for him. He tells me that he never touches stimuli like caffeine and alcohol.

We talk right through to lunchtime about my workload. He tells me that the centre has its origins in 1985 when a pilot project was established by a specialist office of the international agency to determine how the extremely dry conditions and severe droughts of the early 1980s could be monitored and that information used to provide future early warnings to Sahelian governments and international donor agencies. The pilot was set up in 1985 for a two-year period and used to test new technologies to monitor the Sahelian pastures of the northern half of Senegal, encompassing the Ferlo region of the country.

The pilot was composed of two main activities. The first was to import to Senegal the wildlife monitoring activities undertaken with great success in Kenya under the leadership of the United Nations Environmental Programme (UNEP). This involved flying aerial surveys in small aeroplanes to count the different species of large wildlife. In Senegal, the aim was to adapt this technique to estimate livestock numbers. The pilot surveys have proven very successful, partly thanks to the excellent technical inputs of Mike Norton-Griffith, a recognised expert in the field. This year's survey is to begin in only a few days' time; led by my office roommate.

The second activity initiated during the pilot project was even more ambitious. It looked to combine satellite imagery, especially the brand new NOAA satellites, with botanical fieldwork to pro-vide estimates of seasonal vegetation production. The geography team handles the satellite side while 'my team', the ecologists, are responsible for the fieldwork. It was in setting up the field side of the second activity that the Centre had met my old PhD supervisor who had been one of the main consultants for the work. Since I had last seen my old supervisor at Queen Mary College, he had gone to the States for a one-year sabbatical, loved it and decided to stay. After the sabbatical he found a teaching post at the University of Maryland and was brought into the 'GIMS Group' of Jim Tucker, based in Maryland. It was, also, during the work in Senegal that he had recommended me and this led to the international agency offering me the job as an ecology adviser.

As the team leader continues to explain, the relationship between the two pilot activities becomes clearer because once the numbers and distribution of livestock across the country is known and compared with the vegetation available for it to graze, government services should be able to intervene to introduce improved manage-ment of the natural resources. Add in other factors like bushfires and borehole distribution (especially if out of action), and a complex and interrelated picture begins to build up.

The pilot project had completed in 1987, with considerable suc-cess, allowing the current project that seeks to develop the ecology centre to follow on seamlessly. The centre is funded by the Danish Aid Agency, and managed by an independent office based at the agency headquarters on the East Coast. That office is predominantly staffed by Scandinavians who seem to be the most generous of its donors. To add to the complexity – a lovely habit of the agency – the financial and administrative sides, including contracts like mine, are handled by another office of project services.

By the end of my first day, I have received a thorough run through of many of the details of the project and have filled several more pages of my notebook. Now I have to ensure that I understood them and begin to put those details into practice.

The following morning, I hold an introductory meeting with the members of my new ecology team. I start off by explaining that I have not come to tell them how to do their work but rather, especially at the start of my assignment, to learn from them. I also ask everyone to be patient with me if I do not express myself correctly in French, after all this is the first time that I will be working one hundred percent in the language. Each member of the team then describes their work, their plans for the next month or so and whether I can help with any issues they might be facing.

The field botany team tells me that the centre is seeking to expand its vegetation monitoring and aerial survey work to the whole country and, the former, requires the installation of additional permanent field sites where the vegetation production will be measured. Initially we need to add four more field sites in the 'peanut basin' that sits either side of the main road from Thiès to Louga. The installation is to be done in May and my help is needed with the work. Great. After that we need to start adding more sites in the south of the country, south of the Dakar to Tambacounda road.

The aerial survey team then informs the meeting that the next aerial survey is to start in little more than a week and will last throughout the month of April and stretch into May. The centre is awaiting the arrival of the survey plane and pilot from Kenya. The amount of data generated is extremely large and the project has been anticipating my arrival to lead on the setting up of the statistical analysis and map production components.

Finally, the national contractor tells me that his main job is to make sure that I fit into the team quickly and efficiently. He is to be my right-hand man as I try to settle into work. He oversees and lends a helping hand to both the field ecology and aerial survey teams. I also get to meet the two additional technicians who operate in the aerial survey team and will be flying in the plane during the aerial survey work.

Our meeting breaks up and I walk back to my office with the lead for aerial surveys work. As we go through into our room, I ask him how he thinks the meeting went and he tells me that everything went well but that I did not say enough.

Being puzzled by this response, I ask "what did I miss out?"

And he responds "nothing was missed out but you should know that in Senegal we say many words to provide a small amount of information. I know that in the Anglophone world you do not waste words but instead get quickly to the point. Don't worry, you will soon learn to speak like us Senegalese!"

All the activities described to me this morning sound interesting and really pushing the boundaries of my ecological knowledge, to date. I find my three senior colleagues highly competent, knowledgeable and keen to succeed. A good start to my time in Dakar.

The interest of my work aside, I am only too aware that I have just a two-week window before the arrival in country of Véro and the children. During this fortnight, not only must I integrate to the project team but I must also find a house and a car for us as well as purchase the bare essentials of furniture such as beds. Obtaining a car turns out to be easier than I had anticipated. The team leader tells me that he has a friend working for the World Bank who is leaving unexpectedly. The friend has only recently purchased a brand new Peugeot 305 *break* (estate) and must now sell it before his imminent departure. It is for sale at seventy percent of purchase price but I could try to negotiate the price down a bit further. I go to see the vehicle with our project mechanic and he declares the car impeccable with very few kilometres on the clock. I offer just short of two and a half million CFA (about five thousand pounds) and we shake hands on the deal. The local agency office in Dakar advances me a car loan, repayable over six months, and I have purchased a great car at a very decent price.

Finding a house is a bit harder, mostly because there seem to be few on the market and I have so little free time to view those that are. I frankly do not know where to start looking. Eventually I find a four-bedroom house down a short dusty track running off the *Front-de-Terre* road. The location is convenient for the office and so I sign papers with the managing agency and hand over a significant deposit. After purchasing three beds, a table and chairs, a gas cooker, fridge and a couple of air conditioners, the house is getting close to receiving us. The next piece of good news is that my container has arrived from the UK and is whisked through customs by the agency office and arrives at my door a couple of days later. All is unpacked in readiness for my family's arrival.

Véro and the kids arrive on a Thursday evening and we settle straight into our new home. We jointly admit that the house is not perfect and the neighbourhood a little noisy, being so close to the main road, but it will do until we can search leisurely for a more suitable rental. On Friday, I take the family to visit my office and to meet the team. Next, I show Véro where the zoo is, a two-minute drive from my office, and while they look around the animals and feed packets of peanuts to the chimps, I get on with my work. We have just heard that the plane from Kenya has landed at the small airport in Kaolack, a couple of hours drive from Dakar. The aerial survey team has already left for Kaolack, will begin training on Monday, and the survey work itself will start as soon as their training completes. I plan to follow down on Monday afternoon, spend two nights in a hotel, and come back to Dakar by Wednesday midday. Obviously having the family just arrive in town, I feel a little bad about leaving them so soon.

On the Saturday, before I leave for Kaolack, we decide to do a little exploring and shopping and head towards the centre of Dakar to a sector called The Plateau. It is here that the agency's main Dakar office is based as well as our bank and, importantly, le Marché Kermel (market) that my Danish colleague has told me is the best place for food shopping. Dakar is far, far in advance of Calabar with several supermarkets, butchers and bakers as well as wide streets and boulevards. Indeed, Dakar is a city loved by the older, pre-independence generation of French, the so-called '*Dakarois*'. This is partly due to Dakar's relatively mild climate, owing much to the proximity of the Atlantic Ocean, and partly due to the ease and standard of living in the city. Given the pleasant climate and the 'Teranga' of the Senegalese, many French decided to continue to live in Dakar when the country became formally independent in 1960.

Senegal, and particularly Dakar, was once the gateway to France's West African Empire that originally stretched from Senegal and Mauritania eastwards across Mali, Guinea, Burkina Faso, Niger and Chad, southwards to the Ivory Coast, Benin (Dahomey), and south-eastwards to the Cameroons, the Central African Republic and Congo-Brazzaville. That is until the British decided to upset the applecart by occupying the little island of Gorée that sits a kilometre off Dakar and, quite effectively, blocked entry to the Empire. Such shenanigans were settled by the payment of a small strip of land either side of the Gambia River that became known as The Gambia. The Senegalese often tell me that The Gambia is like a worm in the apple that is Senegal; and it does have just about the right shape!

Just across a small road from Marché Kermel is a butcher's shop run by a Frenchman that we have heard sells excellent meat. This is our first stop at the market. We enter the store and are greeted by Pierre, the butcher.

He tells us '*bienvenu*' and offers us a piece of baguette on which is plastered a lovely looking, homemade terrine. I take a bite with Pierre watching my reaction closely. "well, what do you think?" he asks me.

"*Pas mal*," I reply, "*mais mieux avec un coup de rouge !*" (not bad but it would be better with a bit of red wine).

"*T'as bien raison*" and he disappears out the back door of the shop and reappears a moment later with two glasses of red wine. Véro looks on in feigned horror to see her husband and his new friend drinking at 10.30 in the morning. But that bit of fun means that we become regular customers at the shop and Pierre always leaves his other customers to have a chat with us.

Our next purchases are within the market itself. Kermel is a beautiful building that, judging from the architecture, must date from around the art deco period of the 1920s, or perhaps even earlier. It is a round structure with market stalls arranged in concentric circles. On the outside are the vegetable and fruit sellers, inside those are the butchers and fishmongers while on the inside are some stalls selling arts and crafts. As soon as we enter Kermel through the arch across the road from the butcher, a young boy comes across and tells Véro that he will be her basket carrier! Having experienced the same in Calabar, she hands the basket over and the small boy – who progressively grows during our time in Dakar – becomes our permanent basket carrier on each subsequent visit to the market. And woe-betide any other small boy who might try to take his place.

Many of the stalls are manned by ladies of the Peul or Fulani tribe. To be polite, as well as to quote Alexander McCall-Smith's 'No. 1 Ladies Detective Agency' based in Beautiful Botswana, they are all 'Traditionally Built', actually *very* traditionally built!

The first lady, Khadi, we meet asks us how long since we arrived in Dakar. The city may boast a million inhabitants, and many thousands of whom are European, but a newcomer stands out like a sore thumb! Khadi is to become our purveyor of all fruit and vegetables, with the exception of potatoes and onions! These are always purchased from the man who runs the stall next to Khadi's. My memory does not remind me why potatoes and onions are purchased elsewhere, they just are.

Kermel has a fair number of beggars, most are seriously physically handicapped. The presence of beggars is quite normal. After all, Senegal is a predominantly Muslim country and giving alms (or *zakat*) is one of the five pillars of Islam. I notice that a handsome young man with Rastafarian dreadlocks keeps appearing by my feet as we circle the market purchasing our food. The poor guy has withered legs and could never stand let alone walk. He asks me for alms but I have just given all my change to Khadi in exchange for some miniature lettuces and a bunch of carrots.

I tell him that I have no change and he replies in all seriousness "give me a note and I can make you some change!"

Both Véro and I burst out laughing at this cheeky response and he becomes the recipient of our charity each time we visit Kermel. He even tells me that if any other beggar comes to ask for charity that I am to reply phonetically '*aga-na*' that apparently means 'I have already given'.

We arrive back to the house and Mélanie, who is soon to be seven, tells us very seriously "I do not like the market and I do not want to go back. It is too dirty and the beggars frighten me."

In contrast, David now about to celebrate his third birthday tells us "I want to go back to speak with my 'friend on the floor'."

If we are to leave Mélanie at home, we need to find a maid, and quickly. The team leader tells us that he knows a lady who speaks a smattering of French and is looking for a job. The lady, who cannot be more than twenty-five or so, comes for an interview and mentions that she is the first wife of a fireman and that her husband has just taken a second, younger and prettier wife. She has now been instructed by her husband to go and look for work, hence her appearance at our house. Not a good start. However, we decide to give her a month's trial but warn her that she may need to babysit a few evenings each month for which she would be paid extra. She begins work on the Monday morning as I put my bag in the back of the Toyota Landcruiser and begin my journey to Kaolack.

Today my driver is Séraphin, a Catholic, coming originally from the department of Kédougou in the far southeast of Senegal. As we drive out of Dakar, 'enjoying' the traffic jam that always forms as vehicles approach the Patte d'Oie, a roundabout that is apparently in the shape of a goose's foot, Séraphin tells me some of his history.

As a boy and a young man, he grew up in the forests of Kédougou, never went to school and has no idea of his real age. He was, in his own words, 'a bush-man'. Drought and population pressures pushed young men of his region to try their luck at finding work in the closest towns. He found his way to Tambacounda (always shortened to Tamba) in 1970 where he did menial jobs, learning how to speak rudimentary French and finding himself a wife, Delphine. One of his friends had managed to get a job in a garage and, because they needed extra hands, Séraphin was taken on as a driver; notwithstanding that he did not know how to drive. After a bit of practice, he found he had a talent for bush driving; perfect since Tamba had few proper roads. But he needed a licence. No problem. He visited the correct ministry office in Tamba, paid slightly more than the requisite fee (the civil servant explaining that the difference was a charge for him to fill the form instead of the then illiterate Séraphin).

When they reached the section 'date of birth', Séraphin explained that he had absolutely no idea in which year he was born, let alone the day and the month.

The civil servant looked at him and said "oh, you look like you are twenty-one years old so we will put that you were born in 1949, and your birthday can be today."

Séraphin proves to be a treasure and he certainly saved my life on at least one occasion. He is also a brilliant driver, especially in the forests and boggy lands where we are obliged to work for the botanical side of our monitoring. But today, the driving is easier as the road through to Kaolack, Senegal's third city, is tarmacked and relatively wide. We quickly pass through Rufisque, one of the original colonial towns of Senegal, where several large buildings are constructed of limestone, rather like that of my home in Cordon.

As we travel, we listen to a French language local radio and hear that tension is rising between Senegal and the neighbouring Mauritania. Mauritania lies to the north and north-east of Senegal and the two countries are separated by the River Senegal. But the differences between the two are not just geographic. Mauritania is a predominantly Arabic country and many ethnic Senegalese who live there are sadly treated as traditional slaves. Quite obviously this has been a bone of contention for Senegal, and distrust and dislike has frequently boiled up on both sides. Furthermore, the Mauritanians are herders, like the ethnic Peul of Senegal, but the difference being that the Mauritanians have large herds of camels with sheep / goats while the Senegalese predominantly herd cattle. The droughts of recent years have hit Mauritania much harder than Senegal, although Senegal has suffered severely too. Those droughts have forced the Mauritanian herds to seek pastures further south and they have poured across the border and set up camps in the Ferlo; Senegal's traditional grazing area. To try to push back the herds and reduce grazing competition, Senegal has recently announced that camel herds are not allowed into the country and this has lit a tinderbox in Mauritania. As the newscaster tells us, civilian disturbances are occurring in Mauritania and there have been casualties on the ethnic Senegalese side.

Dakar and other Senegalese cities count relatively fewer Mauritanians and those that are in the country are particularly active in the artisanal gold trade and jewellery manufacture or run small corner shops but they are nowhere near as numerous as the ethnic Senegalese living in Mauritania.

On arrival in Kaolack, we head straight to the hotel to check in and drop our bags before driving off towards the airport that is located to the south of the city.

As we drive along the rough road that leads to the tiny regional airport, we see a group of young men with sticks and iron bars that have forced a minibus off the road. They have broken some of the windows and are trying to drag the young Mauritanians out. Instinctively, I say to Séraphin that we must stop to help the passengers but he ignores me, accelerating away.

After we put a safe distance between ourselves and the minibus, he pulls on to the side of the track, turns to face me and says "the quickest way to get killed in Africa is to interfere with a mob. I know that you wanted to help but we cannot. I'm sorry but my first job is to keep you safe."

In the news from Kaolack that evening, we learn that the Mauritanians had been beaten up and robbed but no one killed. That is in sharp contrast to the news and pictures that are coming out of Mauritania. There are stories of killings and sexual mutilation of ethnic Senegalese. Many, perhaps hundreds, are reported dead. The President of Senegal, Abdou Diouf, has put the country on a war footing and the air force is sent to 'buzz' the frontier. All-out war is avoided by the statesmanship of President Diouf and the intervention of French diplomats who try to calm the rising storm.

Our work is now at serious risk since the aerial survey is programmed to fly across the entire north of the country using the Senegal River in the north and the tarmac road from Dakar to Tamba in the south as its turning points. The only positive is that the plane is flying in the agency's bright colours. Nonetheless, the pilot has been warned by the team leader to ensure that he keeps strictly to the southern side of the Senegal River.

We arrive at the airport to find my new colleague working at the aeroplane with his two assistants and the pilot.

The plane is tiny! It is a four-seater Cessna with raised wings and struts that descend from the lower side of the wings to the fuselage below the windows. On to these struts, each side of the plane, have been fixed two parallel rods. I am told that the distance between the rods has been calculated so that two passengers, sitting either side of the plane, will each see a delimited band (or transect in ecological terms) of one hundred and fifty metres wide when the plane is flying at a fixed altitude of four hundred feet. The two assistants will occupy these seats and only count livestock seen within the bands. Should there be too many animals to count accurately and quickly, they will estimate the number while taking numbered photos that will be reviewed at the end of the survey.

One of the principal roles in the plane of the lead technician is to time the distance flown and, at the end of every minute, to announce the fact. The pilot's main activities, apart from maintaining the crew's safety, are to keep the plane at an altitude of four hundred feet (why not metres? I do not know) and an air speed of one hundred and eighty kilometres an hour. A mathematical mind will have anticipated that the transect monitored by the two enumerators is three hundred metres wide and the distance flown in a minute is three kilometres. This means that the transect is being subdivided into quadrats (two matching rectangles in this case) of a total of 0.9 kilometre square.

The plane runs parallel transects over the whole distance of the Dakar-Tamba road in the south to the Senegal River in the north, a distance that varies and generally increases as the transect lines move from the west, or coastal, side of Senegal to the east. The transect lines themselves are flown five kilometres apart and the plane's compass system ensures that straight lines are flown.

As a valuable addition to the work being undertaken, the Centre has purchased and installed a sophisticated Hasselblad camera that takes shots at regular intervals of the terrain below and geo-locates them. Later, we are to interpret the vegetation components of these photos by measuring the percentage of each photo that is covered by trees and shrubs, grass and bare soil, water, roads and so forth. These data can then be overlain on to maps of administrative units or ecological zones.

Once the plane is ready to be tested, I go up for a flight of an hour or so with the pilot. What an amazing view we have from just over one hundred metres up. Particularly impressive are the giant baobabs that occur to the north and west of Kaolack and the beautiful mangrove swamps of the Sine Saloum that lie further south. But while impressive, these mangroves cannot compare with those I used to explore in the south-east of Nigeria.

The day's work being finished, Séraphin drives us back to our hotel. Time for a quick shower before he is knocking at my door telling me that it is time for 'Kaolack-by-night'. My virtue remains safe since the only hot spots in Kaolack are the restaurants that have no air-conditioning; which is where we always eat together as a team. Staff may receive generous per diems while on mission but many economise on these in order to top up their salaries.

The next day I spend as much time with the aerial survey lead as he can spare. We start going through the way we will analyse the results that are to come out of the upcoming survey. I have always been taught, and continue to teach, that the means of statistical analyses should be clarified *before* collecting any data. However, currently it seems, the data are simply being mapped and overlain to administrative subdivisions of the country. Apart from calculating average livestock numbers per square kilometre, no effort has previously been made to analyse statistically the data; an error, in my mind, and where I should be able to have a rapid impact.

The following morning, we take breakfast with the aerial survey team, say our goodbyes and drive back to Dakar, arriving in time to drop into the office to debrief the team leader before going home to Véro and the children for a late lunch. The team leader tells me that the news out of Mauritania is not going well and the Senegalese here in Dakar are beginning to get angrier and angrier.

The remainder of the week follows relatively calmly with the news coming out of Mauritania stating that the situation is quietening down. That is until the Friday evening when evacuation flights start to bring planeloads of ethnic Senegalese back to the airport in Dakar. The first flight is met by President Diouf. This impressively tall, slim and dignified man is shown on national television with tears streaming down his face as stretchers carry the injured off the plane and he witnesses the inhumanity of sexual mutilation that has been inflicted on his fellow human beings. This is a truly dark period in West African history; Senegal weeps with the President. Unfortunately, the Senegalese population of the cities, having seen their highly respected President shedding tears openly on television, begins to prepare revenge.

The next day starts calmly enough as we set off for Marché Kermel. We promise the children that we will stop first at the bakery and cake shop to have breakfast. This persuades Mélanie, always the gourmand, to come with us rather than staying with the maid. David has rattled around in his money box and retrieved some small CFA coins that he will give to his 'beggar friend' at the market.

We arrive at the bakery on Jules Ferry road that sits in the shadow of the Sacré Cœur Cathedral and order our coffees, fruit juices and cakes plus a couple of baguettes for the weekend. As is usual, the café buzzes with expats and Senegalese alike; this is a very successful enterprise and I have discovered that their *Jesuits* (cakes not priests!) are superb.

Suddenly we hear mortar rounds going off in the distance proclaiming that the military are using tear gas. This brings the owner of the bakery out of his office at the back and he announces that he has gotten word that anti-Mauritanian protests have started just outside the plateau area where we are sitting. He tells us that it is better to stay put on the plateau, where there is a strong police and army presence, rather than risk trying to drive out of the zone. This is a worrying moment, particularly as we have the children with us, and the thump-thump of mortar rounds increases in frequency and seems to be getting closer.

After thirty minutes or so of anguish, we start hearing cheers coming from the boulevard opposite, where the cathedral sits. I walk carefully out of the bakery, being joined by a Senegalese man who is in the bakery with his family. We first look down the street where I notice three or four Mauritanians nervously peering out of a small shop. I turn my head to look towards the cheering, that is getting closer, and coming from the main road that leads in a straight line to the Presidential Palace. The road is empty apart from three open-back army trucks driving slowly down the main avenue towards the palace and, probably, onto the town centre. As the first truck gets closer, I can see that the driver and others in the cab are white – strange. As it passes, I can now see that the benches in the back of the trucks are also filled with predominantly white soldiers, sitting ramrod stiff and holding their guns between their knees pointed skywards.

We later learn that the French military, on the request of President Diouf, has mobilised its reserve forces based in Dakar. Their appearance, without needing to fire a single round, calms the morning and delights the local population. We are able to return home, though without going to Kermel for our fruit and vegetables.

While I get the children out of the car and in through the front door, Véro takes the bread to the kitchen.

I hear her exclaim in French "but no, you cannot work like that."

I go quickly into the kitchen to find our maid doing the ironing ... topless. While she tells us that most Senegalese maids work topless when it is hot, Véro explains that this is not the case in our home. David comes out to ogle the 'ninis' as he calls them before the maid reluctantly puts back her top.

As Véro is getting the maid to cover up, I hear a harsh knocking at the front door. I open carefully and find three very scared men (are they Mauritanians?) huddling together in the porch.

One speaks to me in pretty fluent French "boss, please can we come into your home? There are a group of men chasing us and we are scared."

I quickly step back to allow them to enter and get them settled in the sitting room.

The speaker goes on to tell me "we are not Mauritanians but Moroccans" and they draw out their Moroccan passports. The speaker holds a diplomatic one and goes on to say "people here are so angry about events in Mauritania that anyone who looks like a

Mauritanian is getting chased, including us. May I use your phone to call our embassy and get them to send a car to collect us?"

After giving them drinks, their car arrives and they are driven back to their embassy. Our good deed for the day.

Our maid does not last much longer in our household. A couple of evenings later, Véro and I are invited to the home of the agency's Resident Representative (a role equivalent to an Ambassador) in Senegal. He wants to meet new staff like me and introduce us to his senior staff that all work in the agency's building on the Plateau. We have forewarned our maid that we need her to babysit the children for a few hours, and she is in agreement. Séraphin comes to collect us at 7 pm but there is no sign of the maid. We wait a further thirty minutes with me telephoning an excuse to the Res Rep but she still does not show. Reluctantly, I have to leave Véro with the children and go off with Séraphin. I spend a pleasant evening with my new colleagues and find the Res Rep, a national of Mali, charming and attentive.

On the way back home I complain to Séraphin about the maid and he, with his perfect logic, asks "why do you not fire her and find someone more suitable? After all," he adds "you certainly pay three times more than local people would pay so there will be many people happy to work for you."

And of course he is right but, as I ask him, how do we go about finding a replacement? Easy it turns out because the following morning a young lady, Lena from the Cassamance, arrives at the door declaring that Séraphin has sent her to be our maid. Véro takes her inside to have a chat and, fifteen minutes after her arrival, our no-show maid turns up at the door. She does not apologise for her non-appearance last evening, saying very flippantly that her husband would not let her come to our house. However, that fifteen minutes is sufficient to confirm to Véro that the two ladies are as different as chalk and cheese. I pay the original maid off by giving her a full month's salary for the few days she has worked for us, and Lena becomes our new maid, and David's new best friend.

Our aerial survey starts and the flights are to continue for several weeks before the team returns to Dakar to begin the interpretation of the photos and record their results into a statistical programme that I am developing together with our computer specialist. During the survey work, the pilot is careful to ensure that he stays a good couple of kilometres within Senegalese airspace every time he comes close to the Senegal River. In reality, the international border between Mauritania and Senegal follows the north bank – although Mauritania permanently disputes international law and wants to place the frontier in the middle of the river – and so the plane *should* be safe providing the pilot does not actually cross the river. To further safeguard our plane, the team leader manages to get a senior official in the Senegalese Foreign Ministry to speak with his counterpart in Mauritania and set up a briefing between senior military officers of the two countries.

Back on the vegetation front, our chief field botanist chats with me about programming our trip to the eastern side of the "Peanut Basin" to establish four or five new vegetation monitoring sites to add to the fifteen or so that have already been established with the help of my old supervisor over the last few years. We are to be four in the monitoring team, including our driver.

The day before setting off, Séraphin collects a little cash from each person in the monitoring team, and goes shopping for provisions. He comes back with several kilos of potatoes and onions, six large tins of corned beef, several bottles of Magi sauce, two tetra packs of red wine (for he and I) and a sack of white rice *brisé* (broken).

I have found that this type of cracked or broken rice is the Senegalese favourite for use in making their national dish of *thiebou-dienne* (fish and rice although the delicious taste and complexity of ingredients in this dish is lost in such a simple translation) and my favourite dish of *mafé* (mutton or chicken cooked in a peanut sauce and served on a bed of rice with lots of vegetables, mm-mm). I have quickly learnt that broken rice truly does have a nicer flavour than whole grain; and is far cheaper to buy.

Séraphin has also been to the petrol station and filled an oil drum with sufficient diesel to last us for the entire trip and has purchased a few small packets of tea and sugar that will serve as gifts in some of the remote villages where we are due to camp.

First thing in the morning he loads foldable beds, foam mattresses, mosquito nets, a camping gas stove and all cooking implements that we need for the trip. Séraphin is the official, self-designated, chef on our trips into the bush, and he is very proud of his ability to turn white rice and corned beef into a delicious meal for hungry biologists!

We are ready to set off on our trip with the rear of the project Hilux loaded with the camping gear and the other necessities, including a full container of drinking water. We are to camp in the wilds of the Sahel for most of the six days and so have to be totally self-sufficient and ready for any emergencies.

Keita, the project accountant, gets the four of us to sign various receipt forms and hands over individual envelopes "your six days of per diem, Malcolm" he tells me. Since my share of the food that Séraphin has purchased amounts to only two thousand CFA (or four UK pounds) and we are to camp in the bush, I am a little surprised at the thickness of my envelope. I am even more surprised when I look inside and see that I have been given the equivalent of almost four hundred pounds. I ask Keita very discretely if there is not an error and he tells me that the daily per diem is the equivalent of sixty-five pounds; but, of course, that is a figure that assumes a hotel stay not camping in the wilds of Senegal.

Being a little perturbed, actually rather a lot, by this large amount of cash that I have just received, I stick my head around the team leader's office door and ask if there is not a mistake in the amount I have just received.

His simple answer said with a smile is "enjoy, it's correct".

Although we set a departure time of 10 am, the other two members of the team finally roll into the office at almost 11 am and make the excuse that they had to take their per diems back to their wives. This statement adds to my concern that per diems are being seen as a salary top-up and not a way of reimbursing out-of-pocket expenses necessitated by field trips.

Once everyone finally gets into the vehicle, we set off, direction Louga in the North of the country. For the first part of the journey, that takes us off the peninsular where Dakar sits, we follow the same route as we had taken to Kaolack. As before, we go through Rufisque and then on past the cement factory still belching white dust from its giant chimneys. The dust hangs in the air and settles as a thick cloak on all the vegetation around the town. This single factory, while providing employment to much of the local population, brings innumerable respiratory illnesses to the locals, especially the children and the elderly. Just past the factory, the road turns sharply to the left and then enters the little town of Bargny. Here we take the left fork heading north, direction Thiès, rather than taking the right-hand road that would take us south and back towards Kaolack.

I have been told by my lead botanist that Thiès is a lovely little town and is considered to be Senegal's second city. This standing is heavily debated by the residents of Pikine, an overflow city of Dakar, as well as by Touba, the Mouride capital of West Africa. In population terms in the early 1990s both Pikine and Touba are approaching the seven hundred thousand mark while Thiès remains at around three hundred thousand. But for development and quality of life, Thiès remains the place to be outside of Dakar.

At 12.30 we are getting close to Thiès with entry to the city marked by lines and lines of ladies, on both sides of the main road, selling the biggest and best mangoes in the world. Every single lady asks exactly the same price for their stacked bowls containing several kilos of this magnificent fruit. Séraphin pulls over to the side of the road to buy some mangoes to take with us on our trip northwards. We pull up and I am warned not to open my window; too late as a cascade of fruit are tipped by the waiting ladies into my lap. No matter, we have the mangoes we need while Séraphin negotiates the price we should pay.

Soon after, we drive into the very pretty town of Thiès and head down a wide boulevard with green spaces on either side and a wide roundabout at the bottom. On the far side to the left sits a Catholic church and to the right is the regional Court of Justice. As we drive past these buildings and head south, we see the large and magnificent Prefecture that is the regional government offices of the Prefect. Past the prefecture is a small side street, and we turn here and, almost immediately, arrive at a neat little restaurant called 'Chez Aisha'. The restaurant is empty of customers and so we anticipate a speedy service so that we can rapidly continue our trip towards Louga. We are seated by Aisha herself and she tells us that the *plat du jour* is chicken and chips; nothing too risky there and so we order four plates plus a Coca-Cola each.

Séraphin practices his charms on Aisha with little success as she seems more interested in chatting to another of my handsome colleagues. Aisha provides the cokes and, as she walks towards the backroom where the kitchen is located, one of the team calls after her and asks that we be served with the food as rapidly as possible. A few moments later we hear the screech of a chicken being dispatched and a couple of moments later, a second screech as its buddy follows. This, as my botanical colleague advises us, sounds like bad news; not only for the chicken but also for the speediness of our lunch. This is Senegal and restaurants always try to serve the freshest of food even if it means catching the fowl from the back garden first. And wait we do, for a good hour; long enough to allow the plucking, cutting and frying of the chicken.

We finally bid goodbye to Aisha as three o'clock approaches and head out of Thiès and onto the Saint-Louis road. We anticipate a drive of some three hours, straight north, until we reach our evening destination in the small town of Louga. We pass many little houses stretched along the verges of the road and Séraphin pays particular attention as he drives because of the multitude of children who play on the side of the road and wave at us as we pass by. More danger-ous still are the donkeys that wander lethargically into the middle of the road and stand there watching us with a disdainful eye as our driver is obliged to drive off the road, onto the sandy verge and loop around the animals before coming back onto the tarmac.

The botanists in the car identify for me the more obvious plants and trees that we see as we drive towards Louga. All villages have an evergreen tree planted along the verges. I am told that this is called the *neem* and it is a multi-use species. Its leaves provide shade under which the elderly place their rickety chairs and *palabre* (chat) with neighbours while watching the world go by. Its wood is very hard and not susceptible to chomping termites, its white berries when steeped in boiling water provide a natural insecticide while its leaves, when picked fresh and again steeped in boiling water provide relieve from malaria.

In quieter moments, I tell my three colleagues about my time in Calabar as an ecology lecturer. On hearing about the termite-resistance of the *neem* tree, I get them laughing by describing the nipped bottoms of the townies among my students who were ignorant about the dangers of sitting on termite mounds; especially when wearing miniskirts!

We frequently see a tall, stunning and widespread shrub, called *Calotropis procera*, a member of the Euphorbia group of plants, and commonly called Milkweed due to the enormous amounts of milky latex that it exudes when damaged. I am warned not to get the milk on my skin as it burns very rapidly and painfully. My botanist colleague informs me that the presence of this plant is a clear indicator of the desertification that is hitting the entire peanut basin, not due directly to climate change but due to the poor farming practices of the past several decades. *Calotropis* has little value apart from the shade it casts and the fact that in times of famine its dried leaves can be fed to goats. He also points out to me a small green bush called *Gueira senegalensis* that he warns is another indicator of desertification; and we see thousands of the bushes by the roadside. Desertification is clearly on the march here in the Peanut Basin of western Senegal where peanut monoculture has destroyed the soil structure and trees have been removed to make mechanised cultivation easier. A similar looking bush to my, as yet, untrained eyes is identified for me as *Boscia senegalensis.* I am told that the species is considered a useful bush by remote Sahelian communities while Séraphin chips in that the seeds are used to make coffee and, during our trip, we will certainly tastc it!

In return, I give my colleagues a few tips about the bird life we see along the route. Several species perching on the electric lines and taller trees are the same as I saw in Chad, including the different rollers, bee-eaters, weaver birds and some of the dove family. I also frequently notice a stunning little bird, not much bigger than a common sparrow, that has brilliant red and black plumage and likes to sit atop the remains of millet stalks so that everyone can admire it. This is the red bishop and it is the male that puffs up and displays its striking plumage for any female bishops that might be lurking in the vicinity. We also notice a group of six vultures marching in an ungainly and lopsided fashion while bickering over the partially eaten corpse of a dog that had obviously chosen the wrong moment to attempt to cross the road. I find it strange that vultures are so awkward on the ground but so magnificent in the air. They are to be seen on most days flying over the port area of the city of Dakar, usually in the company of black kites, making use of the thermals emanating from the hot tarmac streets below to soar, pirouette and practice loops far above our heads.

At a little after 6 pm, just before the daylight begins to disappear, we drive into the compound of the Department of Forestry for the department of Louga. We will stay the night here before moving into the field tomorrow. Our car is met by a number of foresters; who all know my botanical colleague and several address him respectfully by his rank of Captain. We are also met by a pale-haired man, of about my age, who hails from Sweden and is the team leader of another agency project that is concerned with reforestation around the department. He works with the Forestry staff and has an office within the compound. He shows me where I will be staying: a room with a very aged air conditioner, but apparently it works with a continual loud clunking. I move my bag into the room, grab a washbag and make my way to the small side room where there is a shower and a far-from-clean toilet. As soon as I am dressed, I hear Séraphin calling that we are leaving soon for the pleasures of '*Louga by night*'!

I can assure everyone, that Louga has very little to offer! We head off to the single restaurant that is considered acceptable by my colleagues and each are given a dish of rice and mafé. The chili peppers from everyone's plates are passed down the table and find themselves all on mine. My propensity – established during my years in Nigeria – for this condiment is now well known by my team. As soon as we finish eating and split the already tiny bill, Séraphin drives our two colleagues back to the Forestry Department. Then teasing me that it is time for us non-Muslims to check out the Louga nightlife, we drive back into town and park outside a nondescript general store run by two Lebanese brothers.

One of the brothers leads us behind the counter and through a door that opens into a room at the back of the store. The room is empty apart from a couple of chairs and a beaten-up sofa positioned against the walls and a small coffee table in the middle. A single person is already in place and he is taking swigs from a small bottle of Coca-Cola while keeping his head down and not making eye contact. We choose to sit on the sofa and are quickly brought two bottles of Gazelle beer by one of the brothers while our new drinking partner is handed a miniature bottle of whisky. I watch as he pours the contents into his Coca-Cola and hands the empty miniature back to the server but his head remains down. Should anyone now enter the room, only the two strangers will be seen clearly drinking alcohol.

We chatter away in French but, as it has been a hot, busy day, we both empty our bottles in a hurry and Séraphin calls out *"encore deux bières s'il vous plaît"*, but without success.

Our silent and secretive drinking partner decides that Séraphin must also be a foreigner because, to be very honest, he does not look like a typical Senegalese not a Wolof nor a Peul or even a Sérère. Not surprisingly, I suppose, because he does not hail from any of these ethnic groups. He belongs in fact to a small tribe called the Bassari and is possibly the first Bassari that our new drinking friend has ever seen. However, Mr Louga does understand a little French and knows that we have just called out for more beers.

"Give me your bottle tops" he says and, on receiving them, throws them out through the open door so they fall behind the counter where the brothers are working.

A few moments later, two more ice-cold Gazelles are delivered. The explanation given to us is that the brothers are actually not allowed to sell alcohol but this is overlooked by the local police and politicians, on condition that they remain discrete. Shouting out for more beers is not considered discrete at all! After all the local Imam could be in the store buying rice when such a shout goes up, but a simple bottle top clattering through the door is OK. The colour of the top shows the drink being ordered and the number of tops thrown shows how many drinks are required. This system stands the test of time for my infrequent trips to Louga over the next several years as it almost always involves a visit to see the brothers, and the throwing of a couple of beer capsules through the door and into the store.

The following morning, we are 'up with the lark' or rather with a very skinny but insistent cockerel; breakfast on black coffees and chunks of baguette smeared with triangles of *vache-qui-rit,* and then bid farewell to the couple of foresters who come in early to join us for breakfast. We head due south to our first botanical rendezvous.

As we journey along dusty tracks through rather scrubby vegetation dominated by *Acacia* and *Guiera,* my botanist colleague explains how we will establish the permanent monitoring sites.

He states that the principle is simple: we are going to define a total of four sites composed of blocks of three times three kilometres, so nine square kilometres each, in natural forest areas that are relatively untouched by man. As he explains, there will always be grazing by transhumant herds, but we need to choose areas that should not be at risk of clearance for wood or charcoal, and thus we will work in *forêts classées* (so called gazetted forests that are under state protection). Today we are looking to establish the first site that will lie some fifty kilometres south of Louga while tomorrow we will follow approximately the same line of longitude but go another fifty or so kilometres further south, and so on for the two further sites. At each site we need first to mark discretely the boundary trees so that we may re-find them in future years and carry out an initial botanical survey of the tree species present. At this time of year, all the herb species will be unidentifiable so that particular task awaits the rainy season due to start in July.

After slightly more than two bumpy hours in the car, we arrive in the area where we are to establish the first site. We first drive the three kilometres along the north-south boundary and note that the scrubby vegetation is fairly homogenous – a necessity for site selection – and then turn to drive carefully through the bush to check out the west-east boundary for three kilometres and then follow the south-north boundary before returning to our original starting point by following the east-west boundary. All looks good to go. Using the odometer, we drive to the central point of the north-south boundary and turn left and drive a further kilometre into the scrubby bush. The botanist and I descend and start walking, measuring one kilometre, into the block. This distance takes us across the middle of the central square of the nine kilometre square block that we have selected. It is in this centre square of a noughts-and-crosses board that we will work in today and during future botanical surveys. We retrace our steps for two hundred metres and establish a circular quadrat using a metal pin to which we attach one of our surveyor's tapes. Within the defined circle we set about identifying and noting each woody species (trees and shrubs) and estimating their heights and measuring their girths. This is hard work in the heat of the day but relatively rapid since the trees are quite few and far between. We repeat the work at the four hundred, six hundred and finally eight hundred metre marks. We now have several pages of data inscribed to printed sheets that have been developed for this task, and I have begun to learn a few Sahelian forest species. Clearly, these data, repeat-collected over many years, will provide an incredible database for a future generation who might wish to interpret the evolution of Senegalese vegetation over time.

While we are collecting our vegetation data, Séraphin and our other colleague have been busy with a pot of paint that Séraphin produced from the back of the vehicle. About an hour ago, they finished establishing the boundaries of our nine-kilometre square plot with white paint and designed painted arrows at suitable points to indicate the direction to take to reach the central square where we have just finished working. With their fieldwork finished, Séraphin has taken off his painter's cap and replaced it with his chef's hat. Our other colleague has been given a bowl of onions and potatoes to peel while our chef has been washing the dust off of our plastic plates and metal cutlery. By 2.30 pm we are sitting down to a heap of white rice, *brisé* of course, covered by a stew of corned beef, onions and potatoes liberally doused during the cooking process with a magic, African ingredient: the condiment *Magi-Magi*!

After several hours of hard and sweaty work, nothing tastes more delicious than corned beef stew, and I am destined to eat this on several hundred future occasions. Even the mangoes that follow as dessert do not taste as delicious as Séraphin's stew.

Washing up done, we pack the equipment into the back of the vehicle and head south in the direction of our next field site. Since there are no towns close by, we keep a lookout for a small village where we might spend the night. We eventually find one in the late afternoon. A quick chat with the village chief and we are given an empty compound surrounded by rough wooden stakes into which have been woven spiny branches from the *Balanites* tree. Nothing larger than a lizard will penetrate that barrier.

Once the car is parked inside the compound, we each take a camp bed, foam mattress and mosquito screen from the back of the car and begin setting up our beds for the night. This is my first night of bush sleeping and I have chosen a spot under a *Balanites* tree with the aim of tying my mosquito net to a branch. I can hear my two technical colleagues speaking to each other in Wolof but obviously understand nothing; but Séraphin does and he comes over and sits down on my camp bed.

"Malcolm, do you mind if I give you some advice?"

"Of course not Séraphin. Here in the field, I am the novice and happy to learn from you."

"OK, good, because I want to tell you that snakes get tired too. If you put your bed under a tree and the snake up there in the branches falls asleep, he may fall down and decide to spend the night in the warmth of your bed. Always best to put your bed in the open."

That little bit of bush wisdom serves me well over many future camping trips and I was even able to pass it on to other novices that later would accompany me on field trips.

My first night sleeping under the Senegalese stars passes pretty well although another ruddy cockerel acts as nature's alarm clock as soon as the sky begins to brighten in the East.

As we pack up the vehicle, the village chief comes over to greet us and to receive a cup of Nescafé. In his hand is dangling a rooster which he hands over to me. Feeling rather awkward, I manage to say *'jere-jef'* to express our thanks but turn to my colleague and ask how much I should give him for the chicken. He says a few words to the chief, receiving a rapid response, and tells me '*cadeau*'. A gift that will be our meal later today and showing *Teranga* in action.

Chatting about nothing important with the chief, and using my colleague as my interpreter, I suddenly notice a rapid movement towards the horizon about fifty metres away. Looking up, I see that it is a hawk, a Peregrine Falcon to be precise, which swoops down towards a chattering hen and her six hatchlings and grabs one of the young chicks and flies with it onto a low branch and proceeds to eat it. Now there are five.

I can imagine that the children in the village must have a song that goes rather like this:

'Six little chicks scratching in the sand,
Six little chicks scratching in the sand,
Then down swoops a falcon and does his dirty deed,
now there are five scratching in the sand.
Five little chicks scratching in the sand, ...'
(to the tune of 'Ten Green Bottles' of course!)

Our host seems totally unconcerned about the fate of his chicks and instead wishes us farewell and a rapid return to his village. As we take our leave, I pass him a tin of corned beef that Séraphin has surreptitiously handed me, together with a small bag of sugar. As we drive away, my botanical colleague surprises me by saying that the corned beef will be much appreciated by the chief as the villagers eat very little meat, usually only during their main religious festivals. This is a fact that never ceases to amaze me given that the chief owns a large flock of sheep and goats and many cattle.

My colleagues try to explain my lack of understanding, with little success, until Séraphin pipes up and says "there are no banks in the bush. The livestock are their deposit accounts while any milk or new lambs and calves are the interest from those accounts."

Now I understand!

The rest of our field trip goes pretty much in the same manner as the first day and so, after almost a week, we return to Dakar.

It is so nice to get a big cuddle from my family and hear my children say "we missed you SO MUCH daddy."

We have managed to get Mélanie into a French-language primary school close to the *Sacré Cœur* Cathedral but are learning rapidly that this was perhaps a mistake. The traffic is so dense between our house and the centre of town that I have had to hire a driver, by the name of Malik, and our car is occupied almost the whole day ferrying our little girl to and from school. The school does not offer a canteen for lunch and so my car is leaving the house at half-seven in the morning, dropping Mélanie for 9 am, getting back to me at the office at 10.30 am, leaving at 11 am to collect her for lunch at home. The exercise, complete with traffic jams, is repeated in the afternoon. But what to do?

Two things combine to provide the solution. The first is that Véro has met a lovely English lady, called Judith, and through her the Head Teacher of the preschool section of the International School of Dakar, an American curriculum school. The Head tells Véro that there are places for seven-year old Mélanie at ISD if she wants to enrol her. A quick, informal visit convinces Véro that THIS is how schools should be run.

The second thing that convinces us is that, while we are eating dinner *en famille*, Mélanie says "dad, you were a teacher, so is it OK for teachers to slap pupils?"

Of course we are shocked, especially as her teacher is a nun, and I ask if she has been hit by any of the teachers.

She tells me "no daddy, I am good in school but some of the children talk a lot in class and so the lady teacher smacks them. But I don't think it's nice because she only smacks the African children never the foreign ones."

The following day we enrol Mélanie at ISD and she starts there the very next day. A big plus for us is that the distance from our house to the school is only a fifteen-minute car ride. That change of school initiates a snowball effect.

First off, with Mélanie quickly integrated into the second grade, we decide it would be good for Master David to experience the rigours of school life too. Although he is a lovely child, his blond hair, blue eyes, freckly nose and oh so cheeky character mean he gets away with murder; especially with our maid, Lena, who adores him. Try as we might to get him to do simple things like tidy away his toys, he simply goes to find Lena for a cuddle and then asks her to 'help' him tidy. So, school it is. We enrol David into the preschool where he finds himself in Judith's class and quickly becomes great friends with Tasha, Judith's little daughter.

Véro starts to drive the children to school and has found a shortcut that takes her across the old runway of the former Dakar Airport that cuts across from the housing zone called *Sacré Cœur 3* to the school. One day while making the trip she spots a 'To Let' sign at a house right on the corner of the old runway. Long story short, she visits, likes, gives notice on our house on *Front de Terre* and we are getting ready to move. Also, being a regular mum at the preschool to help out (and chatting rather a lot with the teachers!), Judith says that an assistant is leaving and would Véro like the job. My wife is, once again, a working lady.

The date for moving house is fast approaching, and two events occur. The first is that I get a phone call from the British Embassy in Dakar. Through the American school, we have become friends with the deputy ambassador and his wife, and through them with several other Brits working for the embassy and the British Council.

The call comes from Kevin, the head of visas "Malcolm, did you know that Princess Anne will be in Dakar next week? She has specifically asked to meet with any Brits working in the field of international development. That's simple for us because there are only two: you and Judith's husband Peter. So you have to come."

"No problem" I reply.

"Great, thanks. We will be having a practice on Monday afternoon when we will talk you through the protocol, you know, how to bow when you shake hands, how to greet her and talk to her."

"Ehh, Kevin, what's this about bowing?"

"You know, as you shake hands, you will need to bow your head."

"Sorry, but I will happily meet with a member of the Royal Family and show all the respect necessary but I am not bowing to anyone."

A laugh rings out from the other end of the line and Kevin says "don't be so bloody awkward, see you on Monday at 3 pm." He puts down the phone and clearly did not register that I am in fact being quite serious.

The second event is that both our children, along with most of their school, come down with chickenpox, nothing serious there. What is serious is that Judith catches it from her kids and it develops into a rather serious brain infection requiring a heavy course of antibiotics and prolonged rest. A couple of days after Kevin's phone call, I notice a small blister has formed in the middle of my right palm – my handshaking palm, no less. My penance is confirmed the following morning when I look in the mirror and see a passing resemblance to Job; he of the running boils. My head, trunk, arms and legs are covered in blisters and so is the inside of my mouth right across my tongue and gums. Yucky.

With some difficulty, because it hurts to talk, I call Kevin at the Embassy and tell him about the chickenpox and that I am, of course, unable to attend the meeting with the Princess Royal.

I receive, as a parting comment, "anything to get out bowing, Dr Marks".

That same day, Malick, Séraphin and Diagne turn up at the house on *Front de Terre* to help with the removal to our new home in *Sacré Cœur 3*. One look at me is enough to scare them silly, and they tell me to stay in my chair, not to help and, please, do not come near us. I spend a restful day sitting in an armchair reading a novel while my three friendly drivers undertake all the heavy lifting involved in a removal.

Our new home in *Sacré Cœur* is a world apart from our previous place. We have a large rectangular garden with two small coconut trees, already covered in ripening nuts. The entire garden is surrounded by a four-metre high wall and up and over the top of the wall grows a profusion of the most beautiful bougainvillea in every colour imaginable. The plant has been carefully chosen by the owners of the house, not just for the fact that it offers flowers the whole year round but also because its stem and branches bear a multitude of inch-long thorns that would seriously wound anyone foolish enough to try to scale our wall.

Inside, the house has been well designed and occupies a double plot at the top of this very quiet estate. We have three bedrooms and two bathrooms at one end of the house. This section is separated from the rest of the house by a sturdy and lockable door. All its windows are both barred and mosquito screened. There is even a double, sliding glass door leading to the secluded back garden. The other side of the house starts with an enormous garage that could, if so desired, house three cars. There is also a large and comfortable sitting room and a reasonably sized kitchen. Behind the garage is a small but self-contained apartment that is perfect for guests.

The only drawback to the location is the fact that outside our wall at the back of the garden is a wide-open space that was once part of the original international airport and on the other side of the right-hand wall is a recently built shanty town occupied by refugees from the civil wars in Sierra Leone and Liberia. We are a little concerned, notwithstanding our high wall and bougainvillea hedge, that we might attract the attention of burglars. Cue to hire a watchman in the form of Mbaye originating from the Peanut Basin.

On Saturday mornings we continue to go off to different shops and markets. As the children get to know and really like Lena, they usually vote to stay at home while we go off to the town centre, often with Malick at the wheel. Now that we are relatively well established in Dakar, we spend late afternoons and a few weekends at the small beaches and restaurants around the area of Dakar called Les Almadies. I have decided to try my hand at fishing from the beach. I did bring rods and reels from UK in our container but need to buy some basic items like weights, hooks and swivels. The local telephone directory tells me that there is a shop selling fishing tackle just off the rue Felix Faure and so that is our first destination on this particular Saturday morning. Malick finds the right street, just off the Place de l'Independence, but we cannot see the shop. Simpler, therefore, to get out of the car, walk and look in through shop windows. As we wander down the small street, there is a young man selling soft drinks from a hand cart full of ice. We stop, buy two cokes and chat with him for a while; handing back the empty bottles as we finish. We continue wandering down the street, holding hands, and looking left and right for the correct shop. Suddenly, two young men walk right up to us and crowd us both into a wall. One goes for my shoelaces (they always do this in Dakar!) and the other is getting very close to Véro; apprentice pickpockets no less. This sort of thing had happened to us while we were living in Nigeria, so we are not novice pigeons to be plucked by these two kids.

"Get behind me love" I say, and Véro moves promptly to my rear. I raise my fists and say to the men "*OK, on y va*" (let's go).

This response sets in motion several actions. First, the would-be-robbers are obviously taken off guard to be facing an aggressive pigeon, so they take a couple of steps back rather than continuing to crowd me; second, the soft drink seller comes running down the road to our rescue with an empty coke bottle still grasped in his hand that is now raised above his head. And third, Malick seeing his new employer with fists raised comes screeching down the road in my car and blocks the two robbers' only means of retreat. Rather than us all wading into the, by now, rather befuddled youths, I say very loudly "boo" and they run off down the street with their flip-flop clad feet going slap, slap, slap in accompaniment to our laughter.

Back in the office on Monday, the team leader announces that he is to take considerable leave of absence in order to be part of a World Bank team that is looking at desertification in sub-Saharan Africa. This World Bank initiative proves to be the forerunner to the global warming movement that later morphs into the climate change debate. And it was itself preceded by a movement trying to halt man's degradation of the natural vegetation. During the past few months, our chief has frequently been away for a couple of weeks at a time, naming me as his replacement. But this time, he is to be absent from Senegal for around six months, and so I am to step up officially as acting team leader for the entire time, while still doing my ecological work, of course.

I get to meet the other two team members charged with the study. The first is a very senior Canadian diplomat while the second is a young Frenchman. We sit down to chat over a cup of coffee and the young Frenchman asks where I learnt to speak French. When I mention that I am married to a *Lyonnaise* and have a home in the Department of Ain, he tries to draw me to a more precise location, with the conversation progressing rather like this:

"Where in Ain?"

"Oh, in the Bugey."

"Where in the Bugey?"

"In a small commune in the south of the department."

"What is it called?"

"Brégnier-Cordon"

"Where in Brégnier-Cordon?"

"In Cordon"

"Where in Cordon?"

"Opposite chez-Monin."

"I know the place; my wife's family owns the field in front of your house. She is from the neighbouring commune of Izieu. Do you know it?"

And of course everyone in our region of France knows Izieu because it is the site of a Jewish memorial museum 'Les Enfants d'Izieu'. The museum occupies a large farmhouse where a kindly French family tried to hide Jewish children away from the Gestapo during the Second World War. Sadly, the location of the hideaway came to the notice of Klaus Barbie, the notorious and aptly named 'Butcher of Lyon'. The entire community was captured by the Gestapo during a dawn raid and taken away to Nazi death camps. Local rumour tells, that the Gestapo were notified by a resident of Izieu who had an axe to grind with the owner of the farm. That stupid feud led to the death of dozens of innocent children and their guardians and assured the notoriety of the little village of Izieu.

I guess we will never know the truth of who informed the Gestapo but I do know one thing from first-hand experience: the atmosphere of the museum is the saddest I have ever encountered anywhere in the world. To the present day the souls of those poor innocents hang heavy in Izieu.

With or without the team leader's expert guiding hand, work at the project continues, and it always seems at a frenetic pace. We have just recruited a bunch of young and bright technicians both to bolster the different teams and to expand our activities. At least two of the bunch seem to be really outstanding scientists. First, is a young man who will work on rainfall monitoring using the Meteosat satellite, and second, is a technician contracted to use our incoming NOAA satellite images to monitor bushfires across Senegal. The first, dealing with rainfall monitoring, is collaborating with specialists from a UK university and is a kind and gentle young man who I immediately take a liking to. He has a tendency to be reserved, which is in stark contrast to the majority of the local team but is knowledgeable and I feel has a very bright future ahead of him at the project. The second is also a likeable character and very competent in his work. He has a more flamboyant character and quickly obtains a number of friends among the staff. Both are hired on national agency contracts.

Soon after contracts are signed with these new staff members, I receive a delegation of several other staff. All are civil servants detached to work at our project by their various departments and ministries. They have a grouch: why are the new recruits, employed on national agency contracts, paid so much more than them? Looking at the sheet of paper that I am handed, I understand their query.

Local hires on agency salaries are being paid at least two times more than our civil servants but for doing, admittedly, very similar jobs. On the face of it, that does seem very unfair. However, just like me, all agency contractors are on single year, renewable contracts with no pensions, health or indeed few other benefits while the civil servants have several benefits including a pension plus a guaranteed job when the project ends and they return to their ministries with retained seniority. I explain these points to the delegation but know that such an argument can never be won.

To conclude the meeting, I state "I will contact the team leader to discuss this issue and get him to take it up with headquarters in the USA during his time there. Let's see if they can come up with a solution."

And come up with a solution they do. The team leader manages to convince the hierarchy in the USA to add budget lines for training payments for all civil servants in the team. This provides a 'secret' salary top-up ranging from around eighty pounds per month for the more junior civil servants up to more than two hundred and fifty pounds for our Tetris-playing national coordinator. While these top-ups are designed with completely good intentions, they prove to be illegal under the agency system and eventually lead to me having to stop the payment and accept the full ire of a good proportion of the staff. But more of that later.

7

Work and Play

The relatively short rainy season in this part of the world starts at the end of June or early July and comes to an end as we leave September and enter October. And the end of the rains is the signal for us to undertake our annual vegetation monitoring survey. This year, with the several new monitoring sites we have installed to the west of our range, we have a total of twenty sites to visit and so we are allowing just over three weeks to complete the work.

Séraphin is to be our driver; even my Senegalese colleagues recognise his twin skills of bush driving and corned beef stew making! Our work will start at the most south-easterly of our sites and progressively work north and west. The majority of the sites are established in the sparsely populated Ferlo region which was the initial zone of interest during the project's pilot phase.

The Ferlo is an interesting ecological zone that traditionally has had almost no resident population but is an essential grazing area for transhumant herders. The herders habitually move into the Ferlo as soon as the rains begin and the grasses begin to sprout. They stay as long as adequate pastures and temporary marshes, ponds and water-holes remain. In the 1950s, the French started to try to open up this vast zone by installing a number of boreholes driven by diesel pumps. These have allowed small, permanent villages to establish around them and a few herders remain the whole year round.

I am told that livestock can go for up to three days without water. This means that herders are prepared to walk a day away from the boreholes to find improved grazing, stay for a day, and then walk back to the borehole to water their animals. If, during their grazing forays, they should come across a small pond or *mare,* they will camp there until either the grazing or the water runs out before heading back towards the borehole. Notwithstanding the current day presence of the boreholes, the Ferlo's resident population density remains miniscule when compared to the rest of Senegal. There is sadly a frequently unrecognised negative to the boreholes: the area within a day's walk from the boreholes (about 20 km in every direction) is usually grazed bare of edible herbaceous vegetation, and most trees with consumable leaves have long since been felled. Using our NOAA satellite images taken in the rainy season, we can usually pick up the presence of boreholes by the dearth of green vegetation growing around them. When herbaceous vegetation docs grow, it is composed of inedible plants that the livestock mostly ignore.

The Ferlo sits on two distinct geologies. One dominated by sand and the other by laterite. Each has its own dominant flora and response to drought. Much of the Ferlo has been placed under a certain degree of protection. At the northern end is the 'Reserve Sylvo-Pastorale des Six Forages', an area dedicated to grazing with water originally provided by six boreholes. To the centre and going southwards is the 'Northern Ferlo Wildlife Reserve', although wildlife is now sadly lacking. To the south-west is another sylvo-pastorale zone.

I soon come to learn that most of Senegal's many reserves and gazetted forests exist pretty much in name alone. The charcoal trade has seen to that with annual programmes of forest destruction being sanctioned by a series of minsters that enforce their decisions on the upper levels of the forestry department.

We are to begin our work in the south-east and so travel the whole day from Dakar to spend the night close to Tambacounda before starting at our first site the following day, just to the north of the town. We will work progressively northwards and westwards to cover all the sites between the Tamba-Dakar road and the Senegal River, finishing with the new sites we had established this year to the east of the peanut basin.

Each day is very much like the last. We always wake up early, sometimes because of the rising sun but usually because of a scrawny village cockerel. Breakfast is invariably a piece of baguette smeared with a triangle of *vache-qui-rit* and washed down with a plastic mug of Nescafe. I try to shave each morning, using my coffee mug to rinse my razorblade and, one at a time, we go off to answer nature's call. I have a roll of toilet paper in my trusty canvas bag while my colleagues use a plastic kettle of water. I have quickly learnt that old termite mounds are the best spots for answering the call. They are high and broad and so offer at least one hundred and eighty degree of visual protection. The ground around them is scavenged clean by the former termite occupants, and so there is no risk of a snake or a scorpion hiding in the grass. And looking out from the stooped position, it is possible to see if a wild animal approaches from the front. This latter is not really an issue although there are lions and hyenas in the Niokola-Koba national park; and we are not too far away in Tambacounda for one or the other to have decided to take a vacation here! But never stoop down in front of a large hole in the termite mound; one never knows what might come out at such a vulnerable moment!

By a little after seven, while the day is still cool, we drive to the site near-by to begin work. We each have our designated jobs and copies of various data collection sheets to record our results. Séraphin's job is to get us to the painted tree that marks the start of our kilometre square that sits inside the eight squares surrounding it. My job is to follow a pre-set compass bearing from the starting point and roll out fifty-metre long measuring tapes along the compass bearing for a total of one kilometre. Bushes are not a hindrance; I simply go through them while trees provoke a slight detour until I can get back on the correct compass bearing. At every metre along the whole transect, I record the quantity of vegetation using 0 = bare soil, 1 = poor vegetation coverage, 2 = average coverage, and 3 = above average coverage. Before starting the transect, I use a random number generating table to provide forty random points between 0 and 1,000 (metres) and, as I arrive at each of these points along the tape, I leave a large cloth bag.

Our field botanist follows behind me carrying a one-metre square quadrat made of iron. He is accompanied by two local villagers who will be paid pocket money at the end of the day to use small sickles to cut the herbaceous vegetation, inside each of the forty quadrats I have indicated, and place it into the bags, labelled with the number of the site. Before letting the sickle-wielding locals loose on the vegetation, my colleague first lists all the herbaceous species that he can identify in each quadrat. He is an excellent field botanist; as are very many of the graduates of the Forestry Department. As our measuring tapes progress along the one kilometre transect, Séraphin tries to follow with the vehicle, collecting the bags filled and weighed by the botanist and his workers.

Séraphin always tries to stay as close as possible to us in order to provide water as needed. During a typical morning of work, I am quite capable of drinking four litres of water without needing to pee; showing just how much we sweat during the fieldwork. At the end of the kilometre, Séraphin pays the workers and quickly drives them back to their village while my colleague and I move on to the next stage of our work: delimiting four circular quadrats. In each, we list all the species of trees and shrubs, measure their canopy cover and record their heights and girth. We then snip off and collect ten branches of each of the three dominant woody species and strip off their leaves for later drying and weighing. I confess that coming on top of the transect work, measuring the trees and shrubs is one of my least favourite activities. It is a rare day when one or other of us does not need to sit down with our head between our legs to avoid fainting in the hot, humid atmosphere.

After we have recorded the last tree or shrub, we always feel a buzz of euphoria to have finished for the day; well almost finished. We traipse back along our own tracks to the start of the transect, invariably finding Séraphin returned and peeling potatoes while rice is bubbling in the oversized aluminium saucepan he always uses. A relaxed lunch of corned beef stew, with the corned beef occasionally replaced by a chicken or, once or twice, by a wild guinea fowl that foolishly got under the car wheels, a moment of relaxation on our camp beds, washing up done and car repacked. It is then time to move on to our next site where we will pass the night sleeping under the stars.

Each subsequent day passes very much as the previous one although as we travel north so the vegetation thins out dramatically and the plant species change. After leaving Tamba and driving due north, we enter a zone of grassy vegetation dominated by the wretched '*cram-cram*'. This is a species of grass that has large seeds covered with a prickly coat. The prickles invariably catch into our socks, drop into our wellington boots or prick our fingers as we go about our work. Cram-cram is a real pest for us (and for herders and their livestock) and we cannot get out of its zone quickly enough. Once in the north of our range, approaching the town of Podor that sits close to the River Senegal, the vegetation is very sparse meaning that many transect points are listed as '0' (bare soil). My botanical colleague is always delighted when one of my random numbers falls on such a patch!

Today marks the halfway point of our trip. We have just finished work close to the small town of Ranérou and taken the firebreak that serves as a bush road towards Linguère, the so-called 'Capital of the Ferlo'. Linguère has a population of little more than ten thousand people but does have a bar where Séraphin and I can drink a cold beer and some very downmarket restaurants near to the market-place. Most of us prefer to eat at the *dibiterie* (or BBQ shop) where we are served piping hot cuts of mutton, fresh off the grill, that have a pleasant teeth-wrenching character.

We are to stay for the night in an abandoned building belonging to the government and this provides us with a (very dirty) toilet and a bathroom where we can have a little more privacy for our bucket showers. It is far too hot to sleep inside and so we pitch our camp beds on the outside balcony. At around 10.30 pm we all settle down to sleep. I fall asleep very quickly and, after an unknown time, begin to dream that I am at a music concert. My dream revolves around the music of Youssou N'dour until suddenly I wake up and find that I really am hearing this superb artist ... and he is live.

Once fully awake, I get dressed and simply follow the music over to the football stadium that sits handily just a few hundred metres across the road from our compound. The stadium gates are wide open and so I walk in and quickly find a seat in the half-full stadium. Just as I sit down, Youssou and his band Le Super Etoile begin to belt out *Set Setal* (Wolof for 'Clean Up').

This song has quickly become the youth anthem of Senegal and has inspired youngsters to form groups that are voluntarily cleaning up their local environment of rubbish. When I first arrived in Senegal, the joke was that England has the rose, Wales has the daffodil and France has the lily as their national flowers while Senegal has the blue plastic bags that the wind blows off rubbish dumps and into the thorn trees where they provide a pleasing splash of colour!

So eloquent are the youth protests in Dakar that they have managed to rouse parliament to vote a law banning the sale of the blue plastic bags. Youssou, being inspired by the political protests, wrote *Set Setal* and in turn inspired the youth to push forward their clean-up movement.

In reality, my belief is that the *Set Setal* that Youssou sings about is more to do with cleaning up a pretty dirty political scene than the movement that the youth have got underway over plastic bags; but success comes in many forms.

Now here I am listening to him belt it out live. If the listening crowd had been animated by his earlier songs, *Set Setal* gets the party really swinging. All around me youngsters are getting to their feet and dancing extravagantly. I get pulled to my feet by a young Peul girl and her boyfriend and am soon dancing with them. Girls all around us are trying to outdo each other dancing the 'Ventilateur'; this has to be seen to be believed. An eye-watering dance (and eye-catching too), no more said!

We continue our work routine each day, arising as usual on 9th November. We follow the normal procedure of having breakfast, getting ready and going into the field. However, today proves historic, the moment of the decade, as I tune into the BBC World Service at 9 am.

Something is happening in Berlin. On the hour, every hour, we all stop our work and gather around my little transistor radio in the emptiness of the Ferlo. I do a running translation for the benefit of Séraphin while my two other colleagues who speak some English ask for more information when their vocabulary lets them down. At 10 am the hideous Berlin Wall begins to show cracks, at 11 am youngsters on both sides are taking pickaxes to it, and by lunchtime the Russian and East German troops have given up trying to keep control of the movement of citizens from one side to the next.

As a celebration, we decide to take a day's break when we arrive in Podor. Based in this northern town is another Forestry Department project, this time financed by the European Union. The international team is headed by a young Belgian guy who invites me to stay with him and his wife while my colleagues go off to stay with their forestry friends. How nice it is to take a proper shower and not have to go off with a bucket of water for a bush-shower. Also nice, all apologies to Séraphin our master chef, is to escape for a day from corned beef stew and rice and eat a meal that starts with a salad and ends with a proper coffee.

The following day my new Belgian friend takes me for a visit of his project and we travel to an area that he tells me has a rather unique vegetation type that I really must see: a forest dominated by old and large examples of *Acacia nilotica*. This is an interesting species that likes to grow with its feet in water and so is invariably found along the river's edge stretching away from the water as long as the water table is not too deep. Today, after an hour's drive through sparse bush we arrive at his prized forest ... and find a scene of total desolation. In the couple of weeks since the project last visited the area, a gang has come in and chopped down the entire forest with chain saws. All that is left are stumps oozing sap and some bewildered looking simians. Sad, sad and typical of the anarchy that reigns in some of Senegal's forests at this time.

The next day we begin our work southwards taking another firebreak away from Podor and entering some head high bush. As we travel down the firebreak I spot a very unusual sight: a large male ostrich with the most splendid blue thighs and he is standing about fifty metres further down the trail having a good look at us in our blue Toyota Hilux. Séraphin stops the car and we all get our cameras out and take snap after snap. Eventually, the ostrich gets fed up looking at us and leisurely trots away along the trail picking up speed as he runs. He then veers off into the bush, disappearing from sight. We can now continue our journey and manage to spot him once more in the company of a female and several young. This is the only time in Senegal that I am to see these magnificent birds.

We arrive in Louga in the late afternoon and spend the evening at our usual restaurant with the local foresters. After the evening meal, Séraphin and I stop off to see the Lebanese brothers and are accompanied by a colleague who also wants to drink a beer. Several chucked bottle tops later, we return to the regional Forestry Department compound, pass the night and leave for our next site the following morning. Four days later we finish up the last site, taking a group photo entitled '*La Fin*' (the End) and return to Dakar for a well earnt rest.

Fortunately, Senegal is not all about work! The climate is lovely most of the year and, an hour or so drive south of Dakar, are long sandy beaches, the so-called '*Petite Côte*' (or Little Coast) that hosts various international tourist resorts. The best known of these is Saly-Portudal and slightly less well known is the Somone. Slotted between, them is the little village of Ngaparou. We are invited to spend the day there at the '*cabanon*' (beach house) of some American friends that we met at Mélanie's school.

We pack the car with cool box and beach paraphernalia, and leave our home at 8 am planning to spend the entire day at the beach house. On this Sunday morning the road leading to the *Petite Côte* appears pretty empty and so I anticipate only a little over an hour's drive. The children are excited and chatter away in the back of the car.

As I drive around the roundabout at the *Patte d'Oie*, an old jalopy jumps in front of me, completely ignoring my priority and causing me to brake hard to avoid a collision. I flash my lights in annoyance and then decide to wait for a suitable spot to overtake. After the *Patte d'Oie*, the road is rather narrow and piles of sand have blown off the dunes that lie on the seaward side and accumulated on either side of the road, making it even narrower. With horse-drawn carts parked along the opposite edge of the road for market day, this is not the right place to try to overtake. We drive sluggishly for around five kilometres as Jalopy Joe continues his slow progress and then I see the opposite side of the road is clear and so pull out to overtake. He pulls out too, blocking my overtaking lane. I try to go back inside and he cuts back in front of me. I curse and flash my lights in annoyance at his foolishness. To cut the story short, our infuriating Jalopy Joe continues to prevent me from overtaking each time I try. Blast.

We arrive at the outskirts of the town of Rufisque where there is a long, wide and straight section of road. No way can Jalopy Joe block me here, so I accelerate up to the speed limit and move to the left. He accelerates too. After about one hundred metres of this foolishness, he seems finally to give into me and slows down sufficiently that I can pass and pull in front of him.

Oh no, a uniformed gendarme is standing at the side of the road ahead of me and indicates that I should pull over. I do so and Mr Jalopy honks his horn and continues on his way.

"Turn off the ignition sir". I comply and step out of the car. "Follow me," and he leads me to his small office, taking a receipt book off his desk. "Where are you going in such a hurry? You do realise that you were driving across a continuous line?"

"I am going to the coast with my family. And you are perfectly correct *M. Gendarme* that I drove for a short distance over the continuous line but I would ask you to allow that Mr Jalopy Joe did everything he could to stop me overtaking. He has been driving like that since the *Patte d'Oie*. I understand that I broke a traffic rule and I am sorry. I imagine that there is a fine to pay?"

I withdraw 5,000 CFA from my pocket. This being the usual 'fine' for expatriates with the money often going into a gendarme's own back pocket.

He looks at me and smiles and says "It's a lovely day, I'm sure that your children are excited to get to the sea and you look a nice couple, so no fine today. Put your money back in your pocket and have a great time."

No one but no one every believes the end of that story ... except it is true.

Much of the beachfront at Ngaparou has been purchased by richer residents of Dakar, most are Senegalese but there are also many ethnic Lebanese and French. Over the years, they have erected various types of buildings that range from luxury villas to imitation garden sheds as weekend getaways. Our American friends rent a rather tatty but sprawling building that has no electricity except for the small amount generated by a tiny wind turbine that sits on the tin roof. The electricity is stored in a pair of old lorry batteries that provide sufficient power to run two or three car headlight bulbs. These give out a small amount of light during the long, cool evenings. 'Running' water comes from an overhead tank that has to be filled by a small pump attached to my car battery. The pump slowly lifts the very briny water up from a traditional well in the sandy garden. There is a fridge and a cooker that both run on bottled gas, and both have seen far better days! The house has a guardian and odd-job-man, named '*Vieux*' plus a weekend cook, called Khadi. Khadi is traditionally built and a real sweetheart to all visitors but especially to the children.

The *cabanon* is currently rented by three American couples and a septuagenarian Brit, who has made Senegal his home after a long career with the FAO. Each couple uses the beach house for one weekend a month and pays the grand total of twelve pounds each per month. One of the Americans is soon to leave and so would we like to take their place on the rental?

"What do you think kids?" asks Véro of our two little ones as they splash happily in a rock pool.

"Cool" says Mélanie (when did my little girl start growing up?).

"You bet your sweet pizza" adds David, now fully into his Mutant Ninja Turtle phase.

With their 'approval' in hand, we take over the lease and can look forward to one weekend at the beach every month.

Times flies in the office and I am getting used to being the acting team leader and dealing with work and administrative issues in addition to my usual tasks on the ecology front.

We have just received from the head office in the USA a new-fangled colour printer that melts wax sticks and places small dobs on to white paper. The aerial survey team and I spend a whole day designing maps of cattle distribution (from our survey results) and vegetation coverage (from the Hasselblad photos) and print them out to accompany the reports that the aerial survey team and I have been writing. All colleagues gather round to ooh-and-ah at the quality of the maps deriving from our new printer. The only ick that we eventually discover is that cockroaches love to nibble at the wax and so several months later we find that our stock of maps has been consumed!

That is only one of several serious drawbacks to our lodgings in the loft over the Livestock Department building. Our chief sociologist discovers another of them when he arrives for work on a Monday morning and tries to turn on his computer ... it will not work. Rapid assistance from our computer specialist fails to discover the problem. There is electricity getting to the computer and the screen comes on but the computer box stubbornly refuses to boot up. An invasive operation is required.

Our computer technician unscrews the outer cover of the desktop computer and removes it. A rapid squeaking accompanies this manoeuvre as four mice scurry across the table. Over the weekend, so it appears, a family of mice has squatted the computer. But how on earth did they get inside? We discover that they actually managed to squeeze through the opening at the front to the small floppy disk drive. Once they and their nest are removed, the computer goes back to normal ... but we have been warned.

These instances are forerunners to yet more trouble brewing in our battle with nature. We keep getting breakdowns on our network links with the server thanks to rats that have taken a liking to the cable insulation and have started to chew through it. We also discover that the hay store under our feet is not only harbouring a growing population of rodents and other nefarious beasties but is generating enormous amounts of dust that is causing rising cases of hay fever among staff and breakdowns of yet more computer hardware.

The only bright spot with the office and nature appears to be a friendly hornbill that has taken to knocking at my window, right behind my seat, when he is thirsty. As soon as he knocks, I know that I must switch on my air conditioner which causes water to condense and drip onto the windowsill. Once Mr Hornbill has drunk his fill, he flies off and I can stop the machine.

Another issue with the office is that our team is steadily growing in number but we have no additional office space. This means that offices are getting more and more cramped and tempers often flare. We need new accommodation. I mention this to the administrative officers in the Dakar headquarters and there is an agreement that they will speak both to the Senegalese government about providing us with new and better offices and with head office in the USA about providing a budget for such a removal.

My request comes at a complicated moment in the project life cycle. First, we have the end of the current project clearly in sight and the contracted staff, me included, are worried about whether the follow-up project will be confirmed.

Second, the team leader has finally given notice to quit and join another international organisation. This leads a brand-new international staff member naively to try to usurp the vacant team leader position (and the monetary promotion that goes with it) while I am absent in the field and out of communications with Dakar.

The Senegalese project coordinator is not happy at all with this attempt and neither are the agency bigwigs in Dakar. They send a car and driver to try to find my team in the Ferlo and request me to come back to the capital immediately in order to put down the attempted 'coup-d'état'. Meanwhile senior ministry staff and top personnel from the donors step in and inform the wayward colleague to desist in the claims or be declared *persona non grata* from the country.

An embarrassing situation for all of us, especially him, is brought to an end by the new colleague being obliged to sign a statement denying the wish to be considered as team leader and to the donor formally appointing me to the position. Try as I might to convince this colleague that I knew nothing about the mire that he had so easily gotten himself into, we were, sadly, never able to become friends.

Third, as my introductory nasty moment as team leader, the local office of the donors has officially notified me that the project must cease immediately to pay the civil servants their training allowances; judged to be illegal salary top-ups (which of course everyone knew they were). This has understandably caused a real rumpus in the team and the ire is directed squarely at me as the person responsible for cheque signing, and now forbidden to do so. The donor calls a meeting of the civil service staff to explain the situation but no one from the latter group turns up. Stalemate!

As a final disruption, the national project coordinator has been recalled to the Forestry Department and his replacement named by the government. Everyone anticipates the new arrival with some trepidation. The new coordinator was apparently for, a while, also the coordinator of the original pilot project, and he, again apparently, left under a cloud; but best not to be too judgmental just yet.

Technical and administrative staff, both in Senegal and the USA, are working on the design of the follow-on project. This is to be a bigger and more ambitious phase with administrative and financial management passing from the control of the international side (i.e. me) to the government side (i.e. the new coordinator). Thus the role of the different internationals in the technical advisory team will, in principle, soon be purely on the technical side. Our previous roles covering oversight of the administrative and financial side of the project is to be removed and handed to our government counterparts.

Soon after our new coordinator is named by the Government, he makes an appearance in our offices in the Livestock Department building. We introduce ourselves, have a quick chat about the project and then make a tour of the building and staff. He appears to be proactive and quickly states that he sees two actions to be treated as priority. The first is to settle those staff who have just lost their training allowances. I wonder how he will do this and am surprised at his method.

He calls the group of dissidents into his new office and asks them, as one civil servant to another, whether they really believe that salary top-ups are legal and acceptable by their home ministries. Several of the more outspoken colleagues begin to talk of acquired rights and possible strike action and then, as he remains firm, they begin to raise their voices at him. Big mistake. His calm response is to pull his phone across the desk and ask the noisier elements for the phone numbers of the directors of their respective departments. As he begins to dial the first number, he gently states that as some individuals are so unhappy at the project, he will be returning them forthwith to their ministries. He does not need to finish dialling. No-one leaves but the bad vibes continue until and beyond the day I finally leave.

The second action concerns the efforts to find a new building for our important work and sensitive equipment. The coordinator promises to take charge of this immediately. True to his word, within a couple of days, he asks me to accompany him to view a possible building. Unfortunately, it is a thirty-minute drive out of Dakar and far too far to expect the team to travel each day by public transport. But this, I am told, is the only suitable and vacant government building currently available.

Fate steps in. An American friend who has one of the other four weekends at the beach house, invites me over to his home in Fann Residence for an early evening beer. We take our bottles out onto his balcony in this extremely quiet and rather upper class neighbourhood of Dakar, close to the University of Cheikh Anta Diop. From the balcony, I spot the perfect building on the other side of the road.

"Buddy" I ask, "who uses the building over there?"

"No one, the last government people moved out a few days ago. I think it belongs to the Public Works Department."

I ask our new coordinator to organise a visit and the building is rapidly assigned to our project, and, unbeknown to me at this time, they will still be there more than thirty years later.

The coming weekend is our turn for the beach house. I decide to leave work a little early on the Friday afternoon, drive home, pack the car with everything that Véro has prepared and then we leave together to collect Mélanie and David from their schools. By just after 4 pm we are on the road, direction Ngaparou. No mishaps on route this time and by 5.30 pm, we are driving through the rickety gates and into the beach house garden. Vieux awaits us with the keys to the house and helps me to get the car unloaded. Véro in turn loads the fridge with our food for the weekend while the children change into their swimwear. Fifteen minutes after arriving, we are sitting on the sandy beach, right outside our garden fence, while the children splash in the warm shallow water. A cold bottle of rosé for us and something less alcoholic for the children; paradise.

Vieux has noticed that I have brought a couple of fishing rods and a box of fishing material with me to Ngaparou. He asks if I am interested in going out fishing in a *pirogue* since there is an elderly fisherman in his village who speaks pretty good French. Well, why not?

The following day, Saturday, Vieux takes me to his village and introduces me to M. Sène and, as simple as that, a long friendship is born. M. Sène is probably over sixty and possesses both Senegalese and French nationalities. He served in the French army, as a soldier in the Senegal Rifles during the war in Algeria and his reward for services rendered was recognised by the French government back in the 1960s. Sène has innumerable children ranging in age from infants to ones who are older than me. At first we chat about everything, except fishing, but eventually get down to brass tacks. I tell him that I would like to go fishing every Sunday morning that I am in Ngaparou. His sons would come to collect me at the beach house and drop me back there after fishing. I will bring some bait but I would like him to provide some local bait too. This comes in the form of a large sardine-type fish that is called locally *Yaabooy*. Sène tells me that one of his sons, called Pape, will be in charge of the *pirogue* and another of his sons will accompany us to take care of jobs like weighing the anchor. All sounds good. Then we get down to negotiate the price of fishing trips. I stress to Sène that I would like to fix the price of a trip once and for all and do not want to have to renegotiate the price of every future trip. He smiles, tells me that he thinks that is sensible and proposes 6,000 CFA per trip. That works out at twelve pounds for a morning's fishing, the assistance of his two sons, the hire of the *pirogue* and the small outboard, petrol and fish bait. I suggest 5,000 CFA and we shake hands on the deal. My first fishing trip will take place tomorrow morning from 7 am.

(As an aside, I go fishing in M. Sène's boat during the almost five years that we live in Senegal on this occasion. Ten years after leaving my current post, I go back to work in the country and M. Sène's sons take me out fishing once more. They refuse point blank to allow me to pay more than the originally agreed 5,000 CFA despite the passage of so much time and the devaluation of the CFA. M.

Sène and his sons are real gentlemen and I hold much affection and esteem for them.)

Sunday morning arrives and I climb out from under the mosquito net, being careful not to wake Véro or the two children who are sleeping on mattresses on our floor. I pick up my fishing bag and rod, pop a small bottle of water and a frozen bag of prawns (for bait) into the bag and make my way down to the beach. True to their promise, Pape and his younger brother Malick are just arriving at our sandy beach. Malick jumps out and holds the *pirogue* steady, allowing me to get in with relatively dry feet, while Pape has the outboard motor gently ticking over, holding the *pirogue* in place. We exchange our *nan-ga-def* and set off across a calm sea towards some distant hills that mark the Nature Reserve of Popenguine. During the thirty-minute trip, I learn that Pape understands just as much French as I do Wolof; sadly, we are not destined to have too many conversations! But at least the boat trip allows me to get my rod set up and hooks baited and ready to drop over the side.

Pape slows the motor when we arrive some four hundred metres off the headland of the Reserve. He then triangulates the boat's position using large landmarks on shore and, when happy with our position, tells his brother to drop the anchor. A minute later he says "OK" (at least that word seems universal) and we each drop our lines over the side. Pape and Malick are fishing with hand-lines with three hooks, baited with pieces of *Yaabooy*. I am using a small but solid boat rod that my dad had given me for just such moments. I too have three hooks but baited with pieces of prawn.

Even before my bait reaches the bottom, I see Pape jerk his line upwards and begin to pull his line back into the boat. Then Malick joins the act. Not to be left behind, my rod top kicks down and I too have a fish on the hook. Pape swings in two lovely pink *dorade* or sea bream and Malick adds a third. I follow them with two more. Not bad going with five sea bream in two minutes. We continue catching from the shoal but with greater intervals between our catches until Pape mimics to pull in our lines so we can move the boat.

We travel one hundred metres or so and start again. This time, I am the first to get a bite, a very big one it feels, and so I strike and try to reel in. But it would appear that one of my hooks must have snagged a rock as I cannot put any line back on my reel. Pape starts to grab the end of my rod; clearly he wants to tug the line and either dislodge the hook or break the hook trace, but I motion to him to stop – I just felt a small movement. Slowly now I am able to reel in but there is a strange sensation to the movement of the line. The only way I can describe it is as though I have caught a plastic bag full of water and it is very slowly, but without fighting (why should a bag fight?) coming to the surface.

When I get the 'plastic bag' close to the surface, we can all see what I have actually caught – an octopus! Pape leans over the side, grabs my line with one hand and whatever he can of the cephalopod with his other. He sits up straight and then we pass a few moments of complete comedy and madness.

First, the octopus is clearly less than happy to be brought out of the sea and so squirts a pint of sepia in every direction possible. Soon all three of us have the black dye dripping off our noses and staining our t-shirts. Next it takes a grip of Pape's arm with as many of its legs and suckers as possible. Try as he will to pull the legs away, every time one is removed, another takes its place to grip onto him. What a comedy sketch we are witnessing! And we do what everyone else would do, both Malick and I roar with laughter while poor Pape still tries to unhook the legs while the octopus continues to spray everyone with sepia. Finally, we take pity on Pape and each of us take hold of two or three legs and Pape is released. He throws the octopus to the *pirogue* floor, grabs a short thick stick normally used for dispatching large fish and thumps the octopus until it stops moving in the few inches of water that permanently sits in the bottom of his *pirogue*.

When his energy is spent, he also sees the funny side and between gulps of laughter says to me *"t'es plus toubab"* which basically translates to 'you are no longer a white man' because the sepia has given my face a very deep tan!

Happy to say that the rest of the morning passes without any other serious incidents and, as I hear a church bell chiming twelve, I gesture to Pape that we should start going back to the beach house. The anchor is retrieved, the motor started and we head across a sea that is calm and beautiful. As we glide across the water, I take a peep into the white polystyrene box that we have been putting the fish into as we have been catching them. I express surprise to see that it is almost full which brings a lovely smile from Pape. He can see that he has one very satisfied customer on board today.

The children are first to hear the motor and come running down the beach with Vieux. Véro follows calmly behind wearing her bikini and a silky wraparound while Khadi brings up the rear puffing as she moves her traditional frame slowly down towards the water's edge. Pape and I descend from the *pirogue* and Malick hands over the polystyrene box to Vieux. Immediately Pape begins to use his hands to shovel fish into the plastic baby's bath that Vieux had the foresight to bring with him. Our bath is soon full and the large white box is still only half empty. Pape then begins to throw more fish onto the sand but we stop him and get Vieux to explain that we have sufficient fish for today and that he should take the remainder with him. But I do retrieve the octopus!

Khadi then gets to work with a knife and starts gutting first the octopus and then half a dozen of the largest fish. These I barbecue on the old BBQ full of charcoal that Vieux had lit when he saw our *pirogue* returning. Mélanie manages to eat almost the whole octopus on her own – and from this day octopus becomes one of her favourite foods. David picks out a beautiful pink seabream for his lunch while Véronique and I tuck into two other plump fish accompanied by a tomato and onion salad. Khadi and Vieux take the remaining three fish and go off to eat them together with an enormous mound of white rice, *brisé*, of course.

The remainder of our catch goes into the freezer and accompanies us back to Dakar in the cool box. Given my many future fishing trips with Pape and his brothers, we rarely ever need to buy fish during our long stay in Senegal.

But Ngaparou is not my only fishing location. At nursery school, David makes friends with Maxim, a four-year-old French child whose parents run a cute little hotel that possesses a small bay with a sandy beach protected by a manmade rocky promontory. Maxim's mum provides us with a letter to be shown to the beach guard stating that we are to be allowed free entry. Coincidentally, as we receive the letter, Senegal declares that forthwith the country will work a *'journée continue'* meaning that I am able to leave the office on most days by around 4 pm and go straight to the beach with my fishing equipment. I invariably find Véro and the children already on the beach; Mélanie like her mum bronzing on a beach towel and reading a book while David and Maxim have buckets and spades trying to catch the small crabs that live in holes at the top of the beach.

8

Our friendly refugees

Our children adore living in Senegal and they do enjoy a pretty idyllic life. Their school is made for children, they are well looked after by experienced and friendly staff, class sizes are small, rarely going over fifteen, there must be at least forty nationalities represented by the 120-odd pupils, and the school sits in large, well-tended grounds overlooking the sea. The school day ends at 4 pm and the weather is invariably sunny but not too hot. To add to our children's pleasure, they have their mum and dad present for much of their time out of school and, when I have to be away for work, Lena, the maid, is on hand to spoil them both.

David is a lovely, cheeky chap. Blond hair, blue eyes, freckled nose, and a perpetual habit of getting up to cute but not too serious mischief. Mélanie is a bit more serious at school and we hear nothing but praise from her teachers. But we are a little concerned because now at eight years old, she does not seem to be making much progress with reading; in fact, while she is advancing well in all other school areas, in reading she is struggling.

We make an appointment to speak to her form teacher who tells us that we should not be concerned because the reading issue is simply due to her being bilingual. We do not believe a word of this explanation and so have a quiet word with another teacher who happens to have trilingual children. That kind lady speaks to the special needs teacher and we are asked for permission to test our daughter in case there is an underlying issue. After a few days' wait, we receive the news that the issue has nothing to do with being bilingual (of course it does not) and instead, the tests show that our daughter is struggling to remember the correct sounds to put to the groups of letters she sees on the page. The solution is for the special needs teacher to take Mélanie out of class for twenty minutes a day and to provide exercises that target the problem. Within a month, she changes from being a child who was not very interested in reading to one who cannot put books down. And the rest is history.

Another problem then arises at the school. Being based as it is, on the American curriculum, it has a purely English language programme. Many Anglophone parents have informed the school that it is a shame to live in a Francophone country and for their Anglophone children not to learn to speak French. The school has therefore decided to provide French classes for all children, regardless of age or ability. This raises two problems. First, there are insufficient teachers speaking a good level of French to take all the classes and second the French-speaking ability of the children in each class is highly variable. The crunch begins to arrive when we check Mélanie's homework and find that she is being taught a very basic level of French along the lines of *la chaise, la plage, aller, venir,* and so on. Our worries increase when we start seeing basic errors in the work she has been copying for example *le table* instead of *la table*. When we quiz her about the errors, she tells us that she and other Francophone children have tried to tell the teacher when errors arise but that the teacher does not listen.

It seems that we are not the only parents starting to worry because Claude, a French-Canadian dad, stops me one day as we collect our children from their classroom. He tells me that several parents are getting up a petition to protest about the quality of the teaching of French and would I sign it? My counter suggestion is that we should take the issues directly to the American Principal rather than causing open embarrassment by sending in a petition. The parents agree to the suggestion and decide that, as it was my idea, I should be the one to represent them in discussions with the Principal. He, in turn, asks me to meet with the school board composed of five American parents. The board agrees that the school needs to do a little better and instructs that the French programme be reorganised to allow mixed-year classes to be taught at three levels: maternal language (like Claude's and my children), average speakers and beginners.

That pleasant meeting with the school board has an equally pleasant repercussion. At the end of the academic year, a couple of board members are due to leave Senegal and another has come to the end of her mandate on the board. Elections are to be held but first the school needs candidates to be proposed.

The proposition of candidates and then the elections are to be held in a very short time frame and this coincides with a period when I am away on another botanical field trip lasting three weeks. I give the school no thought at all as I work in the Ferlo. But out of sight apparently does not mean out of mind since several members of the board liked the fact that I had cooled down the situation around the French classes. A delegation comes to our house and, since I am absent, persuades Véro that she should sign the form for me to stand as a future board member. Apparently, many parents agree and I return to Dakar to find that, in my absence, I have been elected a board member with the highest number of votes. Claude, too, is now on the board. Having the highest number of votes provides me with a two-year mandate and the position of Deputy President of the Board, now how about that?

The following year, the Board President is assigned by the American Embassy to another posting and I have the honour to step into his role, the first Brit to preside the International School board. But my only real claim to fame in that role is that I won the parent's Space Hopper race three years in a row!

David spends time each early evening sitting with Mbaye, our house guard, chatting about his day at school. He is picking up a fair amount of Wolof; certainly more than me. One day while sitting with Mbaye, he notices a small boy emerge from the refugee camp that sits on the other side of our tall garden wall. This is Saidou who is probably two years older than David but not much bigger. Saidou is extremely shy but very kind and gentle with David. They manage to communicate somehow in broken Wolof or shattered English. David soon pronounces Saidou as his new best friend. I do not believe that Saidou ever manages to understand what Ninja Turtles are about; his life being far less complicated than that of a little expatriate boy.

Mélanie, being the sweet child she is, tells us that she feels sad to see how poor Saidou is, how ragged are his clothes and, did we notice, he even has to play with a flat football. Cue for Véro to suggest to the children that they should sort through their toys and give the refugee camp any they do not play with anymore while we will all sort through our clothes and hand them over to Saidou's dad to distribute in the camp. His dad also becomes a useful odd-job-man for us and a willing recipient of any excess fish that I happen to catch off Maxim's beach. He also appreciates the occasional cold beer!

Now we have been in Senegal for over a year and a half, family and friends begin to plan for trips to see us. We are soon to receive the visit of my mum and dad. This is a big trip for them as they have never travelled to Africa nor have they ever had to organise an entire trip themselves – in the past they have travelled to different parts of Spain but always on package tours that are purchased from a holiday brochure.

Not to be put off, my mum visits a travel agency in Maidstone and becomes the first client that they have ever received who wants a roundtrip to Dakar. The straightforward flights with Air France involve a change in Paris, and the price is exorbitant, far too expensive for them. However, the agent does not want to lose her commission and so looks around for cheaper alternatives. A popular tourist destination for Brits is The Gambia, the little country that the Senegalese consider as a worm in the apple of Senegal. Spare seats are always available on charter flights from London and these can be found at knockdown prices. So the agent can get mum and dad to Banjul but now how to get them from Banjul to Dakar; a distance of only about 100 miles?

The agent does her work and finds that there is a small charter plane that brings groups of birdwatchers from Banjul to Dakar. A quick phone call reveals that they have five spare seats to sell at a low price; and my parents have their roundtrip booked, confirmed and paid for. As it is the school holidays for Easter, Véro and the children are around for my parents visit while I can take a few days off work to create two long weekends during their stay.

Just before their arrival, we decide it best to stock up the refrigerator and therefore drive into the Plateau area of Dakar to visit the market and then the supermarket.

After we pay the 30,000 CFA bill at checkout in the supermarket, an assistant walks across to inform us "the supermarket is giving a free Easter chick for each 5,000 CFA spent. Here are your six chicks."

And just like that we become the proud owners of a group of cute, day old and chirping chicks. While the children are delighted to have the chicks, and they are cute it has to be admitted; where on earth will we keep them, and what do we feed them? A quick trip back to Kermel and we buy a cage and some chick starter food. That will do for a couple of weeks.

My parents finally arrive at Leopold Senghor Airport and I make sure to be inside to greet them as they come through arrivals. I had nightmares of them arriving before me and seeing their bags and them disappearing in different directions with a couple of taxi touts! My parents are real sweethearts but they are over-polite and, all alone, would have been sitting targets for some of the miscreants that frequent the international airport. As it is, they come through arrivals with the gaggle of twitchers that had shared their small plane; safety in numbers.

David has come to the airport with me to meet his grandparents and the first thing he says to his grandfather is "you have to build a chicken run, grandad!"

And that is precisely what grandad and nan spend the first three days of their vacation doing. Mbaye is sent off frequently to purchase whatever supplies of wire netting, wood and nails are needed and, after a couple of days, we have a very nice run with a little house attached. My dad has the foresight to ensure that the run has a wire netting roof although he was thinking of marauding cats rather than snakes or whatever wildlife might get into the garden.

The chicks make their grand entrance to the chicken run and we all look forward to a steady supply of fresh eggs. Within a couple of months, we can see that one of the chicks is growing much faster than the others. He starts to crow with a broken voice as well as 'tread' the smaller birds. Clearly we have a cockerel and, judging by his amorous overtures to the other five, our supply of fresh eggs will not be too long in coming. That is until another bird also starts to crow. Then cockerel number one fights for crowing rights with number two and the battles look ferocious. Véro and I decide that there is nothing to do but to assign one of the two cocks to the saucepan. Mbaye duly obliges, and we eat a very delicious *coq-au-vin*.

But that is not the end of the tale because another bird begins to crow and the process is repeated and repeated and repeated until all six chickens (no, let us call them what they were: cockerels) have been dispatched to the saucepan.

What a disappointment. We have been feeding those critters for three months and they all turned out to be cockerels.

I ask Mbaye for advice on how to be sure to buy female chicks and he suggests visiting the veterinary surgeon who lives four houses down from us. The Vet sells me twelve, day-old chicks and guarantees that they are all hens; which they turn out to be. The birds grow fast and eggs soon start arriving, often we have six to eight eggs a day and, curiously, most have double yolks. But I digress from the topic of this chapter.

For the last weekend of my parents' trip, we go for three days to our beach house in Ngaparou. My dad has always loved sea fishing, in fact he taught me how to boat fish as a child, and so I take him out on the *pirogue* and we have a pleasant time fishing together. That is until, at a certain moment, he starts to get cramp and decides to stretch his legs – by standing up! Suddenly, with the balance lost, the canoe starts rocking wildly from side to side. Luckily, I am able to reach out and grab his hand to pull him back down to a sitting position. But that was a close thing because one of us could very easily have gone over the side – and climbing back in would not have been simple!

But that was only part of the drama because, a few moments later, my dad's rod tip dips down and he has a fish on the line. As he reels-in, he feels an even sharper tug and then nothing.

"Lost it" he tells me.

He continues reeling in thinking to re-bait his hook. However, when he finally gets his weight and hooks to the surface, he discovers that he has not lost the fish ... only half of it!

"*Cax mi,*" says Pape.

"Shark," I translate for my dad, "in fact, most likely, a hammer-head, there are a lot around here."

"Ooph, good job no one fell in," replies my dad in his under-stated manner!

But that was not the only fright my dad had at the beach house. Years later, long after my dear dad had passed away, Mélanie and her nan were looking through an old photograph album of our years in Senegal. When Mélanie arrived at photos of the beach house, she said how much she loved the time we spent in Ngaparou.

My mum shocked us all by saying "sorry to say but dad and I hated going to your beach house!"

"But why nan," asks Mélanie "we all loved going there and we never realised that you did not like it."

"We were always scared" she replied. "At night when the drums were beating, we imagined people coming through our bedroom window and dragging us off."

"Oh nan!" exclaims Mélanie, "those drums were from the tourist resort just down the road from us and they were part of the tourists' evening entertainment!"

While my mum received the teasing from that incident, I am the butt of another family joke. And you will certainly feel sorry for me; that I am sure.

One very hot day when the temperature is in the high 30s and the sun is blinding in its intensity, I arrive home from work and park my car in the garage. As I walk out the back of the garage and into the garden, Véro and my mum say together that I need to check the drains because the washing machine is blocked and the water is not draining out.

Being an obedient man-about-the-house, and despite the fact that I am wearing a black suit and white shirt, I lift the manhole cover that sits in the middle of the garden path.

Big mistake as the million resident and king-size cockroaches are suddenly exposed to the glaring sun. There is only one thing that they instinctively wish to do, and that is to rush to find shade. Logically for them and sadly for me, the shade they choose belongs to my two trouser legs.

Well, what would you do if a million cockroaches swarm up the inside of your trousers? Too right you would, and I do the same. I was down to my boxers before you can say 'Jack Dash give us a flash'!

For a month or so, just before the short rainy season arrives in Dakar, the air becomes humid, the heat sweltering and we appreciate having air conditioners. Today Véro and I are off on a shopping run to Kermel, then to Pierre-the-butcher and finally to the supermarket. Before driving back to our house, we make a detour to the Lagon II, a beautiful hotel that sits on the seafront of the Corniche. A unique feature is that one of its bars has a window under the sea and so one can sit and watch the fish, in their element, on the other side of the glass. We have taken the habit of stopping there for a late-morning coffee or ice cream before going home with the groceries.

Today, is our thirteenth wedding anniversary and we each decide to have an alcoholic drink; white wine for Véro and a draft beer for me; probably a bad idea in this heat as the alcohol goes straight to our heads. No matter, once home and lunch eaten, all four of us decide to take a siesta.

Ten minutes after lying down, four-going-on-five-year-old David comes in, wakes me up and announces "I've slept dad. Can I watch TV now?"

I know that if I want to have a nap, the simplest thing to do is to let David watch a cartoon on *Canal Horizon*. I go to the sitting room with him, turn on the TV, find the right channel and tell him "please do not wake me up unless there is an emergency".

"Okay-dokey *papa*" he replies.

I leave him on the settee staring goggle-eyed at a Roadrunner cartoon. I vaguely notice that the French windows to the garden are open and there is a cool breeze gently blowing in. He will be comfortable and may soon fall asleep himself. For my part, I have no trouble re-entering Morpheus' embrace.

In my dreams I can hear a calm but shrill little voice proclaiming "mum, dad, ... there's a crocodile in the house; mum, dad, ... there's a crocodile in the house; mum, dad, ... there's a crocodile in the house."

My parental instinct pulls me wide awake and there is no dreaming now when I hear once more in the same unfussed little voice saying calmly "mum, dad, ... there's a crocodile in the house."

What on earth is my little man going on about? But better be safe than sorry. I head out of our bedroom and enter the sitting room. Cartoons are still playing, David is still staring google-eyed at the screen, everything appears normal.

"David, what's this about a crocodile?"

"Over there dad," he vaguely points a finger to his right while still staring at the screen, "it just walked in from the garden and has been walking around the room. That's why I called you."

I follow the direction of his pointing finger and come face-to-face not with a crocodile but with the largest monitor lizard (called a *Varan* in French) that I have ever seen. While this gigantic lizard may not have been much concerned by a small boy transfixed by cartoons, it is petrified when this larger human arrives in the room. It attempts to go out through an open window but the metallic mosquito screen and then the burglar bars stop its escape attempt. The commotion brings a bleary-eyed Mbaye running in through the French windows. The next thing I know is that Mbaye is swinging his machete, almost severing the poor animal's head and gouging a large chip out of the tiled floor. He acts quickly because he is scared of its large lashing tail that can inflict wounds.

Mbaye then informs me that he had seen this giant lizard wandering around the garden several times during the morning and always heading for the chicken run. He tells me that he had tried to kill it already but each time he got close, the lizard shimmied up a bougainvillea trunk and disappeared into the mass of vegetation and thorns at the top of the wall.

Well what to do with a giant but dead monitor lizard? No problem. I ask Mbaye to bring the wheelbarrow and we load the poor creature in. To give a rough idea of the size of this animal, it completely fills the large barrow and its tail still hangs down to the ground.

Mbaye asks "should I take the lizard to the rubbish dump?"

But I have a better idea, "let's give it to Saidou's dad."

During field trips, Séraphin has often told me that members of his Bassari tribe adore the taste of cooked monitor lizard as well as python and a few other exotic types of bush meat. I wonder if this culinary object is also appreciated by the forest people of Sierra Leone. And I receive quick confirmation that it is indeed considered a delicacy in Sierra Leone too, as whoops of joy rise from the refugee camp as I wheel the barrow and its load over to Saidou's dad.

This is not the only time that we become popular with the refugees. We have recently made friends with a lovely Filipino couple. The lady works as a teacher's aide at the nursery school where Véro also works and where David is a pupil. Her husband, works for an international NGO as the in-country finance director.

He is fishing mad, as he demonstrates during an evening at his home. "Come and see my office" he invites.

I walk into a room that could easily have been a European fishing tackle shop. He has rows and rows of fishing rods, each with neat and clean reels attached and boxes and drawers full of the paraphernalia that goes with sea fishing. (I would be too embarrassed to show him my own gear).

"I have hired a pirogue to go fishing for swordfish (*Espadon* in French) next Wednesday, a public holiday. Would you like to come with me? I have all the equipment necessary."

Well, I have to admit that I have never fished for any game fish, apart from the odd tuna, and so have little idea what it entails.

"No matter, I will show you how everything works."

And he does.

Wednesday arrives and I drive one of my project's little Suzuki jeeps over to his house and I am soon convinced that we have loaded enough gear to sink the pirogue. We then drive to a little fishing port where our canoe awaits us. It is a little bigger than the one I use at Ngaparou, but then it needs to be because the ocean around Dakar is more violent and choppy.

We set off out into the choppy sea that encircles Dakar and travel a couple of kilometres around the coastline until we are approximately a kilometre off the headland of Les Almadies and in slightly calmer water. As we skim across the gentle waves, my friend rigs two rods and attaches large bright lures that are supposed to imitate fish. He explains that we will cast these into the sea and tow them behind the pirogue as it moves at quite a lick across the water.

He casts both rods to the rear of the boat and I am told that mine is on the left and his on the right. Within ten minutes, we see the rostrum (or the sword) of a swordfish break the surface and it literally hits my lure with its rostrum. With a real fish, this action is sufficient to stun the prey so it can be grabbed and eaten. My fishing partner picks up my rod, releases a little line and then strikes ... and 'fish on' (as Jeremy Wade would say!). He hands the rod over to me.

I know enough to realise that if I wish to get the swordfish to the pirogue, I must play it and tire it out rather than simply trying to reel it in. My friend watches me carefully as I allow line to leave the reel and the swordfish pulls away from the pirogue. Then suddenly it begins to dance a pirouette on its tail – what a beautiful sight.

"Be patient, Malcolm," I am warned, "I will help you if your arms get tired."

But he was never able to help me because as he spoke, I saw another rostrum break the surface and he has a fish on his line too.

Now, I would ask that you try to imagine the scene. We are in a six-metre-long pirogue and both of us are trying to stand up in the choppy waters and play the two fish that are battling at the ends of our lines. On four occasions, we are obliged to exchange rods because the two fighting swordfish are zigzagging to such an extent that our lines are crossing and the only way to stop them tangling and breaking the lines is to pass each other our rods. For fully twenty minutes we each play our respective fish until my buddy says that he feels that his fish is sufficiently tired to bring it into the boat. Our boatman puts on a strong glove and, as the swordfish comes towards the side of the boat, he makes a grab for the rostrum and pulls the head out of the water, I grab its tail with my free hand, while my friend wraps a length of rope around the tail. He and the boatman then swing the fish into the canoe.

Now it is my turn to repeat the process and soon both fish are lying in the well of the pirogue. My friend carefully removes the hooked lure from my fish and inspects its mouth. As there is very little damage, he asks me to help him to pick it up and return it to the sea. It swims off rapidly.

Sadly, the other fish has a large tear in its mouth and so cannot be released. The boatman dispatches it with a sharp thump on its head with a thick piece of wood.

As we congratulate each other on our dual efforts, we hear cheering and clapping coming from behind us. We turn round in the pirogue and see that we have an audience: a Club Med tourist boat filled with a dozen or so French holidaymakers hoping to catch their own *espadons* are cheering the show we have just put on for them!

We each catch another swordfish and that of my friend is returned to the water while mine is dispatched by the boatman. My second fish is the largest of the four but it has obviously, in the past, been attacked by a shark because there is a lump missing from its gut area and the wound has not had time to heal completely.

Our day comes to an end and the boatman steers his *pirogue* back towards the port where my car awaits. As we travel at pace across the sea, my friend asks if I have ever eaten smoked swordfish because he has a smoker at his home and swordfish meat is delicious when smoked.

The boatman helps us to carry the two large swordfish together with the rods and our bags back to the car, receives payment for a perfect day out and leaves us to walk back to his house. It is once we have said our '*Jere-jef*', or thanks, to the boatman that I suddenly realise how long and heavy the swordfish are. Both are in the region of two metres and fifty centimetres long and each must weigh close to fifty kilograms. How on earth can we transport them in the little Suzuki?

I quite literally sit down and think, and then have a brainwave.

"Hey, help me to lift them on to the roof of the car."

Luckily my jeep has a hard top and not a canvas one. We quickly arrange the two fish side by side on the roof with their rostrums hanging down the windscreen and on to the bonnet while their tails hang down over the rear window.

"Jump in and wind your window down," I instruct.

While he opens his window, I open mine. Then I take a coil of rope from the trunk of the car and pass it through the open windows and tie the fish tightly, looping the rope several times back through the open windows until the fish are firmly attached. Of course, I cannot now enter the car through my door and instead have to climb into the driver's seat through the open window. Job done, we set off towards my house in *Sacré Cœur* 3 with two very large fish attached to the roof.

"Malcolm, since this is an official car, what will be said if anyone reports you to the Big Boss?" A very pertinent question, I have to admit.

I reply that I would say "sir, you say two giant fish attached to the roof, surely not? Are you sure that the person who told you had not drunk too much over the public holiday?"

Back at the house, a very excited Mbaye unties the rope so that we can leave the car in the more usual manner and then together we carry the two fish to the large garden sink that sits at the back of the garage. The children come to inspect the catch and we take photos of both of us trying - and failing - to hoist the two fish held in our hands.

Mélanie lifts up the very large dorsal fin and the light passing though shows the fish's beautiful blue coloration.

"Dad, sorry, but it is such a shame that you had to kill this lovely fish."

And I agree totally with my little girl and feel rather sad that we took these noble creatures out of their element. I vow there and then never to attempt to catch swordfish again.

Véro brings out her sharpest knife and my buddy expertly cuts four long fillets from the first fish. He tells me that he will smoke them and give me back half of the meat. But his smoker is not large enough to smoke the fillets of the other fish. What should we do with the other one?

David pipes up in his squeaky voice "give it to Saidou, dad."

And that is exactly what we do.

That evening we can hear the feasting in the refugee camp going on until the early hours of the morning. I send Mbaye with a crate of beers to help with the celebrations and to wash down the cooked fish.

The following afternoon, a bleary-eyed Saidou's dad comes to thank us for being so kind to the refugees and tells us that from now on, we are under their protection. His promise is soon to be tested.

Approximately a week later, late one night (or is it very early in the morning?) I can hear Mbaye calling me from outside my bedroom window.

"Boss, boss, wake up. Come quickly."

I struggle out of bed slipping on a pair of shorts and a t-shirt and go outside to meet Mbaye.

"what is it?" I ask.

"You have to go to the refugee camp because I am afraid that they are killing someone who tried to come across our wall."

I go with Mbaye out of our gate and into the camp where Saidou's dad is awaiting me with a very heavy club in his hands. He explains that a Liberian man had come into the camp last evening and started asking many questions about us, the house and our night guard. The camp had warned the Liberian that the house was under their protection and that he should forget any plans he might have. But he had not listened and one of the young men from the camp had seen him trying to climb over the wall and had raised the alarm.

A group of Saidou's dad's friends had caught him and dished out a very heavy beating. He was now just coming around in one of the shanties. Taking my torch, I went with Saidou's dad and saw the man lying on the earthen floor. His head and face were badly cut and bleeding but clearly his life was not in danger.

That is until Saidou's dad says "we will take him and throw him over the cliffs into the sea."

"No, no, no. I don't want you to do that. He has been more than punished by the beating. When he is able to listen, tell him that I stopped you from throwing him off the cliff and that he should be grateful that he is still alive."

Whether my request was carried out, I do not know, but we never suffered any other burglary attempts from the camp.

But fun and games with the refugee camp do not finish there.

This weekend, in Senegal, elections are to take place. The incumbent President Diouf is being heavily challenged by the opposition party led by Abdoulaye Wade and there are occasional riots and disturbances led by the youth movement of the opposition parties. The youth now want Set-Setal to move into politics.

The message has gone around from the various embassies that it is best to remain at home over the two election weekends and not attempt to travel, for example, to beach houses. We follow the advice and remain at home staying in the safety of our home and walled garden. In the early afternoon, David makes a quick trip to the refugee camp to hand over to Saidou a coconut that had just fallen from one of our dwarf coconut trees. We warn him to be back in ten minutes.

As instructed, he is back in the house within the allotted time and says a very strange thing: "mum, I want to take a bath." This is strange because on any other day at bath time we would be begged "ten more minutes' play, pleeeease."

Well we are, at the least, rather curious and, at the worst, worried about what might have taken place in those ten minutes. As the bath runs, Véro asks in a gentle voice "Do you want to tell me anything, little man?"

"No mummy."

Once undressed and in the lukewarm bath, Véro begins to wash away the grime that David manages to accumulate every day of the week. But as she gently soaps him, she notices an angry red mark on his left side, just below his ribs. "What caused this *mon chéri?*" she asks.

"Nothing mum."

"It's OK love, you can tell me and I promise I will not be angry." She was secretly concerned that someone had hit him with a stick or had thrown a stone.

"A dog at Saidou's place bit me mum."

And true, we can make out the puncture marks and this causes us to get really worried since rabies is endemic in many African countries where stray dogs are in profusion.

Véro remembers that our friend Geoff knows a doctor who works at the Pasteur Institute and goes off to try to get a telephone number for the doctor. Meanwhile I go with Mbaye to the camp to speak with Saidou's dad. On arrival, I find that the men in the camp have managed to capture the dog and have it tied with a rope at a safe distance from their living areas. Saidou's dad tells me that the dog had wandered into the camp only that morning and that he had seen the dog strike out at David as he walked past, but he had not realised that David had been bitten. I ask him to keep the dog tied up but to provide it with access to a bucket of water. I stress that we need to see what happens to the dog.

Meanwhile Véro has managed to get the good doctor's telephone number and – here is where the Marks' luck plays a part – he has remained in Dakar heeding the embassy warning not to travel.

He tells Véro that he lives in the Plateau area of Dakar and instructs "meet me in fifteen minutes outside of the Pasteur Institute, I have a stock of anti-rabies shots and we must get the first one delivered immediately."

We drive like crazy through the deserted streets of Dakar and pull up in front of the Institute. The doctor, true to his word, opens the door and tells us to come quickly. He smiles at a rather scared David whose freckles stand out even brighter today against his nervous pallor and tells him to be brave. He rubs alcohol on to his upper arm and, as quick as you like, injects the vaccine into his muscle. Our little boy says nothing. No ouch, no complaints; at the moment anyway.

We are given a box of phials and a stock of syringes and needles together with handwritten instructions. The next dose is due in four hours, then eight hours then one day, then two days, then four and finally eight days later. Step up a friend from Denmark, who had been a nurse in a previous incarnation before coming to Senegal, to administer the other six doses.

The story ends on a happy note for us, the only howling David did was when he saw the nurse dropping by to administer the next dose. The ending was not so happy for the poor dog who succumbed after four days and its body was taken away for testing by the veterinary laboratory.

9

The Mischievous Minister

The new phase of the project has been approved and all staff, national and international, move seamlessly from the first phase to the second one. Our new project document, always a hefty tome, states clearly that it is anticipated that we must begin to earn a living. Now this is very modern thinking on the part of the project designers since the vast majority of development projects and programmes continue to run while donor money pours in and promptly close their doors when the cash tap is turned off. We, however, it is anticipated, will continue to receive funding for the next couple of years but must seek progressively to generate our own income and eventually become totally self-supporting.

Suddenly, yours truly has to turn from being an ecologist to a business developer. The other big change that has occurred is that I am no longer in charge of the financial and administrative management; this role is passed on to the new project coordinator. While theoretically this removes a big work burden from my shoulders (to be replaced by the business development work), it heaps a large amount of worry in my stomach. I quickly realise that while I may no longer be involved in financial oversight, I will certainly receive the blame from my international employers if anything goes wrong. After all, how can an international agency discipline a national civil servant if he does not do as they instruct?

The intensity of worry is increased when I see in the new budget that there is a large lump sum allocated for refurbishing our new building. There are, in addition, several other significant budget lines for procuring electricity back-up material in the shape of enormous batteries or uninterrupted power supplies; to improve the network capacity, and to purchase more powerful computing equipment, air conditioners and vehicles. Certainly the solid procurement mechanisms we had in place during the previous phase are well known and trusted but will they be used correctly, if at all?

The project accountant, Mr Keita, comes to speak to me discretely and warns that the new bank account, run by our government counterpart, has a sole signatory – the coordinator himself – and Keita warns that, from an accounting standpoint, this can only lead to trouble; intentional or not.

I set up a one-on-one meeting with the national coordinator and advice that it would be both logical and would potentially protect the coordinator himself if a second signatory is added to the account. I propose Mr Keita or the assistant coordinator. I am most certainly not ready for the response I receive.

"Malcolm, tell me your official title."

"Chief Technical Advisor," I respond.

"And there we have it. I look to you with admiration for your technical knowledge and skills, and you may advise me on all things technical. You should get on with improving the products and setting up the business side of the new project but you must not forget that you are no longer in charge of the administrative and financial matters. Those are now my responsibility and you will do well to remember that it is I who requests the Senegalese government to inform the donors whether or not to renew your annual contract. You should also bring this to the notice of the other internationals in the team who might otherwise forget."

And, yes, there we have it: the start of my troubles that will eventually convince me to leave beautiful Senegal with a very, very heavy heart. But not just yet!

I warn my donor counterparts, both in Dakar and in the USA, about my concerns over the financial structure and management and am told bluntly not to cause trouble for the new coordinator. Their message is as clear as the one I received from the national coordinator. I see the end of my days in Senegal coming on the horizon. Let their intransigent positions be on their heads then.

Luckily, I find that the business development angle provides a fresh and interesting challenge to me. I now turn a considerable amount of my time and energy to this side of the project, leaving my national counterparts to get on with their activities in administration and finance; after all the international agency's local and US-based officers are also supposed to be checking the admin and financial progress of the project.

Like all good business development, we realise that we need dedicated staff, one or more tested products and the ability to develop more, plus a sound and expandable client-base. This must be supported by an adequate and well-funded budget, and an executable business plan.

I call a meeting of the senior technicians and lay out my ideas for the future business. There is a satisfying buy-in and a real buzz from the staff present and we realise that key among our current skills that are likely to be the most saleable are our unparalleled expertise in Geographic Information Systems (GIS) and cartography.

GIS skills were brought to the project by a team from the US Geological Survey, starting in late 1989, and those skills have been developed by our local team, backstopped by USGS consultants. We all know that there exists no competition in this area in West Africa and that our team can compete against many similar units elsewhere, even in Europe and the Americas. Our other abilities like vegetation, bushfire and rainfall monitoring as well as aerial surveys will likely receive less frequent interest but the skills we have obtained in these areas can be used to support GIS and mapping work as well as possibly be useful in punctual consultancy work and training.

As far as clients are concerned, we currently only have the Senegalese government but do occasionally provide support to regional agencies like Agrhymet, based in Niger, as well as initiatives such as the Famine Early Warning Systems (FEWS). We also support a growing number of academic and development agencies with copies of our reports and other products and we attend, and often lead, at national and international conferences and workshops.

Obviously, we cannot bill the government for work because they provide us with an enormous counterparty in the form of offices, many staff, tax free status and technical guidance. Thus, in order to obtain clients willing to pay, we agree during the meeting that everyone needs to be involved in building networks, obtaining information on upcoming or actual needs in other projects and feeding the information to the business development management group.

Luckily we have a sound budget that can support our team and its work while we build a bigger client base.

We also need a business plan and, to help us develop one, the donors send first a rather elderly Brit and then a middle-aged French Canadian who has much more relevant skills. Together we draft the business plan and, during his several inputs, he becomes a friend, a sounding board and, as times get tougher, a confidante and advisor.

It is clear that to broaden our business appeal, we need to widen our network and become better known in the development community; both within Senegal and abroad. And here rapidly arrives a bit of luck.

The British Embassy has recently opened a 'community centre cum bar' in a redundant wing of the embassy. The idea is for the British community and spouses of whatever nationality to get together once a week and discuss issues or just generally socialise and relax. I recently met the new Deputy Ambassador and immediately liked him and his wife. As we chat at the bar one evening, he asks if he might pay the project a visit to see the type of work that a British national gets up to in Senegal. We set a visit for three days hence and he comes with another embassy worker to have a look around in our new offices; now well advanced in their refurbishment.

He is impressed not only with the activities and their products that are shown him but also with the eloquent introductions to the different activities that the activity leaders provide; almost all in very passable English. He goes away satisfied with his visit, promises to give a glowing report to the Ambassador and also to congratulate the Resident Representative who is a tennis partner. As he leaves our offices in his official car, I wonder if the Brits will be able to do anything to help us develop our business; after all in Senegal, Britain is only a bit-player and far down the list from the UN family, EU, French, Germans, Japanese and Americans.

I do not have to wonder for very long because on the following Monday, late-morning, my secretary, pokes her head around my office door and tells me that a small team of visitors would like to meet with me.

I recognise a civil servant from the Department of the Environment and he introduces me to two consultants from the United Nations Environment Programme. The first is a Francophone but with an excellent level of English; a Tunisian, I learn. The second is English with less of a grasp of French. It transpires that the UNEP team made a courtesy call at the UK embassy to announce the presence in country of the Brit (always a sensible step). There they had met the Deputy Ambassador, heard about our activities and seen some of our products; hence the visit.

I call a couple of my senior technicians to join the meeting and receive a detailed, and highly interesting, review of the activity of their mission.

UNEP has decided to undertake a pilot 'Inventory of Greenhouse Gases' in four selected African countries: Senegal and The Gambia along with Nigeria and Egypt. Our consultants are starting in the two West African states and have already visited The Gambia. The administration of the project in Senegal is to be placed in the Department of the Environment while my project is soon asked to take the technical lead. As there is an initial budget for both the administrative and technical activities, it looks like we are about to get our first paid job!

Over the course of the next two weeks, myself, a couple of my team plus a number of other people from various government departments and the university, attend a series of lectures and workshops given by the consultants about how the inventory is to be developed in Senegal.

One major exercise we are tasked to carry out under workshop conditions is to draw up a table with plus and minus columns. In the plus column are areas where carbon dioxide and other greenhouse gases are withdrawn from the atmosphere, so called 'carbon sinks'. Here they need information on, for example, multi-year series of vegetation production data and tree canopy cover; and only my project is able to provide them. In the negative column are listed such items as livestock (because of the harmful methane they produce) and vehicle numbers, factory outputs and also land cover losses. The first and last again require work from us.

One of our senior technicians asks very logically whether bushfire data should not also be placed in the negative column. Everyone is surprised to learn that bushfires are considered carbon neutral because the vegetation matter being burnt and carbon dioxide released will have been stored during previous periods of photosynthesis, and so the two sides cancel each other out.

When the consultants are happy with the completeness of the table and its plus and minus columns, the audience is asked to indicate which government departments and structures are best suited to carry out the inventory work. Fully 70% of the data production is allocated to my project and, given so much of the inventory falls to our project, it is agreed that we should also be responsible for collating cost data of the entire UNEP budget for Senegal.

One of my roles as business development manager includes calculating the cost base for future work streams, and in turn this means that I am nominated to be responsible for establishing the UNEP budget for Senegal. Other departments quickly get me their very simple and rather low-cost budgets while our part, involving the purchase of additional and expensive satellite imagery, together with significant fieldwork and staff and vehicle time, ends up representing some 90% of the overall budget. I anticipate the likely need to do some negotiating with the consultants and so build in some 'fat' that can be trimmed as negotiations get underway.

However, I am surprised when the consultants congratulate us on developing a really great budget that falls below their original estimate (obviously I did not add sufficient fat!). They go on to ask if I would be prepared to help The Gambia since that tiny country, equivalent to only 5% of the land surface of Senegal, has managed to produce a budget double the one we have just developed.

My brief is to visit and discuss with the Gambian lead agency, the Ministry of Natural Resources, and specifically the newly established and independent National Environment Agency (or NEA). Senior ministry staff are contacted and await my visit. Our first overseas' assignment!

A week later I set off by road for the journey to our English-speaking neighbours. My driver is our project mechanic, Seck, and we are using one of our little Suzuki jeeps that bears green, diplomatic plates. We estimate a seven or eight-hour trip.

I have made the drive to The Gambia on a couple of occasions with my own vehicle, once for a long weekend with my family and parents and once, a couple of months ago, when we were mooting to target development agencies based in Banjul. On that occasion, a young American working as a junior in the USAID office in The Gambia, had called together a diverse collection of senior development workers and, after I gave a formal presentation of my project's activities, products and ambitions, the group had hosted fish and chips and lots of cold beer on the beach; just below the British Embassy. That evening had been a lot of fun, had provided a number of important contacts and several good leads for possible future work in the country.

I like my driver enormously. He is a very competent mechanic and a lot of fun to be on mission with. He is not afraid to tease me, when teasing is necessary, and does not get huffy when I reciprocate! Our first stop is at a small *boui-boui* that he knows in Kaolack for a lunch of *thieboudienne* before continuing through the Sine Saloum and into the northern half of The Gambia. After clearing passport control, we drive for a further twenty minutes and arrive at the ferry point on the northern bank of the Gambia River.

My driver buys our tickets and announces that we must wait an hour for the crossing. He suggests that we use the time available to exchange some of our CFA for Dalasis, the Gambian currency. We both know the rate is about nine Dalasis for 500 CFA (about £1). Seck wagers that he will get a better rate than me; almost certainly he will. The loser of the bet will pay for our next meal.

As soon as we park the car into the ferry queue, two young money changers approach the car. The one on my side speaks to me in English while the one on the driver's side converses in Wolof; the most common language spoken between the two countries. The rate today seems to me to be on the low side as I am being offered only eight Dalasis for 500 CFA and, listening to Seck's negotiations, he is not doing any better. After a period of individual haggling, where I am insisting on 8.75 Dalasis, I turn to Seck and we chat in French, deciding that it will be better if we wait to get to Banjul to exchange our money.

I try a last time with my money changer and tell him "8.75 Dalasis or we will not exchange money with you."

He replies "no that is not possible," and walks off with his friend.

My driver predicts that "he will be back later."

And that is exactly what happens. Just as boarding begins and we are slowly driving towards the loading ramp, the two young men run up to our windows and say "OK, OK, 8.75 Dalasis."

I want to exchange 100,000 CFA (about £200) and my driver a more modest 25,000 CFA. Bundles of Dalasis are thrust on to our laps through the open windows and, after counting that we have received the right number of bundles, we hand over our CFA and drive on to the ferry.

Being a rather suspicious character, I take three of the Dalasis bundles at random and count the notes in them. Counting from one side there are indeed ten notes in each bundle but when I count from the other side, I find only eight notes. My clever little money changer has folded one note in each bundle thus depriving me of 10% of my funds.

When I tell my friendly driver of the trick, he roars with laughter and teases me that *Toubabs* are so easy to cheat. In return, I suggest that he might wish to count his money too ....

"No, they would never try to cheat a Senegalese," he assures me but since I continue to insist, he also counts and finds that the cheeky youngsters have taken him for a ride too.

For the next few days, he fumes about being cheated and takes every opportunity to tell any Gambian that will listen that he got cheated by them at the river crossing!

We settle into our hotel and I pass a quiet evening at the Bungalow Beach Hotel. The following morning, I have a courtesy visit to the Minister of Natural Resources and so arrive early at a most charming wooden building on the outskirts of Serrakunda. I climb the stairs and enter a spacious waiting room. After announcing my arrival to a young lady sitting in a room marked 'Secretary', I sit down in an armchair and read through my notes. After about five minutes, I am joined by a youngish man who asks how I am and where in the UK I live. When I mention that in fact I live in Dakar, he is intrigued and asks about my mission. Having nothing to hide, I give him a quick resume and say that I am here for a courtesy visit to the Minister.

His response rather surprises me because he tells me that I should be careful because the minister is a rascal and not nice at all.

I reply, "to the contrary, I have heard only good things about him and I am looking forward to my meeting."

"You'll see" says the man. He then walks off, leaving me more than puzzled, and passes through a side door, that I presume to be a toilet.

Very soon after this young man goes to answer his 'call of nature', a distinguished looking gentleman comes through another door, introduces himself as the senior civil servant in the ministry and asks me to follow him to the minister's office.

We pass through another door, into what looks like a conference room. He knocks at the door at the far end of the room, pushes the door open and states "The Minister."

I walk in and my jaw drops; for sitting in the minister's chair is none other than the young man who had earlier badmouthed the minister to me!

"You passed my test Dr Marks, may I call you Malcolm?"

I burst out laughing at his joke, then excuse myself for laughing out loud in his presence and tell him that I am more than happy that he calls me by my first name.

We pass a very congenial hour or so talking about our work in Senegal that I illustrate with examples of reports, maps and other products. I then explain that UNEP has asked me to come to Banjul to help his team develop their budget for the inventory of green-house gases in The Gambia.

"I would be grateful if you can help in this important area but you do know that The Gambia is not as advanced in ecological monitoring as Senegal? Could you propose to our team that they subcontract as much of the work as possible to your project? I know that your satellite images must also cover my country; so we could save a lot on not having to buy them ourselves; and, anyway, we lack the analytical capacity."

Our meeting continues in this very convivial manner over coffee and biscuits but I am aware that a minister's time is precious and that I must not take up more than my allotted amount.

At a convenient break in our long conversation, I say "perhaps I should not take any more of your time Minister but thank you for being so receptive to my presentation."

He nods at me, as he again looks at the maps and reports on his desk, and asks "why do you not come to work here in The Gambia? It would be great to have someone of your experience and capacity working with our National Environment Agency."

"I would love to sir, but first, of course, there has to be a job vacancy."

"There is an upcoming project to be funded by the Americans. Keep an eye out for it and I will keep an eye open for you."

The meeting ends with a firm handshake.

My next port of call is to the senior team at the NEA, the lady director being sadly absent. Without going into the finer details, I show them our budget and the activities that my project is to undertake. They openly admit that their budget is placed at such a high level because they lack the in-country competence to carry out the work and know that they would instead have to hire overseas' consultants.

"And if we did the work for you?" I ask.

"How would your fees compare with our proposed budget?" I am asked.

"I will have to calculate carefully, but probably we could do the work alongside our own and so the costs would be pretty small, say 20% of what you have budgeted."

Some surprised looks, smiles all-round and several handshakes, and the deal is done.

As a nice cherry on top of the Banjul cake, I drop past the US mission to say hello to the young American who had so kindly set up the meeting with several senior development workers from many of the international agencies operating in Banjul during my previous trip.

"Hey, Malcolm, can you do me a favour?" he asked once we had chatted about latest items of news.

"Sure, what do you need?"

"Can you provide me a couple of hours, say tomorrow morning, to write the Term of Reference for a small project to estimate the quantity of bushfires that hits The Gambia in a year?"

"No trouble at all. But you know that this is one of our services, and we can easily and rapidly do the work for you."

"That's my thinking too. But you know that procuring a contract with a single entity is difficult for a donor agency. We are obliged to put it out to tender. The starting point for the tender will be the ToR and, given your experience and proximity to The Gambia, you are pretty much guaranteed to get the work."

"Since we already have the images and have done the analytical work all around the country on the Senegalese sides of the border, no one would be capable of doing it more quickly or cheaply than us. I am not even sure that anyone else has the analytical experience and algorithms to do the image analysis."

The following morning, I take a seat in a small office of the mission and draft out a four-page ToR for the bushfire monitoring work. As I write and refine the specifications, I become more and more convinced that I am in the process of landing us yet another contract.

(Jumping ahead two months, and following several phone calls to The Gambia to ask about the bushfire monitoring contract, I finally receive news via a phone call. However, not from Banjul but instead from a prominent university in the USA. The caller, who I do not know, asks if I am aware that his university has been awarded the contract to monitor bushfires in The Gambia. Of course, this is bad news for me, but what makes it even worse is the caller goes on to ask if I can tell him how the analysis of NOAA satellite imagery is carried out in order to define bushfires! At this point, I am very naïve about the incoherencies that go on within development agencies, but go on they most certainly do.)

Our short stay in Banjul has come to an end and we aim to catch the 10 am ferry across the River Gambia. We drive along the road leading to the port entrance and see a long, long queue of cars and trucks. My driver puts his head out of the window and asks a passenger in Wolof the reason for the queue. He is told that one of the two ferries has broken down and there is an estimated delay in crossing of around six hours. Ouch.

"Malcolm, will you give me permission to try to get us on the ferry a little more quickly?" my driver asks.

"Of course, what do you have in mind?" I reply.

"Just leave it with me," he responds.

He drives along the outside of the queue and turns into the port gates. A lethargic policeman sitting in the shade of a torn canvas tarpaulin raises his hand in a mild gesture of authority to which my driver calls out "diplomat." This apparently has the anticipated effect for we receive a salute.

He then parks the vehicle just inside the port gates, gets out of the vehicle and walks along to the Harbour Master's office, knocks and enters. Five minutes later, he reappears followed by a distinguished-looking older gentleman in a fine but rather dusty uniform.

The gentleman walks up to my window and says "we are so sorry for the delay Your Excellency, please pass to the front of the loading bay. We will load you as priority in fifteen minutes. Meanwhile would you like to sit in my office, perhaps have a cold drink?"

"Thank you for your kindness Mr Harbour Master" is all I can think to reply.

When my driver and I are once more alone in our vehicle, I ask "what on earth did you tell him?"

"Nothing much, just that you are the head of the World Bank (which is not quite correct, I know) and that you have just seen the Minister of Natural Resources (which you did) and that you agreed a loan of fifty million dollars for the country (which I made up to get us on board quickly)."

After a short moment of embarrassment passes, I roar and roar with laughter. My driver is, in his own words, a *saay-saay bombak* (a big Rascal) with the capital letter firmly on the rascal.

As promised, we are the first car to be loaded on the ferry and twenty minutes later we disembark on the north bank.

Once we have driven off the ferry and passed out of the loading area, he turns to me and says "Malcolm, will you allow me fifteen minutes to find those money changers who cheated us?" Knowing that he has been feeling sore about being cheated and a little humiliated that he was cheated by as much as me. His Senegalese pride is clearly at stake here!

"No problem, I will buy a Coca-Cola while you do your detective work. But are you sure you will recognise the youngsters?"

He strides off and disappears into the crowd of passengers and hawkers while I drink from the bottle. Ten minutes later, as promised, he reappears with the left and right ears respectively of our money changers gripped in his two large mechanic's hands. The boys, because they have not yet reached proper manhood, are trotting along either side of the driver in an attempt to keep their ears attached to their heads. As they reach our vehicle, my driver gives me a proud grin to have captured these young petty criminals.

Trotting behind the trio is an older gentleman, small in stature and obviously rather concerned for the ears of the two boys. He sees our car with diplomatic plates and asks, in passable French, what has happened. It turns out that he is the chief money changer and is rather embarrassed to see his staff ear-marched by a large fellow like my project mechanic.

We explain about the cheating that had occurred several days before. The boys do not attempt to deny the charge and the manager is obviously upset that they have been caught since the government of The Gambia turns a blind-eye to the money changing practice but insists on honesty.

"How much did you lose sir", he says addressing the driver, "and you, sir?" addressing me.

We state the correct amounts and the boys dutifully peel off the correct number of notes from the bundles they hold in their hands. My driver's pride is restored, we drive off and I secretly hope that this is the end of our adventures; for a short time at least.

But it is not to be. Once we cross into Senegalese territory and show our passports at the border post, we are approached by a gendarme who asks if we could give him a lift to Kaolack. Why not?

As we travel the approximate one hundred kilometres to Kaolack, we chat about nothing in particular. He asks if I have ever stayed in Kaolack and I mention that I have a good friend, called Alain, who owns and runs the Hotel de Paris.

The policeman suddenly goes quiet and then says "sorry but did you not know; Alain died very recently?"

I am shocked, saddened and in disbelief to hear this as I had seen Alain and his wife in Dakar only some ten days ago while his middle daughter is good friend of our little David and just as much mischief. This revelation causes our conversation to die down.

My driver mutters "*mes condolences patron*" and he too says no more until we reach the southern outskirts of Kaolack. The policeman leaves us in a small village that touches the larger town and waves goodbye.

As we drive past the Hotel de Paris, I ask my driver to stop and let me go into the hotel to pay my respects and drink a last draft beer in the establishment. I enter through the front door and am immediately recognised by the male receptionist. "Ah doctor, give me a moment" and he goes out through a door at the back of the reception that leads into the hotel office.

I turn around as I hear the hotel's front door open and see my driver standing there with his face crestfallen.

"I will drink with you Malcolm; you should not be alone in your sadness."

We both move to the left side of the room where the bar is located and I hear a familiar voice call out "*ah mon copain, tu es venu boire une bière avec moi ?*"

I stand there staring at Alain, who is clearly very much alive. He sees a tear start to run down the side of my face and asks what has happened. When Seck explains, for my voice was breaking too much to talk, he announces that it is a case of mistaken identity (that is now very obvious to me). The *toubab* who died recently was an elderly Frenchman who ran a small tourist lodge down the road in the Sine Saloum.

"But seeing that tear running down your face, shows me that you are a real friend. So drinks are on you!" he laughs.

The business side at the project is starting to go well and within a few short months we have signed and are beginning to execute a reasonable number of contracts; some small but others quite meaty in value. Apart from the loss of the bushfire contract in The Gambia, our list of work requests is growing and the team is reporting leads and similar 'intelligence' from other projects and donors almost on a daily basis. We even have a request come in from the neighbouring country of Guinea-Conakry.

The next agreement to be signed is with my Belgium friend and colleague based in Podor. His EU-funded project needs large-scale land use and natural resources maps of the northern departments where his teams are working. To develop such maps, we must invest in a series of Landsat images as well as some from the European SPOT satellite. The cost of these is significant while we calculate that the analytical work involved is lengthy and will also require many days in the field in order to 'ground truth' the images. The estimate that I deliver to the project runs into the equivalent of several tens of thousands of pounds but, no problem, the European Union accepts our estimate and contracts are signed. Another work project is added to the growing list.

10

Events Come to a Head

Despite the growing list of business-orientated activities, we must still continue to execute our usual ecological monitoring workload. Eighteen months ago we added about a dozen additional vegetation biomass monitoring sites to the south of the Dakar to Tamba road, and most are in the departments that lie to the south of The Gambia. This brings our total number of sites to just over thirty and the distance required to visit every one adds several extra days' travel to the workload. We decide, therefore, that this year we must use two fieldwork teams; our field botanist will lead one and me the other. Séraphin is allocated to my team and Diagne will drive for the second team. That decision is literally life-saving.

In the south of the country the vegetation is much denser and lusher while the trees are considerably taller, broader and of different species to those further north. Around Tamba the vegetation is considered to belong to the Sudan Savanna vegetation type while south of The Gambia we are to work in the so-called Guinea Savanna zone. This latter vegetation type strongly resembles the vegetation that I had known in the north of Cross River State where I had lived for four years, working as an ecology lecturer at the University of Calabar.

Our trip starts off in the Tamba area where we have two established sites. This year's rainy season has been one of the best in recent memories and the cane-like grass has grown to well over two metres high in places. Now, as we enter October, the grass is beginning to dry and we must work quickly to get our sites surveyed before the dreaded bushfire season starts.

Needing two teams to cover all the sites, means that we lack a couple of able-bodied field technicians to make up the numbers. I am allocated a geographer who has never previously done field work to come with my team for the entire three weeks. He has been brought into the team mostly because he has moaned incessantly about it being unfair that the 'ecologists' get to do fieldwork and so receive a per diem while the geographers are forced to remain in the office and receive no extra pay. So this field trip should be interesting. The gentleman is affectionately known by the team as the 'Mullah' because he is a very devout individual. But his Senegalese colleagues have warned him that, on some days, he will likely have to vary his prayer times.

On our first day of work out of Tamba, we leave as usual at 7 am and arrive at our site half an hour or so later. The site is only about 20 km north of Tamba and is connected to the town by an earthen track that has been partially overgrown by the high grasses but nothing that can seriously cause Séraphin any issues with our 4-wheel drive vehicle.

Our new colleague is working with me by helping to pull the surveyor tapes along our predetermined compass bearing for the usual total of one kilometre. Apart from a few moans about the prickles from the various Acacia trees, he gets on with his task pretty well; at least at first. However, as the morning wears on and the temperature and humidity rise, the poor guy begins literally to feel the heat. Being a geographer and working in an air-conditioned room is one thing, putting on an ecologist's hat and working in the field at the end of a steamy rainy season is quite another; per diem or not!

After we have finished our one kilometre transect, the next task is for him to help me establish the circular quadrats and determine the different parameters of the trees and bushes. His role is purely as a scribe. I will do the species identification and measurements while he can sit in the shade of a neighbouring tree and write down the information as I call it out. But 'no' he tells me. It is far too hot, and look at the time. He is going back to the vehicle. Fortunately, another team member volunteers to take his place.

As we are finishing the fourth and last quadrat, we hear a whooshing sound, rather like a train approaching; but there are no trains in the bush of Tamba and we realise that the only other possible source of this sound is a bushfire. We then hear the car horn honking continuously and so we grab our equipment and jog back to the car. Séraphin and another colleague are already inside the Hilux while our two Bassari grass cutters are sitting in the open back of the pickup.

"Where's the Mullah?" I ask.

"Over behind the bushes saying prayers" explains Séraphin.

I hurry over and call out to my colleague "I'm sorry to disturb your prayers but we really must leave, the fire is getting very close." And as I talk, small patches of flame are visible only about sixty metres or so away from us.

"I will come when I finish my prayers"

"Please come now. This is a very dangerous situation for everybody."

And I am completely ignored as he continues with his noon (*Dhuhr*) prayers. I hurry back and tell the rest of the team that we have a situation.

"No we don't," retorts Séraphin. He runs across to our co-worker and says very loudly "you have five seconds to get in the car or we will leave you to the flames. We do not intend to die for you."

He calmly walks back to the car, jumps in, starts the engine and slowly pulls away down the track towards Tamba.

We soon hear our friend calling "wait, wait."

Of course we stop, and he climbs into the back of the car receiving a torrent of abuse not only from Séraphin but also from the other team member, himself a devout Muslim too.

Our journey back to Tamba is, in places, quite scary. By now the fire is burning noisily along several sections of the trail. At some places we are even obliged to drive straight through burning vegetation but eventually we arrive safely back in Tamba.

Séraphin is still moaning about that 'foolish guy' who nearly got us stuck in a bushfire when we arrive back at our lodgings in the town's forestry department. The other team members go off to wash while Séraphin drives me to our favourite place in Tamba: a bar that serves very cold beer and, outside of which, permanently sits an elderly lady selling cows' feet stewed in a very hot chilli sauce. Today, that is to be our lunch.

As we eat, we chat about the fire and Séraphin informs me that he considers the fire was almost certainly started either by a cattle herder or by the Forestry Department itself.

He explains that the dry cane-like grasses that predominate in the south of the country have very little nutritional value when mature and dry. Herders have discovered that by burning the grasses, new and tender shoots will quickly sprout and these are much appreciated by their livestock. But the damage that such uncontrolled fires can cause to trees and bushes is enormous. That is why the Forestry Department has several ploys to diminish the potential damage. For example, they have driven miles of broad firebreaks through the bush – we saw these in the north of the country where the Ostrich family was sighted. Firebreaks can prevent the spread of fires but they must be maintained and cleared of vegetation, and many are not. The foresters also carry out controlled 'early burning' fires that seek to reduce the amount of vegetation but not to remove it completely.

However, the art of setting early fires is not known by all department chiefs and many fires are set too late in the season, when the vegetation is too dry, or the fires simply get out of hand and cannot be controlled. Many of the fires we pick up on our bushfire monitoring satellite images are in fact so-called 'controlled early burns' that have gotten out of hand.

A few days after the bushfire event, we travel south, driving around the perimeter of the Niokola Koba National Park and head into the *département de* Kolda. This is only the second time that I have visited this attractive department. The first time being when we came to set up the new sites. Our two Bassari grass cutters have accompanied us from Tamba. They like the work, are related to Séraphin and are very competent and helpful. But we have lost the services of our Geographer, he has gone back to Dakar to find succour in the air-conditioned office! Séraphin volunteers to help me pull the surveyor tapes because the vegetation at this site is far too dense for the car to follow along with us.

We begin our work like any other day. I set the compass bearing and we begin to pull out the 50-metre-long tapes. Séraphin works with me along the transect but then, after several hundred metres, excuses himself to go and collect a number of cloth bags, crammed full of herbaceous material cut by his fellow Bassaris. He puts the bags in a pile and then hurries to catch me up as I pull out the tape once more.

Suddenly he shouts, "stop Malcolm, don't move."

I stop, holding my advancing foot in mid-air. "What is it?" I ask.

"Look where you were going to put your foot. There is a snake, stay still, don't move".

I look under the direct trajectory of my right foot and there, unseen by me but spotted by Séraphin's eagle eyes, sits rather nonchalantly, what I believe to be, a Puff Adder. Short, fat, well camouflaged and unmistakably deadly with extremely large venom glands protruding from behind the head.

While I stand in the 'heron position', Séraphin calmly snaps off a stout piece of wood, walks across to me and .... wap, one dead snake.

"Thank you but could I not simply have moved backwards?" I ask.

"Don't be deceived by that fat snake. In my village we call them 'bite-two-times' because as soon as you realise that you have been bitten, he will have bitten you again. No one survives those bites, especially as far away as we are from a hospital."

I owe that sweet guy my life.

Our mission completes without further serious incident and we arrive back in Dakar to meet up with the other team. Our vegetation samples are carefully dried in a drying oven, weighed and the biomass for each field site calculated.

These data are put into a rather complex equation that relates the physical biomass at each site with the corresponding measures of reflectivity in selected colour bands taken from several series of NOAA satellite images covering the entire growing season.

With a total of around thirty points located in natural vegetation around the country, we are then able to calculate the *likely* vegetation biomass for every NOAA 'pixel' of one kilometre square across the whole surface of Senegal. By the way, while doing this work for Senegal, we also get the data for The Gambia for 'free' from the same calculation.

While all is good on the technical front, I even have the time to author a couple of scientific papers, the same cannot be said on the finance and administrative front – but as I have been told, this is no longer my business. But of course it is. I cannot sit idly by and pretend that all is rosy.

One Monday morning, I arrive at the office and see, propped against an outside wall, an almost new tyre from one of the Landcruisers. There is a foot-long gash in the side. I wonder how this has occurred. I find out a few moments later as our team of drivers enter my office and all begin speaking in angry voices at the same time.

"Wait, wait," I say "you, explain to me what has happened," I instruct the project mechanic.

He draws a deep breath and says "boss, it has to stop. We cannot be made to drive across to Tamba every weekend and receive no pay or per diem, little food and no place to sleep."

"I agree that should not occur, and it doesn't on this project. So what are you telling me?"

"The national coordinator makes us go on the campaign trail for the President's Party. He makes us drive project vehicles and carry dozens of militants in the vehicles. We all have to drive to different villages out in the bush where the politicians hold rallies. Did you see the tyre that got damaged on Diagne's car?"

One of the other drivers then adds "I even overheard one politician tell the coordinator that he must contribute a very large sum, millions of CFA, to the campaign funds if he wishes to get a seat in the National Assembly. And he replied that there was plenty of money in our project. This is not good boss!"

I tell the drivers to leave it with me, but in future they must stick together and refuse to drive if the work involved is not for the project, and especially if they do not have the correct mission papers authorising their trips.

I wait until 4 pm, when I know that staff will be in the US offices, and ring through to the lady who is technically in charge of our project. I explain the reason behind my call and am shocked to be told that I am a troublemaker.

The following day, my secretary comes into my office with a very concerned look on her face. She tells me "please sir, do not report me for telling you but the national coordinator has ordered that your international phone line be cut."

I try to dial through to the USA and receive a computerised voice telling me that my phone can only be used for national calls.

The situation goes from bad to worse. Keita comes to my office, locks my door behind him and sits down in front of me.

"Work orders and contracts are not following procurement guidelines. One of the national coordinator's friends has been given considerable rebuilding and decorating work without the work going out to tender. The coordinator is also ordering me to make large cash withdrawals so that he can make payments to this friend. Other work has been given to a company that no one here has heard of before and the head office is in a small village in the Peanut Basin where, coincidentally, our desk officer comes from."

I instruct Keita to show me the incriminating papers and I am left in no doubt at all that serious dishonesty is occurring. I have to be the whistle-blower; I can see no other course of action.

That evening, since I no longer have an international phone line in my office, I drive to the post office at the International Airport and make a call to the head of the office in the USA that controls my project. We speak at length and I tell him of the issues I am facing and that when I reported other incidents to his office, I was accused of creating trouble.

"Sir, it is important that you call an internal audit. What is going on is far beyond my capacity to deal with it and now outside of my job description too," I insist.

I am assured that an audit will occur but getting a team to Senegal will take some time.

Meanwhile bad things turn to horror.

After being in the field for so long on the recent biomass campaign, I have a lot of paperwork to catch up with. I decide to go to the office on a Saturday morning when I know that there will be no staff around to distract me.

At 10 am I drive through the gates and into the compound at the back of the office that serves as a car park and note our Landcruisers and Hilux are parked in neat rows. Obviously the drivers have refused to take part in any more political campaigns. However, I see one of our little Suzuki Jeeps, bearing diplomatic number plates, start up and then drive towards me. I do not recognise the driver. I flash my lights and drive towards him, forcing him to stop. He opens the driver's door and walks towards me. He is a total stranger, a Lebanese man.

"Good morning," I address him "what are you doing driving one of the project's vehicles?"

"Good morning, you must be the team leader. I have just purchased this vehicle from your national coordinator." He holds out a handwritten receipt for two million CFA *cash* (the equivalent of four thousand pounds).

"I am sorry but no individual can sell one of our vehicles because they belong to the donor, not to our project. Come with me and I will get your money back."

We walk into the coordinator's office and he first says something in Wolof to the car buyer and then tells me to sit down.

"Hold on a moment, Malcolm, I will be back in two minutes." He walks outside with the gentleman and a few moments later I hear the high pitch whine of a Suzuki engine as it drives off.

Blast!

The national coordinator walks back into his office and explains to me "I had to let him go because I handed his cash over to Keita and he has already left the office to go home. I will go and fetch the money and take it to that gentleman and get the car back. Can we meet here tomorrow at lunchtime to put your mind at ease?" I have to agree.

Very early on Sunday morning, at around 5 am, I can hear Mbaye calling me urgently from outside my bedroom window. "Come quick boss, come quick."

I dress quietly, leave the bedroom and pass through the kitchen and garage to the front gate. Séraphin is waiting with a project vehicle and he greets me with a sad expression on his face.

"M. Keita est décédé cette nuit. On m'a dit d'un infarctus."

Poor, gentle and troubled Keita has just passed away with a suspected heart attack. I smell real evil in the air and a cold chill works up my spine.

We drive the couple of kilometres to Keita's home, coincidentally on the *Front de Terre* where I used to live, and I find many of the staff already in attendance. I greet Mrs Keita and give a hug to her young son, only twelve, who has just lost his dad. The national coordinator is there, of course he would be.

"Don't worry," he tells me, "I have confiscated his briefcase, the one with the combination lock. That is where he put the money from the car sale."

In my softest voice, I curse the coordinator for his unfeeling stupidity and say out loud to the colleagues standing nearby "we need to request the police do a blood test to show whether he was poisoned."

One kind colleague comes across and wraps his arms around me in sympathy.

"We know that you were close to Keita and we understand what you are saying, his death was very sudden, but our religion requires that burial occurs at sunrise and he has already been taken to the Muslim cemetery for burial. There is nothing we can do."

Any evidence of foul play is buried with Mr Keita on that Sunday morning. And, on that same morning, I make up my mind that we should start to make plans to leave. I have never felt so unprotected both for my family and myself.

The audit does occur ... at the end of 1992 and, not surprisingly (since I spend many hours with the auditors giving as much information as I can), finds that there has been a woeful lack of procedure leading to considerable dishonesty within the financial administration of the project. The written report mentions that I am held partly responsible for failing to notify the local and head offices in sufficient detail. Of course, nothing is said, at least at this time, of the fact that I was pushed away by the senior people that were supposed to support me and that I had been told on several occasions that I was just a troublemaker for raising issues.

During the audit feedback meeting, I realise just what 'closing ranks' really means. As soon as I return to my office, I write my resignation letter to the Resident Representative in Dakar. This starts with the words:

"You will be aware that my annual contract is due for renewal in the coming July. I take this opportunity to inform you that I will not be seeking renewal ..."

I feel sick to the heart to receive a reply the next day that says "We regret your decision not to renew your contract ...".

"Hypocrites" is all I could think to mutter under my breath.

11

Time to Go

Véronique is always gentle and kind but I know that the wrench of leaving Senegal is very hard for her. While she sympathises with my predicament and will support me to the very end, having to give up the near-perfect life that we have as a family is hard. And this is made even harder with the knowledge that we are leaving without a job or indeed without any well laid plans.

Of course the Marks' luck is sure to step in at this dire moment; and it does.

First, I hear via the British Embassy that the IUCN are seeking a new Regional Director for West Africa, to be based (yes that's right) in Dakar. I get the application forms filled and faxed to Switzerland and, within a few days, am called to a preliminary interview with the outgoing director in Dakar. Apparently, I do well because I am then given a return plane ticket to Geneva and from there take a train to Gland where both the IUCN and WWF headquarters are located. I am to undergo a second, more formal, interview there.

After a restless night's sleep, I walk to the headquarters for the interview and am shown into a waiting room. A quick double-take because I know most of the other candidates. A couple are French and have visited my project in the past, three are from Belgium and all have worked as consultants on the EU project in Podor, and the one I do not know is Dutch.

I make a round of the room, shaking hands and introducing myself to those who have not met me in the past.

One of the Belgians says kindly "with you here, time for the rest of us to go home!" Such is the international respect held for my project.

Before the formal interviews begin, a lady from the Human Resources Department comes in and informs us "as you know, the West Africa office covers both Anglophone and Francophone countries. This position is strictly for a bilingual candidate and therefore you must all be prepared to be interviewed in your second language."

With a certain amount of humour, the Dutch gentleman says "great. My first language is Dutch so I should be interviewed in English because my French is very poor."

My turn for the formal interview eventually arrives and I enter a conference room with a long oval table with six ladies and gentlemen arranged around the table. Everyone introduces themselves in turn and all speak in French although I note that there are at least three English or Americans at the table while the others are Francophone, I presume, hailing from France and Switzerland.

We soon get down to talking about my different work experiences in Senegal and the ecology work that I carried out across the country. I also remember to plug the years that I spent in Nigeria and the fact that I ran the botanical gardens and nature reserve. Some of their questions are highly technical but since I have done the work in French, I have little difficulty in explaining the details in that language. But this leads to a humorous moment when an English interviewer admits that he cannot understand and asks one of the French speakers to translate for him. The response, with much good-humoured laughter, is to request me to explain again but this time in English.

Time passes quickly and it seems that I am soon being thanked by the interview panel for coming to Gland at such short notice. I am instructed now to report to the HR lady that had spoken to us all earlier. I say my thanks and, after I walk out the door, look at my watch and see that my interview has in fact lasted a full hour.

Following the instructions to take the stairs to the next floor up, I knock on the Human Resources door and enter. The lady greets me with a broad smile and says a single word 'congratulations'! She goes on to explain "all the other candidates have been interviewed and you are our preferred candidate. I should not really be telling you but our outgoing West African director gave you high praise and you scored far higher than any of the other candidates in our initial assessment. Also, you were the only candidate who interviewed exclusively in your second language; that impressed everyone. We would like to offer you the job, I can give you some of the details now but we will send you full details at a later date."

I travel back to Senegal feeling happier than I have felt in many months. Véronique wears a big smile too, when she hears the news from my trip.

But that is not the end of the story because a few evenings later, the young American that I knew from the US office in The Gambia calls me from Washington DC. He has now left The Gambia and taken up employment with an American consulting company. His *excuse* for calling me is to ask my advice on a new US-funded project to be based in Banjul that his company wishes to bid on. This is, therefore, the project that the Gambian Minister had referred to during my meeting with him some months previously.

The young American goes on to list large areas of work that will be required under the contract and asks how I would suggest that his company explains those details in their technical proposal.

After spending an hour or so going from one technical area to the next, he apologises for taking so much of my evening time and finishes with "it's a real shame you are not available to be in our team."

"Who says I'm not?" I reply.

At this point, I sense that his hand covers, well partially covers, the telephone speaker because I hear a muffled voice saying "I think we've got him."

A different voice then comes on the line, introduces himself as the company chairman and does an excellent job of selling me the position of 'Environmental Information Specialist' in the team.

So there we have it. It seems like the IUCN will be making me a serious offer as their new Regional Director for West Africa while the American company wishes to put me in their bid for the Gambian contract. The first seems the most certain but Véro and I both consider that we should keep the Gambian possibility as a just-in-case fall-back.

We enter June 1993, and my birthday will soon come around again. But this year is special; can I really be coming up to forty? It only seems a moment ago that Véronique and I were spending my thirtieth with a host of friends in Calabar. Now I am about to spend the next big '0' in Senegal. Not only am I getting older but so are my kids. Mélanie has recently had her eleventh birthday and David, handsome in his Ninja Turtle outfit (of course) celebrated his seventh in April. Time is passing at an ever increasing rate and soon our life will change too.

My final day arrives at the office in Senegal and I cannot wait to finish and get aboard the plane back to France. Sob's Law, unfortunately, dictates that I must first undertake a full project annual review on my very last afternoon. I find it hard to concentrate and this becomes even harder when it is apparent that the donor staff present are not interested at all in the number of fee-paying contracts that we have won and executed in the last several months. They prefer to read through the project document and count the number of aerial surveys carried out, the number of reports produced, what percentage of the budget has been spent, and so on. Bureaucrats to my last day.

Goodbye!

12

After the Fact

We are back in France and have taken up residence at our home in Cordon. The children have settled straight back into French life and their village friends seem to be drawn like magnets to our home; we must be doing something right!

Véro and I are seeing a lot of her family and even more of our local friends. The summer weather is beautiful and I have heard that our bid for the Gambian contract has won, so I have an assured job. But I have heard nothing further from the IUCN (and actually never will). The last, unofficial information I received was that the West African headquarters was going to be moved from Senegal to Mauritania; and that is a country I am not prepared to expatriate to with my family. The memories of early 1989 are still too fresh in my mind.

On the surface, then, everything is going well. But I am not. I know that I am going through a bout of depression. I have not been to see Dominique, my doctor and friend; I just know that I am not feeling right. I am trying hard to be seen by everyone as the happy, funny, loving husband and father that I enjoy being so much. Sadly, however, I feel anything but funny and happy. When depression arrives, and this is the first time in my life that I feel this way, it is not a simple task of clicking fingers and telling oneself to snap out of it. Once in that hole, something needs to happen so that one may slowly climb out; life needs, somehow, to change.

I know that the reason behind my depression is that I blame myself for my self-perceived weakness in not dealing better with the corruption and dishonesty that went on in the latter stages of my old project. I wonder, to this day, how a project could have been so technically successful but, latterly, so administratively dire; how I could be so proud of the technical side and so ashamed of the administrative.

Somewhere in this black period of self-criticism, I make the promise to myself that should I ever be faced with a similar situation, I will face it full on and do whatever is needed. No backing down, no taking 'no' for an answer from superiors, no crossing my fingers and hoping that things will work out for the better. And, in a future job, this does occur and I do face it squarely and successfully. Senegal taught me a lot and helped me grow up and, I believe, become a better manager and a much better person.

I knew that the national coordinator's days were severely limited and while he still sat in his chair on my final day at the office, there were intense machinations behind the scenes, at the very highest levels of state and donor, to have him removed from office. This soon occurred.

Also, in previous months before leaving, I had helped the French-Canadian business consultant to draw up the terms of reference for a new hierarchy to run the project when donor funding for the current phase came to an end. We also worked hard to find the correct legal status for the future structure and came up with a possible entity entitled 'Association of National Interest' which was based on a law of 1904. Our thoughts were that the new association should be led by a Managing Director and I pushed hard – and, as it turned out, successfully – for the appointment of a former Forestry Director who had impeccable credentials, was a talented leader and well respected in both government and civilian circles.

During my last two weeks in Senegal, I wrote a 'For Your Eyes Only' document that analysed everything that could be analysed about the project. From staff strengths and weaknesses (even which individuals should be retained and others released) to the individual unit costs of driving a vehicle for a kilometre or the price of printing a map. There was also a section dedicated to salaries both for private contractors and any civil servants who might remain. I always believed that there was a need to get away from the dual salary system that had caused so much jealousy and anger in the past. What I also came up with was a form of profit-sharing to be based on level of seniority and individual roles in generating that profit. Indeed, the document contained anything that I felt might help the new managing director to find his feet quickly and run the association profitably.

But I think that my most inspired section was an analysis of the key personnel and the suggestion of the person I thought would be best suited to lead the technical side of the new structure. The reserved but brilliant young technician who had joined us in my early days at the project to develop the rainfall monitoring activities was my first choice. And he did get the job and, as I write these words is still there ... because several years later he became, in his turn, the managing director.

That document was sealed in an envelope and I entrusted it to Aisha, our senior secretary, to keep it safe. She handed it over to the new Managing Director on his first day in the office and, when I met the new MD several months later, he assured me that he had read my document through several times over and that it was now locked in his office desk. He told me that whenever an issue arises, he checks to see what I might suggest should be done.

As the summer in Cordon wears on so my depression seems to lift a little and I am making plans for a first input to The Gambia which should occur within the next month or so. I have installed my office on the top floor of our house in Cordon and this brings some privacy and peace to undertake bits and pieces of work in preparation for my new project in Banjul.

One afternoon, as I am concentrating on the background to developing a strategic plan for the Ministry of Natural Resources in The Gambia, my phone rings and, on answering, the speaker introduces himself as a new desk officer from my former donor agency and employer based on the East Coast of the USA.

"What can I do for you?" I ask.

"There is a new team in place in the US and we have been going through notes and files from Senegal and we are very concerned by what we are reading. We feel that you were unfairly treated and understand why, but regret, that you resigned. Not only did you leave but so did the team leader of our forestry project in Louga. He quit at about the same time as you and his leaving notes bear a strong resemblance to what you have written into the files. We are shocked to see that the team leaders of our two flagship projects left at the same time for very similar apparent reasons. We believe that some of our staff in Dakar and the US who were supposed to backstop both projects may have broken our internal rules. We have already asked the other team leader and wonder if you would be prepared to write in detail the events that led to your resignation?"

My response was short, bitter and drawn out from my frustrated and depressed state.

"Let's be very clear. When I worked for you and tried to talk to different people within the hierarchy of the organisation about the problems, I was called a troublemaker, and no one would listen. Now I have left, you are eager for me to talk and to help you. My message is simple: you can all f**k off!" and I slammed down the phone.

Now, that burst of fury actually has a soothing effect. Many months of depression, stress and frustration start to lift, and I come to realise that I have just said, in the last short sentence, something that I should have said, indeed needed to say for a very long time.

I confess that I do feel a little sorry for the guy at the end of the line. He was not around when all the problems arose in Dakar and so cannot really be blamed for the turmoil that entered into my work and life. And, as if sensing this latest sentiment, the phone rings again.

"Dr Marks, Malcolm, please do not hang up just yet. I understand how you feel and I am so sorry for what you went through and I really sympathise with you."

I manage to spit out, "you guys ruined my career, do you know that?"

Looking back, I suppose that was a bit melodramatic – but it is how I feel at this time. After all, I loved the technical side of the work, the business development had been proving to be an enjoyable challenge, the family loved living in Senegal and, in another couple of months, I would have tied into the donor's pension scheme, and that is not to be sniffed at.

He responds very sympathetically, so I let him continue talking.

"What happened should not have happened and we are doing some house cleaning here at headquarters and we have already started in Dakar too. There was a lady in our accounting department in Dakar who was complicit with the old national coordinator; I won't go into details, but she is already out. The real issue we have is with the desk officer whom we know made your life extremely difficult, and there was that suspicion about him having profited from contract awards. Please help us to nail him. Give us all the details that you have on his behaviour towards you and the project, together with any deals you think he made with the old national coordinator; especially if you have any evidence. The team leader from Louga has already supplied us with information from his side. Will you do that please? I know you care about development, about the project and about Senegal. We need to get rid of the bad apples and we cannot do it without your help. Please help us."

I pause and then surprise myself by saying "OK, I will get started and fax you the details as soon as I finish." The caring about development, the project and Senegal were the bits that hit the right spot.

The call ends and I sit down at my computer and, almost literally, pour my heart out into the text starting with suspicious contract awards, passing via tricks to block my reporting of those contracts to the headquarters and finishing with his personal attacks against me. For example, when I officially became the team leader, the personnel department at the US headquarters had promised me promotion from P4 to P5. Such a promotion comes with a very nice salary increase and was a recognition that I was actually doing two jobs since my role as lead ecologist was never filled. Just like anyone else would have done, I filled in the forms that very same day. However, the desk officer in Dakar had persuaded the Resident Representative to decree that no team leader in Senegal should communicate directly with the East Coast office. Rather, everything was to pass via his, the desk officer, desk for onward transmission. This included my promotion forms and unbeknown to me, he took the opportunity to hide my forms under lock and key in his office.

The only way I ever knew that head office had not received the forms was when, several months later, I got a very odd fax saying, quite bluntly, that 'no one at headquarters can understand why you do not send in your promotion forms. Are you not interested?'

Eventually, under pressure from me, the forms did finally get sent off and I received the promotion from the *date the forms arrived* on the East Coast. I lost over six months of promotion due to the nastiness of that fellow.

When finished, my text runs to four closely spaced pages, and I rather enjoy faxing them off to headquarters in the USA. I subsequently hear that the 'gentleman' was removed from his position and that this was in fact the second time that he had been fired by one of the sister donor agencies.

Just to finish off these bad memories, many years later I happened to run into the gentleman himself, coincidentally eating a plate of *thieboudienne* in a *boui-boui* in Kaolack. He greeted me as though butter would not melt in his mouth and told me that he is now working for another one of the donor agency's offices ... The mind boggles.

That autumn of 1993, I start to work on the project in The Gambia but, apart from a short trip to Dakar to run with the Banjul chapter of the Hash House Harriers, I do not manage to get back to the city until two years later.

The joy of seeing all my old colleagues at the ecology centre and to meet up again with the management team was negated by the news I receive from Aisha, the secretary.

"Malcolm, I'm really sorry but I don't think you know that Séraphin passed away peacefully, very recently."

During the turbulent years that I spent in Dakar, dear Séraphin was the one person that I knew I could trust, one hundred percent. A true friend.

As a final word, in this year of 2023, my old project has not only survived, it has flourished. That small business seed that I helped to sow in the early 1990s did manage to take root, occasionally it needed pruning back but finally grew, under the tutelage of an excellent new management, into everything we could have hoped for. I like to think that all the crap that occurred during those early years actually served to manure the young sprout and help it become the strong and successful structure it now is.

www.ingramcontent.com/pod-product-compliance
Lightning Source LLC
LaVergne TN
LVHW050857200726
843508LV00011B/2039